EUROPEAN CABINET
and
FURNITURE MAKING

Byron W. Maguire

Prentice Hall
Englewood Cliffs, New Jersey

Library of Congress Cataloging-in-Publication Data

Maguire, Byron W.
    European cabinet and furniture making / by Byron W. Maguire.
        p.   cm.
    Includes index.
    ISBN 0-13-292061-1   ISBN 0-13-292053-0 (pbk.)
    1. Furniture making. 2. Furniture—Europe. 3. Cabinet-work-
-Europe. I. Title.
    TT194.M335 1989
    749.294—dc19   88-10107
                                                         CIP

Editorial/production supervision: WordCrafters Editorial Services, Inc.
Cover design: Lundgren Graphics, Ltd.
Manufacturing buyer: Mary Anne Gloriande
Page layout: Karen Salzbach

 ©1989 by Prentice Hall, Inc.
A Division of Simon & Schuster
Englewood Cliffs, New Jersey 07632

This book can be made available to business and organizations
at a special discount when ordered in large quantities. For
more information, contact:

> Prentice Hall
> Special Sales and Markets
> College Division
> Englewood Cliffs, NJ 07632

Printed in the United States of America

10 9 8 7 6 5 4 3 2 1

ISBN 0-13-292061-1

ISBN 0-13-292053-0   PBK.

Prentice-Hall International (UK) Limited, *London*
Prentice-Hall of Australia Pty. Limited, *Sydney*
Prentice-Hall Canada Inc., *Toronto*
Prentice-Hall Hispanoamericana, S.A., *Mexico*
Prentice-Hall of India Private Limited, *New Delhi*
Prentice-Hall of Japan, Inc., *Tokyo*
Simon & Schuster Asia Pte. Ltd., *Singapore*
Editora Prentice-Hall do Brasil, Ltda., *Rio de Janeiro*

This book is dedicated to my wife and children. It was through the research and development of this book that many pleasant memories of our experiences in Europe and England were recalled.

Contents

Preface

In so many ways our American heritage is linked with the cultures of other countries. This concept is really true when we study the furniture and cabinets of Europe and compare them with the furniture and cabinets in our homes.

This idea became one of the most interesting studies I have ever made. As you will study, almost everything we design and build has its roots in the countries of Europe many years ago. I hope that many of you will have the opportunity to live in England and on the Continent as my family and I did. In this way you too can experience, first hand, the cultures and styles of the people and their furniture and cabinets.

As cabinetmakers and furniture makers we almost always design and build each piece according to a style or include certain characteristics which we are really comfortable with. This book will aid you in many ways with accomplishing this task. As you study the chapters on France, Italy, Denmark and others you will be studying the history of styles and origins of characteristics of cabinets and furniture.

If I were to cover each of the developments of style and characteristics of each country to an indepth degree, it would require something like an encyclopedia. What I have done is editorialize and condense the events, facts, styles and characteristics in such a way that with careful study you will readily recognize the style and period of furniture and cabinets by their characteristics. In

Part 1, the focus is on style and character and how to construct these cabinets, tables, stands, chests and so on.

I assume that you know a type of joint, for example, by its name and what it looks like. Therefore, the description of construction techniques in these chapters is very technically written. If you should need better descriptions of joints and other technical data, you should read Chapters 1 and 2 and all of Part 2 first, then study Chapters 3 through 9 on England and the other countries.

The first two chapters in Part 1 are designed to make you aware of the principles of cabinet and furniture design that have been in existence for more than 500 years. You are encouraged to closely study these chapters before studying those on European countries since foundations disclosed in these chapters are recalled frequently in following chapters. Throughout my research I read many different ways of expressing the principle shape of cabinets. These included using the terms "units," "proportionalism", "mass", "line", "character", "element and sub-element", "period" and others. There were good and bad points in using any of these terms. Further, several manufacturers label their cabinets as modular units or just units. So to avoid confusion I chose the word *mass* as the point of principle to discuss a cabinet design characteristic.

In Part 2 technical subjects including materials, tools, techniques, and methods are covered in detail. You may find several different lessons that could improve your overall skills. For example, Chapter 11 on drawing shows and explains several techniques that make cabinet drawings easier to make. Later chapters discuss the different parts of joinery, sanding, bonding, and finishing.

Good luck with your projects.

                                                                    B.W.M.

Acknowledgments

The following contributors have added much to providing understanding through visual aids. Their photographs clearly show by example the characteristics and styles of the furniture and cabinets they represent. I would like to thank Drexel Heritage Furnishings Incorporated, Drexel, North Carolina; Karel Mintjens, Furniture International, Incorporated, U.S. division Leesburg, home organization Belgium; and A/S Hundevad & Company, Ulfborg, Denmark, American Plywood Association, and Western Wood Product Association.

Several figures listed at the end of this paragraph were photocopied from a book written by Herman Schmitz in the early 1920s entitled "Das Mobelwerk", and published by Verlag Ernst Wasmuth A.G., Berlin W8, Germany. I have researched to determine that the publisher of this 65-year-old book still is in business and have found no record to that effect. However, I do feel an obligation to acknowledge that the author procured the original photos from several European institutions. These may be found in figures 3–1, 3–2, 3–3, 3–4, 3–11, 4–1, 4–2, 4–3, 4–4, 5–1, 5–2, 5–4, and 8–1, which represent antique cabinets from England, France, Germany, and Spain.

A special thanks to the members of my family. They have assisted in the preparation of this book with reading, word processing, editing, and in locating stores that market furniture and cabinets from countries other than the United States.

PART 1
European Cabinet and Furniture Making

1

Fundamentals of European Cabinet and Furniture Making

While walking through several furniture showrooms recently, I could not help but admire the skill and artistry of the various manufacturers, both American and European. As I stopped time after time to admire tables, chairs, chests, desks, dressers, bars, and numerous other pieces, I observed the details included in their construction and finish, and the variety of skills and techniques used to create them. This casual study led me to begin this book with an introduction to European styles of cabinetmaking by first discussing the approach one should take to understand the art involved in reproducing the European styles of cabinets, and then examining the skills and knowledge needed to create and build cabinets and other pieces of furniture in the European style.

Objectives

1. To better understand the art of cabinetmaking.
2. To grasp the significance of the knowledge and skills needed to build beauty into cabinets and furniture.

1.1 APPRECIATING THE BEAUTY OF A CABINET OR PIECE OF FURNITURE

As cabinetmakers we have a special appreciation for the beauty of a cabinet we make because it is a part of us. For most of us, myself included, our first project was crude by most standards. Proportions may have been wrong, poor woods may have been used, construction techniques may not have been the best, finishes may not have been well done, and our planning may have been flawed. However, as we matured as cabinetmakers, our appreciation for each part of the cabinet and the process of creating it increased. This growth period may have taken years.

Even though our projects may not have been of the quality created by top-flight manufacturers such as Drexel and A/S Hundevad, to name just two, some feature did attract us and caused us to try again and again. Many of us studied and kept trying until the mastery of combining design, technique, materials, and skill became very real. Now when we browse through furniture showrooms we can appreciate the real beauty of furniture and cabinets, not just the surface features.

Since some readers may not be as experienced as others, we proceed slowly with the discussion and take little for granted. Of course, we discuss factors relating to European styles, specifically how the characteristics and techniques built into the piece bring about its beauty.

Masses must be proportioned correctly. Consider the computer work station shown in Figure 1–1, which is actually two stacked units. This cabinet includes vertical and horizontal masses. Notice that the principles of vertical and horizontal lines and areas are without error. Although it is difficult to see from the figure, I have seen this unit, and all joints are perfectly made. Wood grain is carefully used in the design. The oak wood veneers are carefully selected. The base wood is strong, well dried, and straight. Adornments are not used in this piece, but when adornments are used they must be used properly. Finally, finish and color must be correct for the cabinet or furniture piece.

Beauty is not limited to Danish-style cabinets. It is expressed in every European country in many different ways. England produced some master cabinetmakers such as Chippendale, Hepplewhite, and Sheraton. William and Mary and Queen Ann styles are especially beautiful. France gave us the Louis IV, XV, and XVI classical styles. The Italians, Germans, Belgians, Spanish, Morrocans, and others each contributed in many ways to the beauty of cabinetry. Throughout this book, you will see many examples and learn more about this artistry.

Cabinet and Furniture Functionality

Cabinet and furniture functionality is a very old subject. It dates back well over 3000 years in the Western and Middle Eastern societies, and well over 5000

Figure 1–1 Computer work station. (*Courtesy of HU Wall Systems by A/S Hundevad and Co., Denmark, with permission*)

years in Eastern cultures. However, since our main interest is in European cabinetmaking, we restrict our discussion to that part of the world.

Oddly enough, one function of cabinetmaking was brought about by taxation. At one time Europeans were taxed according to the number of rooms in their houses. In some locales this type of taxation still exists today. To save on taxes, landowners built houses with a few large rooms, and hired cabinetmakers to build schranks, chifforobes, and other cabinets for storage. In this way taxation brought about the need for functionality.

Other needs of the wealthy, which included the desire to display personal possessions and express personal tastes and individuality, also called for functionality. The secretary cabinet is a good example. For milady it was small, delicate, and richly ornate. For milord it was large and contained pockets and sometimes secret compartments.

Another functional requirement was satisfied by the sideboard or china closet (cabinet). Since European homes for many centuries had no built-in cabinets, free-standing cabinets were used to store and display dining room supplies such as silver, gold, pewter, china and crystal, and linens and silks. China closets are still in use today, but they are much smaller and are proportioned to fit in rooms with eight-foot ceilings. Scaling down some of these cabinets does not affect their functionality, but it does make them fit more attractively into the modern home.

Combining Functionality with Beauty

One of the most difficult and demanding aspects of building the European styled cabinet is combining functionality with beauty. Characteristics must be strictly followed to maintain the period style or designer's original intent. In some instances, downsizing must be designed in, which makes the task of proportioning a vital yet difficult one.

The builder must also choose woods whose grain is appropriate for each part being made. This means that a knowledge of wood must be used in the design. The wood used for planing, carving, and shaping may not be easy to work with, but these processes must be done correctly so that each piece adds to the whole in terms of functionality and beauty. A simple example is the matching of wood grain on side-by-side doors. Each door is an equal mass area and each needs to be similar or duplicate in grain to complement the other. They must be hinged properly to function as doors, and the grain must match to create visual balance and harmony.

Recognizing and Using Design Principles

Building materials are very expensive, but paper and pencils are not. Therefore, designing on paper is superior to repeated practice with expensive wood. Most cabinetmakers have a feel for design principles; they recognize them instantly and use them repeatedly. In Chapter 2 we look at a wide variety of design principles, so we shall save our study for there. But the principles are important. You must recognize how design affects the outcome of the project.

A suggestion that may prove useful is to visit to the local furniture showroom and see if you can recognize the design principles that went into each piece. Practice recognizing vertical and horizontal lines and mass. Observe Figure 1–1 again. Note that everything is rectangular, yet each part has symmetry.

Study the way pieces are joined together. These techniques are important. Even though you cannot tell if a joint is doweled or mortise-and-tenoned, you still can learn much. Are all parts flush? Are some recessed? If so, how much? Which way do grains run?

Notice the overall effect when the grain on the sides and top of a cabinet run in the same direction. Also notice the effect when a cabinet has some drawer fronts with the grain running horizontally and others with the grain running vertically. Notice how the sizes of drawers vary within a cabinet and from cabinet to cabinet.

Next notice how adornments are used for effect. Some are placed for style and others for function, such as door pulls. Some are add-ons, others are carved into the surfaces of pieces.

Using the Beauty of Wood To Bring Out the Art of Cabinetmaking

Every piece of cabinet wood has natural beauty, especially in the eyes of the cabinetmaker. Therefore, it is up to each of us to select those pieces that will create the built-in beauty.

Cabinet dimensions and character are altered by the selection of wood and its use. The most common example of this art form is the veneered dining room tabletop. Matched pieces of veneer are cut in radians (wedges) from the center outward. The work is always beautiful. The grain in each piece complements the other pieces. The result can never be duplicated exactly. Doors are another part of cabinetmaking in which wood is used to create dimensions and character—the grain pattern in veneer causes the appearance to be symmetrical, yet they never match exactly.

Wood grain ranges from stark and bold to soft and muted. Where great mass is desirable, the bold grains found in oak, ash, and some elms are used. Where mass is needed, but not necessarily for dimension, muted wood grains such as those found in birch and some mahoganies are used.

Cabinet pieces used for their grain must be cut on *flat grain patterns* as opposed to edge-cut and quarter-sawed, where the grains are parallel and close. The flat grains produce the more appealing patterns, which is why they are used most often.

Heartwood, sapwood, and crotch and burl woods produce different characteristics, each of them unique. Heartwoods are frequently dark in color. Sapwoods are lighter, with close grain patterns. Crotch and burl woods are almost indescribable in their uniqueness. Since most are relatively small sections of trees (seldom over three feet in length), they are usually reserved for fine veneers.

Knot-free and knotty woods also have special character. Most cabinetmaking work is done with knot-free wood. Sometimes furniture is styled to make use of knots, in which case woods with tight knots are selected. A tight knot is one free from decay between the knot and wood holding the knot.

These are a few examples of the ways that the beauty of wood can enhance the art of cabinetmaking. Another way is to use the natural color of the wood. We know that oak is white, red, and black; walnut is medium and dark but almost never light. Birch and ash are light woods; birch is the lighter of the two. Elm is more of a honey color and, of course, mahogany is brown-red to deep red.

The Power of Observation

What do you notice about the Bombé style chest shown in Figure 1–2? This hall chest was designed and made by Drexel as part of their Grand Villa collection. What can we observe?

1. The legs reach from the floor to under the top. They are carved, curved, and grooved to receive the side panels. They are probably doweled to the rails at the bottom, between the top and middle drawer and at the top under the cabinet top.

2. The lower side panels are curved veneer plywood. The upper side panels are flat.

3. The aprons on the sides and front generally follow the same curvature, but the front, which is longer, has a central surface enrichment of ribbon design.

4. Notice that the top has quite a few miters, along with a gentle outward curve. The complex design is probably made from hard wood. The center stock is probably made from lumber core, and the top is made from veneer or veneered plywood.

5. All three drawer front grains run horizontal, in contrast to those on the sides. The top drawer is grooved so much that its grain is almost overpowered. But the grain on the lower drawers is fully visible and bold.

6. Notice the ornate delicate hardware. Knobs are backed with a plate. Drawer pulls are the drop variety, and each lower drawer has its own lock.

7. The overall grain of the cabinet is bold; this creates a great deal of character.

8. Look carefully at the joint of the rails to the stiles (legs). Notice that they are flush. We should except this, since the carving in each leg mates with the carving in the aprons.

9. Hidden from view but always a feature of chests of this type are the dust covers between the drawers. These aid in cabinet stability and functionality by providing separation between drawers.

1.2 SKILLS AND KNOWLEDGE OF CONSTRUCTION TECHNIQUES NEEDED

Cabinetmakers must possess a variety of skills and a great deal of knowledge about construction techniques. These must be used over again and again, but technique is often modified ever so slightly according to the unique needs of the cabinet being made. In this section we discuss a variety of skills and techniques, beginning with *design training* and *drawing*.

Figure 1–2 Hall chest from "Grand Villa." (*Courtesy of Drexel Heritage Furnishings Inc., Drexel, North Carolina*)

Design Training and Drawing

When a cabinetmaker must meet a customer's or his or her own specialized needs, plans prepared by others are seldom appropriate. The need for sketches and full-scale plans for cabinets still exists, but they must be done by the cabinetmaker. Several alternatives are available to the cabinetmaker. He or she could enroll in a night class or self-study course in mechanical drawing first, then follow this training with a course in architectural drawing.

The mechanical drawing course should provide some of the following skills and knowledge. First, drawing lines and lettering are studied. Next, three views of each drawing are made: frontal, top, and cross-sectional. The lines and lettering are readily usable in drawing cabinet plans. The mechanical drawings are simplified examples of the more extensive cabinet front, side, and cross-sectional drawings. Mechanical drawing training also includes the technique of drawing hidden data using dashed lines. This technique is useful for cabinet drawings. Another technique called "scaling" is also learned in mechanical drawing classes. However, the scales are usually in decimal or metric measurements rather than fractional parts of inches or feet.

The architecture drawing class continues the training. Several significant techniques are directly transferable. First, all architectural drawings are made to a scale or set of scales. Some are shown in Figure 1–3. Some scales represent fractional parts of a foot: "$\frac{1}{4}$ in. = 1 ft." means one quarter of an inch on the drawing equals one foot of actual building length. Likewise, "$\frac{1}{2}$ in. = 1 ft." means each $\frac{1}{2}$ inch on the drawing equals one foot of building length or height, and so on. Notice that one scale shown, "$1\frac{1}{2}$ in. = 1 ft." represents an enlargement greater than actual size.

The use of architectural scales is basic to drawing cabinet plans. Since almost all cabinets are larger than their plans, scales are used in their drawing. Notice the example in Figure 1–4. The scale is included so that the cabinet-maker is able to use the drawing later during the building phase. Notice that the dimensions are provided so that the builder can merely read them and then use them for the actual layout. The numbers in each dimension (between arrows) are actual or true—numbers not scaled down or up. But notice that this scaled drawing shows us the relative distribution of shelves and base as well as thicknesses of shelves. We see that the proper proportions are planned well.

Enlarged, scaled drawings are useful in cabinet drawings, too. These frequently show the detail of moldings, and intersections of complicated or complex joints. On architectural plans these might be called "detail" drawings. This same term is used for cabinet drawings. The use of enlarged detail drawings on cabinet plans makes it easier to set up tools such as saws and routers to make precision cuts.

Figure 1–3 Architect scales.

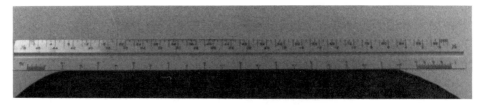

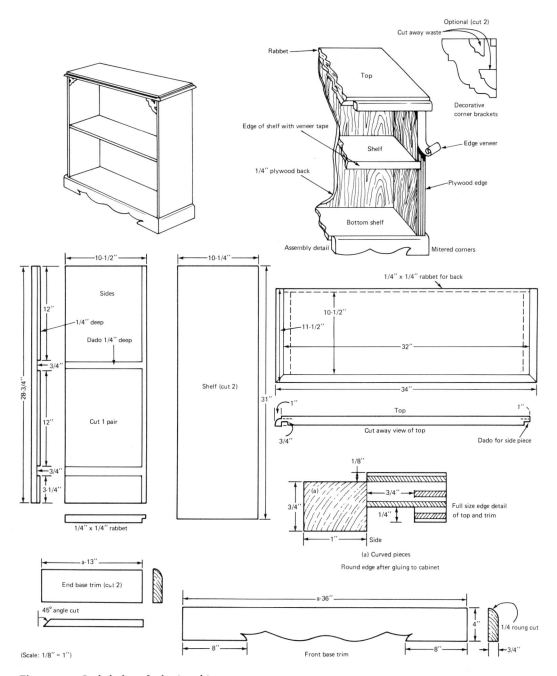

Figure 1–4 Scaled plan of a basic cabinet.

Optional (cut 2)

Cut away waste

Rabbet

Top

Decorative corner brackets

Edge of shelf with veneer tape

Shelf

Edge veneer

1/4'' plywood back

Plywood edge

Bottom shelf

Assembly detail

Mitered corners

10-1/2''

Sides

1/4'' deep

Dado 1/4'' deep

12''

3/4''

Cut 1 pair

12''

3/4''

3-1/4''

28-3/4''

1/4'' x 1/4'' rabbet

10-1/4''

Shelf (cut 2)

31''

1/4'' x 1/4'' rabbet for back

10-1/2''

11-1/2''

32''

34''

1''

Top

1''

3/4''

Cut away view of top

Dado for side piece

1/8''

(a)

3/4''

3/4''

1/4''

3/4''

Full size edge detail of top and trim

1''

Side

(a) Curved pieces

Round edge after gluing to cabinet

a-13''

End base trim (cut 2)

45° angle cut

a-36''

4''

1/4 roung cut

8''

Front base trim

8''

3/4''

(Scale: 1/8'' = 1'')

11

Another skill learned during architectural drafting classes is that of *developing specifications*. Specifications must be thought through and listed. They collectively set parameters which the builder must follow. In architectural drawings many specifications are call-outs from various building codes, types of windows, doors, appliances, and so on. The parallel to a cabinet drawing specification listing is similar in purpose but dissimilar in content. The contents list specifies the types of wood, glue, finishes, hardware, and adornments to be used.

Organizational Ability

The skills and knowledge gained from courses in drawing are invaluable in enabling the cabinetmaker to visualize each piece as it fits into the plan. This is a fundamental part of the organizational ability to plan the cabinet. As the drawing is made, decisions are made to provide specified functional uses of each part of the cabinet. Spacing of shelves, providing for drawer supports, allowing for a baseboard or base support, and adding design features are just a few of the elements that go into organizing the plan.

When European cabinets are planned, more organizational ability is needed. Many of these cabinets require special pieces for various purposes that must be prepared and assembled in certain sequence. Moldings and adornments and specialized joints also complicate the organization of the plan.

Organizational ability extends to shop activities. The work in the shop is much more rewarding if properly organized. An example of good organization is to do all ripping first, followed by crosscutting on a radial arm saw. Otherwise, the guides in machines must be reset repeatedly. Each time a saw guide is reset, the likelihood of making an exact duplicate piece becomes more remote, and time is lost.

Organizational ability also influences the efficiency of obtaining materials. If many trips to lumberyards, supply houses, paint stores and hardware stores are made, waste and poor organizational planning are evident. Proper planning should allow for a minimum number of trips to pick up supplies.

In summary, a cabinetmaker's ability must be broad based. Each part of building a cabinet, from design to finish, requires careful organization.

Adaptational Training

Adaptational training involves learning how to adapt old principles to new uses. There are only two methods to obtain adaptational training. One is the coach-pupil method. By observing the coach, the pupil understands each adaptation: a detail drawing, the new use of a joint, the new use of molding or trim, or even another way of gluing. Many adaptations are also useful in the finishing processes.

A second method is through self-development. This requires a great deal of study and experimentation, which can be quite time-consuming. An adaptation that is found through study must be tried before the skill is learned. The knowledge becomes enriched only through experience. From the experience gained through adapatation, further adaptations are easily learned.

The experimentation type of self-development is more subject to failure, but repeated tries can overcome poor planning and errors. In the shop, an adaptation should be made with scrap wood until it is done successfully at least once or twice.

Each technique of adaptation is appropriate to custom cabinetmaking. Ultimately, each adaptation must be applied to a cabinet in order to be fully understood.

Fundamentals of Joinery

Obviously, wood must be joined together to build a cabinet. But a decision-making process must be used in selecting the correct joint for the job. Success in this is proportional to one's knowledge of joint fundamentals.

This section of Chapter 1 will not illustrate the various joints. They are explained in Chapter 12. Any cabinetmaker who needs examples of joints to copy from should use those shown there.

The primary fundamental of joinery is to use a proven way to join two or more pieces of wood in a particular configuration. These include:

- butt joint
- dado joint
- miter joint
- rabbet joint
- mortise-and-tenon joint
- shiplap joint
- keyed shiplap joint
- dovetailed joint

A second fundamental of joinery is that the surfaces being joined must be parallel. A perfect joint is achieved when two surfaces to be joined are "closed" or match perfectly. In other words, no gaps are evident when contact is supposed to be made. It does not matter that the grain of each piece runs parallel, at right angles, or at other angles (see Figure 1–5).

A third fundamental of joinery is that the joined pieces' outer surfaces are level or "flush" with each other, which is difficult to achieve. Making a butt joint is the least difficult. As the surfaces are glued and clamped, they can be held in place with surface clamps. The more difficult joints are the miter,

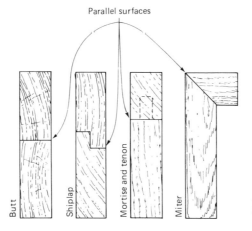

Figure 1–5 Joining surfaces must be parallel: (1) butt joint, (2) ship or mortise-and-tenon joint, (3) miter joint.

shiplap and mortise-and-tenon. If one miter is cut at 44.9 degrees and the other at 45.1 degrees, the joint will not fit correctly and is "mismatched," even though a 90-degree corner is made. The difficulty in mating outer surfaces in a shiplap joint is in making the rabbet in each piece exactly correct. If either is a hair too thick or thin, the joint is incorrect. The difficulty with the mortise-and-tenon joint is compounded by the variety of mistakes that can be made. First, the mortise can easily be offset from the exact center of the board. Next, the tenon can be cut off-center. This often occurs when a bandsaw is used instead of a radial arm or table saw.

A fourth fundamental of joinery is that the surfaces to be joined must be smooth. Glue is a bonding agent, not a gap filler like paste wood fillers. Glue forms a complete film that anchors both surfaces to each side of the glue. Where gaps or irregularities exist, no bonding takes place.

A fifth fundamental of joinery is to make practice cuts on scrap pieces of wood that have the same dimensions that the final pieces will have. This technique saves wood and enables the cabinetmaker to set each machine as finely as needed.

These are the most basic fundamentals of joinery. There are many other, less significant ones. Most of them entail the use of very sharp blades on saws and planes and sharp drills and bits, and making sure that all fences on machines are set exactly at 90 degrees or, in the case of miters, at the proper degree. Other fundamentals include principles of depth of cuts, depth of shoulders on cuts, depths of grooves and mortises, and so on.

Skill with Hand and Power Tools

The cabinetmaker needs skill with both hand and power tools. In the past, many cabinets were made entirely with hand tools. However, today using power tools makes the various jobs easier.

Some hand tools cannot be replaced by power tools, which is one reason for obtaining skill in their use. The hand wood chisel is one such tool. It must be used while cutting with the grain and across the grain. Turn it one way and it digs into the board; turn it over and it glides along the surface, much like the action of a block plane.

Block planes are indispensable. Rather than set up a router or joiner, a block plane is quick and easy to use to chamfer edges on smooth, small, or narrow surfaces.

The handsaw is another indispensable tool. Every cabinetmaker must learn to use this tool very accurately. A craftsman is able to cut a piece of wood along a line and leave the line on the usable piece. The angle through the wood cut must be 90 degrees, or another angle if a compound miter is made.

Power tools include hand-operated and bench-type. It takes considerable practice to become proficient in their use. Hand power tools are the more difficult to learn to use with skill. They require considerable hand and eye coordination. For example, the apparent ease of boring a hole in a board with a portable power drill is deceptive. One must develop an inner instinct to keep the drill bit precisely 90 degrees perpendicular to the surface and at the same time parallel to the outer edges of the board (see Figure 1–6).

Another hand power tool that appears very easy to use is a belt sander. One merely grasps the two handles and sands away. It's not quite that easy! The skill that must be learned is one of balance and pressure. A slight tilt of

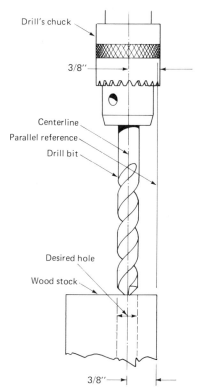

Drill's chuck

3/8''

Centerline

Parallel reference

Drill bit

Desired hole

Wood stock

3/8''

Figure 1–6 Hand drilling a hole with precision.

the sander creates a groove in the surface of the board being smoothed. Sanding the thin edge of a long board requires the same inner instinct of balance that one uses with the drill. A tiny tilt and the 90-degree relationship of surface to edge is gone. Unequal pressure causes deep and thin sanding. Imagine the need to sand a piece of veneered plywood with a belt sander. The veneer is only 1/20th of an inch thick. Feather-like sanding pressure is needed. Just a bit too much pressure and one will have sanded through the veneer. At $35 or more per sheet of 4 × 8 plywood, or at several dollars per square foot for veneer, this could be a costly mistake.

Another hand-held power tool almost every cabinetmaker feels he or she must have is a router. It looks simple, but actually it is quite difficult to use. There are so many variables that must be learned: first, depth adjustments are difficult to duplicate; second, balance of the machine is difficult; third, the bit, rotating at 25,000 RPMs, is unforgiving; fourth, the operator must thoroughly understand the grain pattern of the wood. Sometimes small cuts must be made over and over; other times a full cut can be made with one pass. Very long and deep slivers of wood can be torn free if the machine is used improperly. Routing the edge of a board with the router base requires balance and perception.

Probably the easiest hand-held power tools to use are the saws. Yet experience must be gained to follow a line and have it remain on the finished piece, and to hold the saw so that the cut is perpendicular to the surface at all times. Circular saws are heavy (6 lbs. or more) and awkward. Saber saws, although light, are difficult to use to make exact cuts, due to the freedom of the blade and variability of hand pressure while cutting.

Obviously, hand-held power tools are not as easy to use as it would appear. Their skillful use requires years of practice.

Bench power tools are easier to learn to use than hand-held ones. More references are fixed. More surfaces are calibrated, which makes setting them up and using them easier. For example, the angle of the blade on a table saw can be verified easily with a square or protractor, due to the fixed position of the table top. Once the exactness is carefully set, no further adjustments need to be made for some time. One soon learns the range of reliability of each bench machine.

The most significant skill a cabinetmaker needs to develop when using portable or bench machines is a sensitivity to 90-degree and 45-degree angles. Once achieved, this skill is invaluable. The sighting of a board or the positioning of a fence or hand-held tool are done instinctively by the experienced woodworker.

Knowledge of Layout

The more a cabinetmaker understands the principles of layout, the more efficient he or she is in every aspect of the construction and finishing phases. A simple definition of layout is "a method of planning or actually performing the act of planning for efficient use of materials."

We could say that once the design phase of a cabinet is complete, a material layout can be made. This concept is accurate to a degree. Let's explain. Furniture manufacturers have design sections and layout sections, plus a mill with very large machines capable of cutting any size piece of cabinet needed. Therefore, a worker in the layout section will use design drawings to make a model piece. The model piece is then used in the mill to set each machine to cut hundreds of pieces according to a scaled detail drawing which was obtained from the design shop. In this example, the design phase can be done completely before the layout begins.

For most cabinetmakers, entrepreneurs, hobbyists and others, the design stage includes layout considerations. This is due primarily to the varied availability of materials. Lumber, which we shall learn more about in a later chapter, is available in limited thicknesses, widths, and lengths. Plywood is also limited in size and thickness. Therefore, these constraints must be accounted for in the design phase.

Once the ideas are on paper and the design is finished, a paper-and-pencil layout should be made. Each side, bottom, top, and shelf of a cabinet must be laid out on a rectangular sketch of about 4 × 8 inches as shown in Figure 1–7. Notice that this layout technique shows how many pieces of a cabinet we are able to get from one sheet of plywood. It also shows the waste. It also permits us to arrange the pieces so that the grain will run properly on the actual piece cut from the sheet. A plywood layout such as that shown in the figure also permits us to determine clearly and accurately how many sheets will be needed for the entire project.

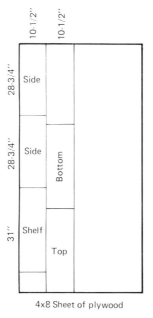

Figure 1–7   Hand sketch of plywood layout.

4x8 Sheet of plywood

Lumber should also be laid out carefully with paper and pencil to determine the most economical size of boards to buy. For example, when 12 facing trim pieces measuring $1\frac{7}{8} \times 28 \times \frac{3}{4}$ inches are needed, the rough-cut width must be $2\frac{1}{8}$ inches, or not less than 2 inches if a medium-set combination or ripsaw blade is used. The extra width is, or course, needed to dress both edges. So now we know the width per piece. The length is 28 inches finished, so we can round off the length to 30 inches. This helps determine the length of board needed. Consider the alternatives:

1. 2 lengths @ 30 in. = 5 ft.	Lumber is seldom sold in 5-foot lengths. A 6-foot board results in one foot of waste.
2. 3 lengths @ 30 in. = $7\frac{1}{2}$ ft.	Lumber is sold in 8-foot lengths. An 8-foot board results in $\frac{1}{2}$ foot waste.
3. 4 lengths @ 30 in. = 10 ft.	Lumber is sold in 10-foot lengths. This results in no waste.
4. 5 lengths @ 30 in. = $12\frac{1}{2}$ ft.	Boards are sold in 12-foot lengths (*too short*), and 14-foot lengths. This results in 18 inches waste per board.

Our best length is, of course, 10 feet. Next we determine the best width. Since one strip of lumber 10 feet long produces four 28-inch pieces, and we need twelve for the job, we will need 3 strips $2\frac{1}{8}$ inches wide. So:

$$3 \times 2\frac{1}{8} \text{ inches } = 6\frac{3}{8} \text{ inches.}$$

But do not forget that the board must be ripped at least twice to obtain 3 strips $2\frac{1}{8}$ inches wide. Each saw cut is $\frac{1}{8}$ inch wide. Therefore our total width is:

$6\frac{3}{8}$ in.	for three strips @ $2\frac{1}{8}$ in. each
+ $\frac{1}{4}$ in.	for two saw cuts
$6\frac{5}{8}$ in.	for a total width

Now we know the width. But boards are not sold $6\frac{5}{8}$ inches wide. Hardwood is sold in random widths, usually rounded to the nearest inch of width. In our example, we would plan to buy a 7 in. $\times$ 10 ft. $\times$ $\frac{3}{4}$ in. board.

You can see that paper-and-pencil layout is very important. It translates to error-free work and maximum use of materials. It is also useful for estimating costs. To most of us, money is an object of serious concern, and we should control expenses wherever we can. Skill in layout will help us achieve this.

Layout is also important during the cutout phase. It is during this time that plans made on paper are put into practice. With paper sketches of our layout in hand, several cutout techniques are used.

The first very important technique is to set up a saw only once, if possible, for all the pieces needed for the project. Let's provide an example. A Danish-styled wall cabinet has sides, tops, and vertical dividers $11\frac{7}{8}$ in. deep and shelves $11\frac{1}{2}$ in. deep. When the table saw is set for $11\frac{7}{8}$ in., all the sides, tops, and vertical dividers should be cut at one time. This single saw setup ensures that every piece will be exactly the same width. Next we would set up the saw for $11\frac{1}{2}$ inches and cut each shelf and bottom piece. Hence, with just two setups all pieces are cut for width.

Next we need to plan the layout for all crosscuts. Crosscuts are made most efficiently on a radial arm saw, but they also can be made on the table saw, with a portable power saw, or even by hand, although that would be unlikely. A technique to follow when making crosscut pieces is to begin by making the longest ones first. By combining the techniques of making as few adjustments as possible to fences or stops and cutting longest pieces first, we obtain great efficiency.

These layout and cutting techniques apply equally to sizing stock lumber, since the fewer the setups of machines, the better the overall accuracy of trim, facings, panels, rails and stiles.

As we shall see later, sideboards and many other European cabinets were large and were made without the use of plywood. The stile, rail, and panel assembly was used to make the backs and sides, and frequently the front doors. Since wide boards tend to split, many cabinetmakers used several narrow pieces. If you build a European cabinet using the stile, rail, and panel technique, you will require many pieces. Therefore, it is extremely important to cut sufficient pieces to allow for some mistakes. In the long run, it will save time at a very nominal cost.

The layout for cutting stock lumber for the type of cabinet just described may require the use of crosscuts first, followed by ripsaw requirements. If this is done, the crosscut pieces should be rough-cut slightly longer than needed and trimmed to exactness once their width is determined. This technique is not always necessary, especially when design drawings are made to the finest detail. Frequently adjustments must be made when the panel pieces are ready to trim to final size and squareness or assemble. If the pieces are a little long, they can be trimmed to exactness with one or two additional saw setups, but they can never be made longer!

Laying out irregular shapes requires considerable skill. Cabinet tops that are oval, hexagonal, or octagonal must be done with exactness to avoid costly errors. If possible, a template should be made from inexpensive $\frac{1}{8}$-inch hardboard. The framing square should be used, along with string, dividers, and the bevel square. These tools aid in layout in different ways. First, the more expensive framing square has tables stamped into it for various irregular, geometric shapes. Dividers are essential when using the square and making hexagonal and octagonal tops. The bevel square is also useful when making these angles. String is useful in making an oval.

Once the pattern is made to exacting detail, machine setups should be made. Always maintain a reference line; that is, ensure that after the cut has been made on a side or around the oval, *the pencil line is visible throughout the cut line.* Only when this is correct can you be assured of the accuracy of your work.

Irregular shapes may include beveled pieces such as 45-degree angles and raised-panel beveled edges. In these instances, scrap wood must be used to set up the saws accurately and then the finished pieces can be run through. The layout must be accurate.

Layout carried over from the design to the shop may also include dadoes, mortise-and-tenon and shiplap joints, or rabbets. The rules for using a single setup apply here as strongly as before. All dadoes of the same width and depth should be made at one cutting. If some require different widths or depths, they should be done systematically. Let's examine these concepts a bit more fully. Suppose the sides and dividers in the wall unit we read about earlier had fixed shelves at 24 inches, 36 inches, and 48 inches. How many fence or stop setups would be needed to make all the cuts? Since each board requires three dadoes, the answer is three. If six or nine pieces needed to be cut, only three setups would be needed. Once the first setting of 24 inches is made, *every* piece is dadoed for the 24-inch shelf. Then the stop is moved to the 36-inch position and all pieces are dadoed. Finally the 48-inch dado is set and all pieces are cut.

Tenons are treated the same way as dadoes. Use as few setups as possible to make each tenon. Make at least one extra piece of rail with tenons on it. Mortises are ready to make with a mortise rig on a bench drill press. Again, lay out the mortise on scrap wood of the same size as the finished stile, and in some cases, rail. Once the machine is set up, make all the cuts at one time.

Miters should be laid out and made with two setups. First, the pieces to be mitered should be rough-cut for length, with one end mitered. Then the fence and machine should be reset for the exact length and the opposite miter. When pieces are required to be various lengths, as in rectangles, the fence will need to be adjusted several times, but the saw should not.

Economy of Materials

Throughout our discussions, we have directly or indirectly considered *economy of materials.* This important aspect of cabinetmaking should never be taken lightly. For most cabinetmakers, the problem is twofold: money to purchase materials is a limited resource, and so are woods, veneer, and other building materials.

Before we discuss techniques that enable us to use materials economically, let us consider the factors that contribute to expense:

- Hardwood prices range from $1.80 to more than $5.00 per board foot.
- Softwood prices range from $1.20 to more than $6.00/per board foot.
- Standard 1-inch boards are cheaper per board foot than 2-inch lumber.
- Standard 3-inch and thicker boards are more than twice the average board-foot price of 1- or 2-inch lumber.
- Veneer prices vary according to both the availability of the type or species and the cost of obtaining the material.
- Veneer prices also vary according to the type of match patterns needed for the project. Size and dimensions such as width, length, and thickness each contribute to cost.
- Trim materials such as edge moldings, plant-ons, and carved scrolls can cost more than $3.00 per linear foot or individual piece.
- Hardware prices range widely.
- Support materials such as abrasive paper, glue, and screws vary considerably in costs.
- Finishing materials such as stains, fillers, lacquers, polishing compounds and others vary considerably in costs.

The following two techniques or methods of economical use of materials are appropriate for cabinetmaking.

Positive Control

Positive control of cost of materials can be defined as the technique used by a cabinetmaker from the conception of a cabinet through its final completion to avoid unnecessary expenses related in some way to costs or uses of materials. Let's be sure we understand this concept of positive control, which involves not only the actual use and costs of materials, but all indirect uses and costs attributable to materials.

Recall from our earlier discussions that a cabinet should be designed to use materials readily available, and that the various pieces should be cut from stocks that result in minimal waste. The technique of positive control, therefore, begins with the design phase.

Positive control continues through the layout phase. Recall the discussions concerning paper-and-pencil layouts and model and pattern layouts. Each of these practical applications avoids the cost of miscutting boards, plywood, or other parts of cabinets. Recall also that in most situations that involve making facings and trim, the best advice is to allow for some waste.

Positive control in the use of moldings is another area of serious concern. As already indicated, trim moldings and plant-ons are expensive; their proper use is important. European styled furniture and cabinets, with the exception of Danish modern, make extensive use of these materials. Therefore, positive control requires using the appropriate style and size molding, trim, or plant-ons. A study of the furniture examples provided in chapters that follow may help the cabinetmaker control the uses of these materials.

Positive control of materials also includes selective use of finishing materials. The proper selection of stains, fillers, and top finishes is critical. This control is considered from a different viewpoint. Whereas wood should not be wasted, finishing materials must be controlled to create the proper final surface color and protective coating. Lack of control not only wastes the stain, filler, and lacquer, but could ruin the entire cabinet.

Along with proper staining, appropriate sanding must be done. Sometimes partially sealing the grain with shellac or sizing is required to inhibit deep staining. Rough sandpaper (100 grit) roughs the surface of wood to allow deeper penetration; conversely, extra fine sandpaper (220 grit) almost polishes the wood surface, which restricts stain penetration.

Control of top finishings, whether lacquer, varnish, or plastic, is essential for a quality finish. The improper control of plastic-type wood filler can be disastrous to the finish of a cabinet, since it fills the wood pores completely and the surface is impervious to stain penetration. Lacquer must be thinned to allow for proper evaporation of its thinners and to preclude the "orange-peel" effect. Varnish must be applied in thin coats to avoid the uneven build-up of air pockets and picking up impurities. Plastic finishes must be pure to avoid air pockets and impurities that destroy the penetrating quality of the sheen.

Positive control of materials involves indirect uses and costs as well. Every experienced cabinetmaker knows that each trip to a supply house, lumberyard, or paint store costs money. Therefore, as few trips as possible should be taken. This ties in directly with properly estimating materials and allowing for waste. Continuously setting up machines wastes time and utilities. Improper storage of materials creates waste. The use of dull or fractured tools wastes materials due to splits, splintering, non-true cuts, ragged holes, and so on.

Avoiding False Economy

Still speaking within the framework of materials, we need to understand something about false economy, which can affect the use of materials and both direct and indirect costs. This subject always involves trade-offs. Some of these include whether or not to:

1. Allow for waste at 5 to 10 percent.
2. Allow for a miss-cut of trim or molding.
3. Preplan for purchase of all materials during one trip.

4. Preplan for support materials.
5. Prepare a model of custom-made moldings.
6. Prepare a model of a complex joint.
7. Stain a scrap piece of cabinet material.
8. Premix enough stain to allow for restaining if necessary.

The list could be extended further, but we can see that false economy can be costly. As you may have interpreted from the list, there is some direct cost associated with each decision, such as buying a little more lumber and finishing materials or molding. On the other hand, choosing not to do so and making a mistake or having a piece of the cabinet marred by hand or machine means added indirect costs. More shop time and machine use are needed. Hours of direct labor increase. Transportation costs increase because more trips to suppliers are needed.

We see from this discussion that economy of materials is a serious subject. Each cabinetmaker must take every precaution to avoid waste and misuse of limited resources.

Knowledge of Assembly

Once again we go back to the design phase to understand another aspect of cabinetmaking. To assemble a cabinet, table, chair, or other type of furniture, we must perceive how the pieces will ultimately fit. Unlike the production line shown in Figure 1–8, we are model makers when we build a one-of-a-kind cabinet.

The shop cabinetmakers take each piece provided from the model shop and duplicate it many times. We, on the other hand, cut only those pieces necessary, and to do this we must understand how they are assembled.

As a general rule, the basic cabinet is assembled first. The sides, shelves, and bottom are joined. The back may be fit, but is usually not installed until later to allow for other tasks to be done more easily. Next, the cabinet facings and trim are applied, but in some situations the base is built first. Moldings are added if planned. It is possible at this point to assemble and install drawers and doors. Then hardware can be installed.

The description you have just read may be an oversimplification of the actual assembly process. There will be many intermediate steps before a major assembly can be connected to another part. For example, early European cabinets were made from solid sawed lumber, not plywood. The panel-and-frame construction technique was used extensively for sides, back, and dust covers. Once the stiles and rails were properly mortised-and-tenoned and grooved for the panels, they were assembled section by section. In other designs, corners were glued (assembled) first. Usually, boards had to be cut to widths that limited cupping and warping. Then they were glued to make wide planks for tops of tables, cabinets, and similar pieces. More often than not, cabinet bases were

Figure 1–8 Production line in a cabinet factory. (*Courtesy of Karel Mintjens n.v., Belgium*)

assembled from parts that, when united, made a subassembly. The same was true of cabinet crowns.

Another aspect of assembly carried forward from the design stage is the cutout phase. Models made of pieces to be joined provide understanding of assembly. During this period, prefitting of pieces leads to decisions which affect assembly.

A critical decision that affects assembly is whether to make cuts, grooves, decorative scalloping, and the like in separate pieces before major assemblies are joined. This is because smaller, partial assemblies are easier to handle when working with the machines. Adding these characteristics to smaller assemblies reduces the costs incurred should an error be made in cutting.

Finally, limited availability of clamps or other such constraints may affect the assembly process. Although clamps are expensive, most shops are equipped with several bar clamps, several wood clamps, and a variety of C-clamps. Another problem that I have experienced on numerous occasions is that the overall dimensions of a cabinet are greater than the door openings through which it will be removed. Needless to say, major decisions must be made when this is the case. Sometimes, built-ins must be constructed in sections, delivered to the place of installation, and assembled.

Assembly planning is important in order to anticipate and avoid problems.

Knowledge and Skill in Finishing

Knowledge and skill in finishing a cabinet are as vital as any other parts of cabinetmaking. This is never more obvious than when stain goes on unevenly, or lacquer turns white, or varnish runs. Hours and hours of construction can be wasted. Those of us who experience failure can study and learn how to correct or camouflage our mistakes and make the final job beautiful.

Chapters 14 and 15 deal specifically with finishing cabinets. For now, though, we need to understand the knowledge and skills that must be learned.

The most important areas for knowledge and skill in finishing are *control* and *characteristics of the materials to be finished and the finishing materials.* Control can be studied, as you are doing now and when you read manufacturers' directions. For example, stain penetrates end-grain wood more deeply than surface wood, and since sometimes end wood shows and must be stained, control is needed to ensure uniform coloring. How does one control the penetration? One effective way is to partially fill the end wood with a shellac wash. Shellac thinned with denatured alcohol is applied to the end wood *only.* It sinks in and dries quickly as it partially fills each of the wood cells. Once dry, the wood is rough because the thinners make the wood fibers stand up. Sandpaper not only smooths the surface but also rubs away the surface shellac. Then when stain is applied, it only penetrates where the wood is not sealed with shellac. The trick is this: Too little shellac means poor control and darkly stained wood; too much shellac means no control, since stain will not penetrate.

Similarly, the control in sanding wood surfaces determines the coloring. Sanding with 120-grit sandpaper allows deeper penetration and darker coloring. Sanding with 240-grit sandpaper almost polishes the wood surface, thus restricting stain's penetration so that light coloring takes place.

Water can also be used to control the color of wood. Spill a drop of water on a scrap piece of wood and then stain it. You will see a deeper penetration and darker color at the water spot. Why? Because the water caused the wood fibers to enlarge and stand up, so they absorb more stain.

As you have just read, control can be studied, but almost never without considering both the character of the finishing material and character of the wood to be finished. Since European cabinets are made largely from oak, ash, elm, walnut, and mahogany and veneers that include oak, teak, mahogany, and some birch, the characteristics of these materials must be studied to understand finishing. Table 1–1 explains how the characteristic of the wood affects the finishing process.

TABLE 1–1 COMPARISON OF WOOD CHARACTERISTICS
WITH FINISHING TECHNIQUES

Wood	Stain penetration	Filler/ Sealers	Wash	Top finish
Oak	deep	usually	yes	hard
Ash	medium	sometimes	no	hard
Elm	medium	sometimes	sometimes	hard/hand rub
Walnut	light	no	no	hand rub
Mahogany	medium	yes	seldom	hard/hand rub
Teak	light	sometimes	no	hand rub/hard

Now let's shift our attention to the harder finishing materials, which include lacquer, varnish, and plastic (polyurethane), and softer finishes, which are oil rub and lacquer/oil rub mixtures.

The hard finishes require knowledge and skill related to their desired consistency for application, thickness of application that permits thinners to evaporate, preparation before application and between coats, and final buffing techniques. The softer finishes require considerably more hand work, since most involve the use of handrub oils or a mixture of oils and 5 to 10 percent lacquer. These require seven to twelve applications to create the desired appearance.

Knowledge and skills also are needed to select a finish durable enough to withstand abuse. Though handrub cabinets are great for bedrooms, they would never withstand use in a den, office, or other high-activity room. The cabinets in high-activity areas must withstand abrasive objects sliding across the surface of shelves and tops. Sometimes, alcoholic drinks, hot coffee cups, or just plain water in a glass are placed on surfaces, and the finish must withstand these as well. Table 1–2 shows some relationships.

TABLE 1–2   COMPARISON OF FINISH TO TYPE OF ABUSE/SUBSTANCE

Finish	Quiet room	Active room	Abrasive materials	Liquids
Oil rub	good	poor	scratches	stains
Lacquer	good	good	some scratches	stains (white)
Shellac	poor	poor	scratches	stains
Varnish	fair	good	scratches	fair
Plastic (polyurethane)	fair	very good	few scratches	very good

Both temperature and humidity play a significant role in understanding the finish material and finishing techniques. Finishing materials are available to meet most temperature and drying conditions. Dryers or retarders can be added that combat humidity, for example. Each cabinetmaker must understand how the climate alters the characteristics of finishing materials and take steps to make sure that they are properly prepared for use.

Our final subject in this area concerns application concepts and techniques. As already mentioned, many thin coats of top dressing are preferred to few coats. With polyurethane finishes, however, two are usually enough. Equally important are the tools used to apply the materials. Some must be sprayed, others must be applied by hand, and on some occasions fine brushes may be used. Manufacturers' recommendations should always be followed. I personally believe all hard finishes should be sprayed.

REVIEW EXERCISES

1. Cabinet and furniture functionality dates back well over 3000 years in the Western and Middle Eastern societies. (T/F)
2. One of the most difficult and demanding aspects of building the European styled cabinet is combining functionality with beauty. (T/F)
3. Designing on paper is wrong; repeated practice with woods is better. (T/F)
4. Heartwoods are frequently light in color. (T/F)
5. A cabinet drawing specification listing is similar in purpose but dissimilar in content to a house specification. (T/F)
6. Organizational ability extends to shop activities. (T/F)
7. Where great mass is desirable, the bold grains found in _____ are used:
    a. maple, fir, pine
    b. oak, ash, some elms
    c. maple, oak, redwood
8. Making which joint is the least difficult?
    a. butt joint
    b. dado joint
    c. rabbet joint
9. Cross cuts are made most easily and most accurately with a:
    a. portable power saw.
    b. table saw.
    c. radial arm saw.

ESSAY

10. In a short paragraph of 30 to 40 words, show some knowledge of layout.

ANSWERS

1T, 2T, 3F, 4F, 5T, 6T, 7b, 8a, 9c.

2

European Styled Cabinets and Principles of Their Construction

In this chapter we explain how the principles of making European styled cabinets create their uniqueness and symmetry. This study is not a new subject; rather, it is so old that the ideas can be found in practice and in writings several hundred years old. The principles we examine are extremely evident in Renaissance through modern furnishings. Other authors have labelled these principles as design features, cabinetmaking principles, guides to better cabinetmaking, guides to better cabinet design, or just plain rules. Even though they have been stated often, it is important that we state them again here for cabinetmakers such as yourself who intend to venture into creating European styled cabinets. To make the study as interesting as possible, we provide samples of European furniture and cabinets that incorporate the principles.

Objectives

1. To understand how to apply the principles of mass.
2. To learn to deal with stress and force.
3. To use line and curve principles.
4. To understand how unlike materials work together.
5. To learn to use decorating principles to maintain style and period.

2.1 USING THE PRINCIPLES OF MASS
IN DESIGN OF FURNITURE AND CABINETS

One of the key principles applied by European cabinetmakers was their use of *mass*. This principle is fundamental in the design of all cabinets, and modern-day cabinetmakers must emulate earlier craftsmen if we hope to incorporate their concepts into our own work.

Let's briefly begin with the principle of *dominant line* in mass, and later return to this principle in more depth. The server shown in Figure 2–1, from the Drexel "Tryon Manor" collection, illustrates by its design both vertical and horizontal dominant lines. A dominant line in a mass should lead the viewer's eye in a vertical direction in a vertical mass and horizontally in a horizontal mass. Let's apply this principle. In the figure, the dominant line in each of the three vertical panels is up and down. In contrast, the base section and drawer have horizontal dominant lines.

Another principle of mass also used in the server design is *major mass*. The cabinet is designed with three mass units. The base is the first, the center section consisting of three vertical panels is the second, and the drawer and top is the third. The *major mass* is the middle section. Notice that the end of the cabinet carries the same theme of major mass as the front.

Figure 2–1 Server from "Tryon Manor." (*Courtesy of Drexel Heritage Furnishings Inc., Drexel, North Carolina*)

The two other sections of the cabinet are *minor masses* because the major mass assumes such a large percentage of the vertical height and dominates. The base is one minor mass, and the drawer and top assembly are the other minor mass.

The three sections constitute a *primary mass*. Primary masses should always be composed of major and minor masses. Subdivisions can be included within each mass. Look again at Figure 2–1 and:

1. Appreciate that the principle of primary mass is used as three vertical masses consisting of a major and two minor ones.
2. Observe that the major mass can be subdivided into three minor masses of equal dimensions.
3. Observe that when the principle of primary mass is used vertically the masses or sections are all different dimensions. The base is the smallest, the center is the largest, and the drawer and top are between the two.
4. Observe that when the principle of primary mass is used vertically the larger mass (major) is always sandwiched between the others.

Figure 2–2, a china cabinet by Drexel, also from its "Tryon Manor" collection, is another example of a vertical primary mass. However, another principle is used in this design. There are two major masses, the solid lower unit and the glazed upper one. When a primary mass is vertically subdivided into two major masses, one must be taller or larger than the other. It makes no difference where the larger one is placed. In the case of the china cabinet, convention dating back several hundred years places the larger mass on top.

Let's explore the use of dominant line and subdivision. Beginning with the upper mass, it has three dominant lines: two sidelight panels and the glass framed door. We should consider these as mass sections. The center mass is most dominant and is therefore considered a major mass within a major mass. The sidelight panels, which are narrower and less dominant, are minor masses within the larger mass. The dominant line is vertical. The three sections with their vertical dominance demonstrate the principle of subdividing a major mass into three parts with one wider than the other two. The rule is: place the wider section between the two narrower ones.

Although the lower mass (section) is made entirely of wood, it follows the same subdividing rules as does the upper one. Within the subdivisions there is a major mass in the center consisting of three drawers, each of which is a minor mass with a horizontal dominant line, and two doors on either side, each of which is a minor mass.

In review, the china shown in Figure 2–2 shows us how

1. The principle of two major masses in a vertical arrangement has one larger than the other.

Figure 2–2   China from "Tryon Manor." (*Courtesy of Drexel Heritage Furnishings Inc., Drexel, North Carolina*)

2. The masses are subdivided employing unequal sizes with the largest one centered between the other two.

3. The drawers create further subdivisions with a change in dominant line direction.

A variation of the two vertical masses in the primary vertical mass is shown in Figure 2–3, a chest by Drexel from its "Tryon Manor" collection. The upper mass is equally divided into three vertically dominant minor masses. But here is an adaptation: the drawers in the lower mass are horizontally dominant. This is a rule that is used frequently with European styled cabinets.

Figure 2–3 Chest from "Tryon Manor." (*Courtesy of Drexel Heritage Furnishings Inc., Drexel, North Carolina*)

The Thomas Chippendale Chinese styled low chest in Figure 2–4 is by Drexel from its "Vintage" collection. What principles can we apply to this piece? Closely observe the vertical dimensions of the various drawers. The principle of designing chests and similar structures is that when drawer heights are different, the largest one must be on the bottom. Each drawer above must be smaller, and the top one smallest of all.

Another example of this principle is shown in Figure 2–5, the lowboy in Queen Anne style fashioned by Drexel from its "Vintage" collection. The height of the lower drawers is significantly greater than that of the upper drawer. In addition, the design makes use of the principle discussed earlier. Notice the division of mass. The three lower drawers are equal in horizontal width, but which is dominant? The center one, because of its shell carving.

Let's continue with more principles employing vertical primary masses. Figure 2–6 is a secretary from Drexel's "Vintage" group. The principle we examine here is one that involves vertical divisions. When a primary vertical mass is to be divided into more than three pieces, the major masses should be unequal in size. Further, each major mass should be subdivided with its own individuality. The secretary fits this principle well. There are three major masses and two minor ones. Each is different in size, which demonstrates one part of

Figure 2–4 Low chest from "Vintage Cherry." (*Courtesy of Drexel Heritage Furnishings Inc., Drexel, North Carolina*)

Figure 2–5 Lowboy from "Vintage Cherry." (*Courtesy of Drexel Heritage Furnishings Inc., Drexel, North Carolina*)

Figure 2–6 Secretary from "Vintage Cherry." (*Courtesy of Drexel Heritage Furnishings Inc., Drexel, North Carolina*)

the principle. Each mass is individualized, thereby meeting the other part of the principle.

The lower mass consists of three drawers. Except for the hardware, the drawer fronts are veneered and contain no adornments. The second major mass is the desk section, with its drop-leaf desk top, compartments, and small drawers. This second mass section is totally individual compared to the drawer section. The third major mass is the glass door bookcase with two subdivisions, each one a door. Here the style includes not only curves but different materials as well. The dominant minor mass is, of course, the split pediment with curved rosettes and turned center finial. The other minor mass is the base unit. The secretary applies all parts of the principle where more than three vertical masses are used.

Thus far in the study of mass and principles of cabinetmaking, we have been concerned with vertically designed cabinets. Now we shall identify some principles used in horizontally designed cabinets.

Figure 2–7, a sideboard styled and crafted by Hundevad & Co., of Denmark, provides us with an example of a horizontal mass that is divided into three parts. Since there are a major center mass and two minor masses, the rule used here is this: Place the major horizontal mass between the two minor ones. The leg assemblies on this Danish modern sideboard define the limits of the center major mass. The lower part of the sideboard is, of course, styled with a dominant vertical veneer. The upper open-shelf design also employs the same horizontal mass arrangement as the lower section.

Now let's apply a principle when a horizontal styled cabinet is divided into more than three sections or masses. Figure 2–8, a buffet by Drexel from its "Grand Palais" collection, shows such a cabinet. This example illustrates the technique of giving equal importance to each of the four doors (sections).

Figure 2–7   HU sideboard. (*Courtesy of Hundevad & Co., Ulfborg, Denmark*)

Figure 2–8 Buffet from "Grand Palais." (*Courtesy of Drexel Heritage Furnishings Inc., Drexel, North Carolina*)

Also notice that the earlier rule of dividing horizontal sections in three is applied in this cabinet—in the drawer sections, the middle one is major and the outer ones are minor. In the lower section there are no minor sections. Several variations of this principle are possible:

1. Two center masses can be major and thus are dominant; the outer ones thus are minor.
2. Two outer sections may be major, thus making the inner ones minor.
3. In a five-section cabinet, all sections may be equal, or one may be dominant and the rest of equal importance.

The sewing desk shown in Figure 2–9 from the private collection by Maguire illustrates the principle of horizontal mass where one area is larger than the other, yet there is balance and harmony. The drawers make up one mass and the seating mass section makes up the other one. This design is commonly used with desks and computer work stations.

There are many principles involved with mass. We have examined most of them. But let's close this section by adding one more principle closely associated with mass. It's called *proportion*. You are familiar with the standard dimensions of picture frames. They range from 3 × 5″, 5 × 7″ and up. If we evaluate these proportions, they generally fall within the "golden mean rectangle" shown in Figure 2–10. This rectangle has proportions approximating 1:1.618.

Figure 2–9   Sewing desk by Maguire.

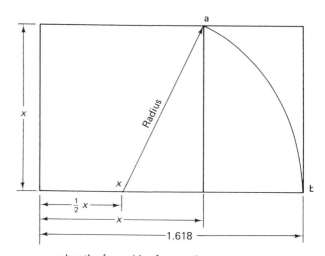

Figure 2–10   Golden mean rectangle.

x = length of one side of rectangle
1.618 = length of adjacent side of rectangle times x
Ratio of sides is 1:1.618

The illustration is simple to construct and employ. Let's say that you need a credenza for the entrance hall. You want it to be a horizontal primary mass and about 36 to 38 inches high. How long should it be?

- With a height of 36 inches, it should be $58\frac{1}{4}$ inches long:
  $36 \times 1.618 = 58.25$ inches.
- With a height of 38 inches, it should be $61\frac{1}{2}$ inches long:
  $38 \times 1.618 = 61.48$ inches.

These dimensions may not be exactly what you need; there may be some restriction. Slight variations are permitted. However, if you deviate drastically from these proportions, rectangles take on an odd look.

The golden mean rectangle proportions may be used horizontally or vertically as primary masses. They may be used, in combination, all vertically, all horizontally, or one vertically and one horizontally. Figure 2–6 shows the use of one horizontal and one vertical primary mass.

This concludes the study. If you make it a special project to gain practical experience with mass, a long visit to the local furniture showroom should prove helpful.

2.2 DEALING WITH STRESS AND FORCE IN DESIGN OF FURNITURE AND CABINETS

Stress and force are properties that must be reckoned with both while building and when using cabinets once built. These properties are especially important with European styled furniture and cabinets since reproductions of antique styles are made without the use of plywood. However, even those made with modern styling features and materials still have problems with stress and force.

Experienced cabinetmakers are familiar with stress and force from two points of view, internal and external. The internal types are *compression and tension*. The external types are *stress and pull* and *push force*. Let's first deal with compression and tension.

In every board, compression or tension is present in varying amounts, from extremely slight to very powerful. Figure 2–11 illustrates these properties from two views.

Every board cut in the plane-cut method will have the tendency to cup, warp, or deform into unusual shapes during the drying process. As a rule, compression occurs in softwood and tension occurs in hardwood.[1] Both compression wood cells and tension wood cells are thicker and harder than normal. Therefore, they respectively exert greater force on adjacent normal cells. In both cases, shrinking along the grain is greater for compression cells in soft-

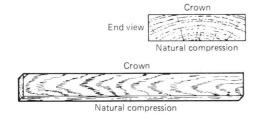

Figure 2–11 Tension and compression in wood.

---

[1]*Classroom Demonstrations of Wood Properties*, US Department of Agriculture, Forest Service, PA-900 (Washington, DC, April, 1969), p17

wood and in tension cells in hardwoods than in normal cells. In hardwood especially, when the wood is machined the fibers in tension tend to pull out, resulting in a fuzzy surface.[2]

Figure 2–11 shows several problems that we must be concerned with. Boards which have been dried and display characteristics of compression or tension must be planed or cut to eliminate those characteristics. As they are cut, some added reaction can and often does occur. The boards may warp or bow due to the disturbance caused by the cutting action. This most often happens when ripping the board into narrower pieces. From my experience, it's best to have this happen before the cabinet is made than to watch a split start in a finished piece.

The third illustration in Figure 2–11 shows a technique that identifies when and sometimes where compression or tension exists in a board. Where support from the use of a board is desirable, the edge surface with the crown should be placed upward. If force or dead weight is placed on the edge, the board will straighten.

So what? Let's see! Except for oak, which is usually *quarter-sawed*, all other cabinet woods are plain or flat sawed. Further, the boards are generally sold in random widths. This means that both items (1) and (2) in Figure 2–11 will be present in a stack from the same tree. Add this to the fact that plywood is not used in authentic reproductions, and the boards will be either too wide for stiles and rails or too narrow for panels, sides, or tops. Thus we have to expect that ripping the boards will cause them to deform, so by cutting the boards we can reduce further deformation.

If we rip the boards to the needed width, we can anticipate some warping (crowning), which must be removed with a joiner once the approximate lengths are cut. So we must allow for waste, which costs money.

We can also rip boards to reduce tension or compression, then glue them back together to make wide boards for tops, shelves, sides, and panels. This is costly in materials and time, but in this case it must be done.

Some pieces used to make posts and legs need to be three to four inches square in order to turn them or shape them into Queen Anne or cabriole legs. These pieces may have had internal forces of tension and compression that can cause warped and split legs. Properly cut and dried lumber can minimize these possibilities. *Close-grain* and *straight-grain* woods should always be selected for legs. Quarter-sawing wood produces close grain uniformly through the piece. Straight grain usually occurs in quarter-sawed wood.

Now let's shift our attention to the subject of *external* forces and stresses. The first consideration should be the force and stress created by loads. Figure 2–12 provides several illustrations for us to examine.

Item (1) in the figure shows that a load, if heavy enough or concentrated in one place, causes the shelf or top or bottom rail in a cabinet to experience compression in the top fibers and tension along the bottom fibers. If the load

[2]Ibid, p18

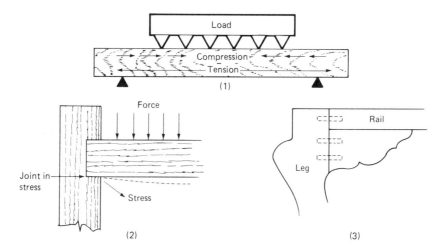

Figure 2–12   Force and stress in wood.

is left on, the deformity of the wood may become permanent. How many times have you seen a bookcase shelf or cabinet with this condition?

In item (2) in the figure, a dado joint is shown. The "a" in the illustration shows the part of the joint that has the greatest force. All the force placed on the shelf from its midpoint to the left is borne by this heel of the dado. This heel remains intact due to the modulus of elasticity inherent in every piece of wood. Each species of wood has its own modulus of elasticity. The stiffer the wood, the higher the modulus of elasticity, so if hardwood is used, there will be little chance for shearing off the heel. With pine and other softwoods, there may be a chance of a shearing.

In this figure, we see that as a load is placed on the shelf, the joint is placed in stress. Normally, the joint is close-fitted and bonded with glue. The combination of the glue's holding power, the joint's fit, and strength or elasticity of the wood used minimize the possibility of rupture. But if the joint is poorly fitted and bonded with glue, an excessive load will rupture the joint because the stresses and forces are too great.

Now draw your attention to Figure 2–12(3), the sketch of a cabriole leg's upper unit. In many applications of cabriole and Queen Anne legs, one must use two pieces. The first is the full-length leg, which is frequently cut from a solid stock of about four inches square. But to continue the curve into the rail section, other pieces must be added to the front and side. These pieces are usually fastened with dowels and glue. Since the joint is not capable of withstanding severe weights for any length of time, additional support is added by using a rail section which may be either doweled to the leg or mortise-and-tenoned into the leg.

Cabinet legs in general are in stress when fastened to a cabinet bottom. This couldn't be more true than when attempting to move the cabinet by sliding, turning, or walking it. The problem is overcome by creating a base unit capable of withstanding the force and stress. If legs must be used, then they must be designed into the cabinet structure, thus overcoming the inherent weakness of mounted legs.

In another design where a primary horizontal mass with two or more major mass sections is used, the sides and back are sufficiently strong to preclude sagging, but the front is not. Normally the front is a network of small trim pieces that form dimensions for drawer and door openings. The drawers and doors add stress to the joints, thus causing sagging. Figure 2–13, an example of this potential problem, happens to be a three major mass, horizontal primary cabinet. The Drexel Company uses a "turnbuckle" between each outer mass and the middle one. The tension created by tightening the turnbuckle lifts the bottom front rail. This compensates for all weights applied to the cabinet front. This technique is very simple and relatively inexpensive, plus it does not add much weight and does not occupy much room.

We have identified a variety of principles associated with force and stress. Some are internal to the wood that we select for cabinets, and some are external qualities that affect the way wood and joints respond. As we have seen, each cause of stress and force must be dealt with.

2.3 LINE AND CURVE PRINCIPLES IN FURNITURE AND CABINET DESIGN

Line principles are usually associated with characteristics of a cabinet that cause a certain feeling or cause the eye to follow the line. Line principles can be used independently from curves, and we shall examine several applications. Curves, on the other hand, are usually related to natural, geometric shapes and cannot be excluded from lines, since the eye will always tend to follow the curve. Further, true curves in cabinets are not a continuation or arc of a single circle. We shall examine several applications of these.

The breakfast china shown in Figure 2–14 from Drexel's "Eighteenth Century Classics" collection provides us with several adaptations of the use of lines. All of the major dimensions of this cabinet employ straight lines, so the overall feeling is one of straightness. In the upper section, straight lines are used in the pediment. The shelves are straight across the three subsections, thus creating a parallel symmetry. Each minor mass is vertically oriented. The straight lines are created by the raised flat molding/trim on each side of the glass. The partitioning of the door in the major subsection creates both vertical and horizontal lines.

The lower section contains several adaptations of the rules for lines. The raised border molding/trim on the doors plus the line created by the raised panel define the straight-line characteristics of the doors. The border molding/trim around each drawer in the major middle section creates the dimension line of each drawer.

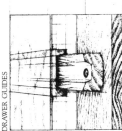

DRAWERS

...re crafted from solid hard... ...d at all corners by precision inc... ...g dovetail cuts. The drawer is then placed in a special press to insure tight fitting square corners.

The drawer interior is sanded smooth and finished with a sealant to protect fine clothing and linens from snags and tears.

DRAWER GUIDES

The unique Drexel Heritage drawer guides are perfectly milled and planed from select hardwoods for straightness and fit. The top and bottom pieces are hand-sanded, sealed, then waxed to provide continual ease of use.

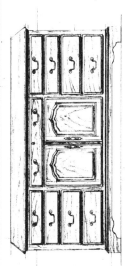

Drexel Heritage case goods reflect an enduring tradition of excellence. Select hardwoods and top quality materials are shaped by caring craftsmen into some of the finest furniture available. From rough cut lumber to fine finished furniture is a long journey involving many steps that may not be obvious. The essential steps are illustrated here.

Every collection features custom hardware accents, knobs, latches, drawer pulls and hinges.

A quality feature, between the floor and drawer level of each piece, is the dust bottom. This special feature, along with side and back panels, keep Drexel Heritage case goods as air tight and dust free as possible.

The top and lower rails are then securely joined to the corner posts completing a durable frame promising years of use.

The finest hardwoods, such as pecan, oak, maple, cherry, and mahogany are used in Drexel Heritage case goods. Under controlled conditions, select cuts are air and kiln dried to a specific moisture content.

This careful attention in the early stages prevents cracking and splitting while maximizing the wood's strength and stability.

A new finish is developed for every collection. As many as 38 steps may be required for a finish that enhances the wood and compliments the collection design.

TURNBUCKLE LEVELING DEVICE

The turnbuckle prevents sag and keeps the furniture square. Adjusted at the factory, the device is used in furniture over 60" wide.

Other levelers are also used in the base to keep the pieces steady on uneven floors.

SOLID CORNER CONSTRUCTION

At the base of each piece, stout pieces of hardwood are carefully mitered, doweled, and glued to the corners. For additional support, blocks of hardwood are glued and screwed into the bottom rail and attached base piece, creating a solid foundation for the verticle corner posts.

Figure 2–13 Cabinet structure. (Courtesy of Drexel Heritage Furnishings Inc., Drexel, North Carolina)

Figure 2–14 Breakfront from "Eighteenth Century Classics." (*Courtesy of Drexel Heritage Furnishings Inc., Drexel, North Carolina*)

Straight-line rules or principles are relatively simple to incorporate into cabinets. Cabinets are usually relatively narrow in width, which causes the viewer's eye to follow the line. Lines extending across sections create symmetry. This rule is used most frequently with sectional bookcases, room dividers, and similar pieces.

Curved lines follow certain principles too. There are generally five principles for curves:

1. A curve in one direction has no straight lines in its composition.
2. Free-hand curves resulting from human art forms should be graceful and contain rhythm.

3. A compound curve must contain at least two curves of different arcs. When the reverse compound curve is used, one must have a sharper bend than the other. (*Note:* Table legs generally conform to this rule.)

4. Turned curves should be full to be attractive, and well rounded versus scant or flat.

5. The point at which a curve in molding connects with a flat adjacent surface (filet) should create an almost 90-degree angle.

Now let's find some examples of these principles. The entertainment center in Figure 2–15 from Drexels "Cabernet Classics" collection illustrates several principles. Every curve applies the principle of a continuous arc with no straight line breaking the curve. The rule for compound curve (3) is followed in the cabinet crown and several times in the base. The curves reverse and one has a slightly sharper bend. Rule 5 is also used on each door and in the base. Where there is a break created by a straight line, the curve and straight line meet to create an almost 90-degree angle.

Figure 2–15 Entertainment center from "Cabernet Classics." (*Courtesy of Drexel Heritage Furnishings Inc., Drexel, North Carolina*)

(a)

(b)

Figure 2–16(a) 1.2.3. Program; **(b)** Combi. (*Courtesy of Karel Mintjens, West-malle, Belgium, and Leesburg, Virginia*)

Figure 2–16(a), 1.2.3. Program, and 2–16(b), Combi, both designed and crafted by Karl Mintjens of Belgium show several curve principles applied. In part (a) of the figure, the reverse-curve principle is used in the doors—one is sharper than the other. Also in this figure, the pedestal of the table illustrates very well Rule 4 for turned curves. Notice the full, well-rounded turnings. The chair legs also display this principle.

In contrast, part (b) of the figure shows an interesting adaptation of a single curve. Each door, except the drop-down door in the center, has a single curve. When created in pairs, such doors provide balance.

Free-hand curves are very much like French curves. They are sculptured curves drawn by penciled sketches. Although there are many examples of these in Greek and Roman architecture, most free-hand curves used in furniture and cabinets are found in pediments and in table, chair, or cabinet legs and bases.

Two examples of free-hand (or French) curves are shown in Figure 2–17, a china cabinet from Drexel's "Eighteenth Century Classics" collection. Part (a) shows a reverse-curve principle—the shaping along the sides of the curve is also made across the exposed ends. It is filled with a solid and accented with a fluted center finial. In contrast, part (b) is much more steeply curved and ends in a circular carved enhancement. It is filled with fretwork grilles, all in the Chippendale style.

Lines and curves are very important to the design of European styled furniture and cabinets. When you study further chapters devoted to specialized furniture from various European countries and master cabinetmakers, recall

Figure 2–17 (a), (b) Chinas from "Eighteenth Century Classics." (*Courtesy of Drexel Heritage Furnishings Inc., Drexel, North Carolina*)

(a)

(b)

these rules or principles. Study how they are used in the various pieces, and thereby learn more about them. Then plan to include the principles in cabinets you build.

2.4 HOW UNLIKE MATERIALS WORK TOGETHER IN FURNITURE AND CABINET CONSTRUCTION

European styled cabinets sometimes were made with a combination of woods or with entirely different types of materials. Where either of these techniques are used, several principles must be considered and used.

Different species of wood have distinctly different growth patterns which cause different cell structure and porosity. For example, birch and maple are quite alike in composition and color, so they are frequently used in one cabinet. They take stain about equally and finish to a very smooth surface. Walnut is like these woods, except that it is much darker. These woods grow in northern climates, grow slowly, and therefore have close grain patterns and small wood cells.

In contrast, oak wood cells are much larger and the wood is much more grainy. Staining oak is much different than staining maple, birch, and walnut woods. Stain applied to oak soaks in much deeper, so the result may be much darker. Here's a rule: If a cabinet is made combining oak and maple, presealing the oak is necessary to have a uniform color.

The open grain of oak requires care when sanding, since the springwood (softer, lighter colored wood) sands away more readily than the late wood.

Pine is a softwood that was used to build cabinets in Europe. Since it is soft, its surfaces are easily marred and subject to deep stain penetration. Poplar, a soft hardwood, was also once used in cabinetmaking. Pine and poplar can be combined in a cabinet, but they take stains differently, so watch out for this and use preseal or wash coats of thinned shellac on pine.

Wood veneers and solid woods of the same species are totally different when the veneer is rotary-cut from a log. The grain is *open* and it sands and stains differently from adjacent stock wood. On the other hand, slice-cut veneer and its companion stock wood are quite similar and thus work well together.

Mahogany was widely used for European cabinetmaking at one time, especially during the *age of mahogany*. The harder varieties were used rather than the softer, more porous species. Mahogany can be carved more easily than most other woods, so many carvings were made in mahogany and then glued onto cabinet surfaces as adornment. Since the wood is usually red to dark brown-red, its color will affect the overall color of a cabinet.

Let's review:

1. Woods that have different pore structure, growth patterns, and grain texture require special care when combined in one cabinet.

2. Woods of different colors combined in a cabinet must be treated with preseal or wash coats to minimize the difference in color stains will make.

3. Woods of the same species but cut with different grain patterns will accept finishes differently unless pretreated.

One common material combination used in cabinets is glass and wood. Glass adds considerable weight to a cabinet. When glass is used as a panel in a door, the design generally calls for the wood frame to be slender and decorative to allow for maximum visibility into the inside of the cabinet. Since this reduces the amount of wood in the door, the corner joints which bear the force of the door's weight are in stress. Unlike the wood panel, the glass cannot be glued into the frame, so it does not add support for frame joints. Therefore, joints in glass panel doors must be soundly made. Specifically, they must be perfectly fitted, properly glued, and reinforced where possible by design.

Another material used in combination with wood is porcelain. When porcelain is inlaid into a wood frame for a cabinet top, for example, it should be slightly higher than the frame. (*Note:* This same principle applies to glass inlaid in a cabinet top.) The edge of the porcelain needs to be beveled to prevent chipping and scarring.

Marble is also used in cabinets of European styling, most frequently as a top. Natural marble is extremely heavy, so it creates a severe downward force on the cabinet corners and surfaces it contacts. Since the force must be transferred to the floor through some means, the best method to use is to transfer it through the cabinet legs or cabinet ends which extend from the underside of the marble to the floor. This technique results in full transfer of the force of the marble's weight, since the marble is generally sufficiently rigid to sustain itself. Hence, other parts of the cabinet under the top do not experience any pressure. An exception to this fundamental would be when the marble top is too thin to support its own weight and therefore sags, or when the marble is man-made.

2.5 DECORATING PRINCIPLES FOR MAINTAINING STYLE AND PERIOD THEMES

From earliest times, cabinetmakers have been faced with adding characteristics to cabinets and furniture to create unique, one-of-a-kind pieces or sets. In times when European styles were dominated by a few master cabinetmakers in each of the countries, all were skilled in hand carving. Today there are many more cabinetmakers than in the past, but few possess the skill of hand carving.

In the past, guilds of craftsmen were formed that permitted members many years of apprenticeship in which to learn the skills they needed. In Germany, for example, an apprentice would spend ten years or more learning his craft before becoming a journeyman.

For some of us today, it would be impossible to carve the adornment into a cabriole leg as was done with Louis XIV table legs. The artist required years of practice to become proficient. We can overcome this limitation in various ways:

1. Avoid using adornments requiring skills not learned. Obviously this solution would cause an undesirable outcome.
2. Purchase a set of carving tools and dedicate several years to practice, then carve the adornments where they are needed. This would mean an extremely lengthy delay in finishing the piece.
3. Use modern electrical machines such as flexible shaft with carving bits, or a hand-held drill-type tool with carving bits. These tools make carving possible, but considerable practice is still required before the needed degree of accuracy is achieved.
4. Purchase commercially available adornments (plant-ons) that can be either applied as overlays or inserted into the cabinet. This solution is an easy one, but does not enrich the cabinetmaker's skill.

Before discussing the numerous types or classes of adornments, let's make a short list of where they are most frequently used.

1. cabinet doors and door frames
2. cabinet drawer fronts
3. table legs and or aprons
4. panels
5. pediments
6. outlines around important openings
7. borders separating mass sections
8. bases
9. crowns other than traditional pediments.

The first of several classes of adornments is the *naturalistic*. These are copies of nature including plant, human, animal, and sea life. The adornments copied from plant life include carved leaves, acanthus vine, and leaf, palm, olive branch, honeysuckle, and numerous flowers and their leaves. Of the flowers, roses and the rose bud carving predominate. Look again at Figure 2–15 and notice the use of plant carving consisting of honeysuckle leaves and vines. In this example and others like it, the adornment is carved into the board before it is assembled into the cabinets, which makes good sense. This carving is also machine made using assembly-line machines. However, the original from which all others are made may have been hand carved.

Human and animal-like adornments have been used for thousands of years, more often in architecture than in cabinets. Hundreds of examples of carvings representing human and animal forms can be found in Greek and Roman architecture. It is therefore natural that carvings depicting humans and animals were also included in cabinets. Naturalistic adornments include busts, animal heads, legs, feet, the ball wrapped with claws, griffins, and cherubs. (The griffin from Greek mythology was a fabulous beast with the head and wings of an eagle and the body of a lion. A cherub was a winged celestial being, frequently displayed in castles in Germany as a winged child with a round face.) Figure 2–18, a cocktail table from the "Heirloom" collection by Drexel Heritage, illustrates the use of the ball and claw. The overall shape of the leg is that of a goat. The remaining carvings are plant representations.

A third class of naturalistic adornment includes those from sea life. The most copied are the seashells. Look again at Figure 2–5, the lowboy which employs the shell carving. During the time of Queen Anne, the seashell carvings symbolized wealth and happiness.

Another category of adornment used extensively in European cabinets is the *abstract* variety. This category includes geometric designs, inlaid bands of veneer and other materials, and other applied ornaments such as lozenges, dentils, and bosses.

The circle, square, and rectangle are used extensively in European styled cabinets. We discussed most of these in the section on masses. One, though, was not mentioned and should be. The use of veneer for cabinets and table tops is frequently designed in geometric patterns such as pie shapes, squares, and rectangles to create a distinctive appearance. The use of veneer grain patterns in geometric shapes on door surfaces and especially in panels is common.

Inlaid bands are extremely decorative and are done in several ways. Builder's supply houses usually offer a wide variety of bands for inlay ranging from $\frac{1}{8}$ inch to 1 inch wide. A very shallow routing is made where the inlaid band

Figure 2–18 Cocktail table from "Heirlooms by Heritage." (*Courtesy of Drexel Heritage Furnishings Inc., Drexel, North Carolina*)

is to be placed, then the band is cut for length and glued in place. Return again to Figure 2–13 and observe the different techniques of veneer banding. Around the perimeter of each door, the veneer grain runs crosswise to the length of the door side, top, and bottom. Also note the raised banding just inside the border banding. It too shows a crosswise grain pattern.

A *lozenge* is an applied adornment that is diamond-like in shape, as in Figure 2–19. In geometry it would be a rhombus rather than a square. The term is very old, dating back to the middle English and old French era. The term is not used frequently today, but the concept is still in use. More frequently fretwork overlay-type adornments in a variety of sizes are used to decorate doors and sides of cabinets. They may be applied vertically or horizontally.

A *dentil,* a term associated with architecture, consists of a series of rectangular blocks which form a molding that is placed under a cornice. They were used in European cabinetmaking. Of course, the dimensions were much smaller than those used on cornices, and they were more decorative. Figure 2–19 shows an example.

A *boss* is a circular, knob-like protrusion used as an ornament. One example is a finial. Another is similar to the ball-like leg or foot base on a chest, as shown in Figure 2–19.

A fourth category of adornment is the *artificial object.* These include carved and sculptured variations of vases, musical instruments, and ribbons. All shapes of vases have been reproduced in wood and applied to cabinets or carved into them. Naturally, the full vase is not carved, but only the face view. The most frequently used representation of a musical instrument is the lyre. We have seen this used on numerous chair backs, especially in English and Italian furniture. Ribbon-like carvings have been used as adornments, sometimes without the bow.

Now that we have identified the categories of adornments, we should apply a few principles for their use. First, the cabinetmaker must consider the ratio of the dimensions of the adornment to the section or mass that will be adorned. Adornments should never overpower the mass. They should provide

Figure 2–19 Lozenge, dentil, and boss.

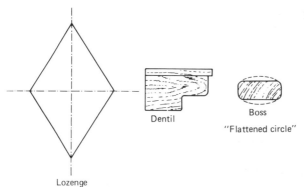

Dentil

Boss
"Flattened circle"

Lozenge

a distinctive character, visible, proportional, and carefully placed. Border adornments such as bands should be sharply distinctive. They should capture the eye and cause it to follow the border. Thought of another way, border trim should develop a perimeter encasing and creating a dimension in a door panel or drawer front.

Enrichment of panels should cause the focal point to be the adornment. Fretwork carvings, seashells, vases, and geometric designs such as circles and squares can be used to create interest. However, the size of the adornment must not be so small so as to be overpowered by the mass surface of the panel, nor so large as to overpower the panel mass. If a panel is rectangular, then the adornment must have a rectangular proportion. The adornment must follow the ratio of height to width of the piece.

As you study future chapters which deal with cabinets and furniture from European countries, these principles will be illustrated time and again. This chapter provides one of the foundations needed for a clear understanding of design of European styled furniture and cabinets.

REVIEW EXERCISES

1. The dominant line in a cabinet will always be either vertical or horizontal, but seldom both. (T/F)

2. For a mass to be labelled "major" it must be the largest of all masses that make up the cabinet. (T/F)

3. If a cabinet has three equal masses side by side, it is called a primary horizontal mass. (T/F)

4. In a primary vertical mass with masses of different sizes, the major mass is located on top or bottom of all other masses. (T/F)

5. When a mass is subdivided horizontally into three minor unequal masses, the center one should be dominant by its added width. (T/F)

6. Where should the drawer with the least height be located when all drawers are of different heights?
   a. top   **c.** bottom
   b. center   **d.** anywhere

7. In order for a cabinet to be classified as proportional, when the height is 54 inches, the width should be:
   a. 29 inches.   **c.** $37\frac{5}{8}$ inches.
   b. $33\frac{3}{8}$ inches.   **d.** $47\frac{1}{8}$ inches.

8. A board cut from a tree has built-in compression and tension. Which statement is correct?
   a. Compression is often visible as the crown curve of the softwood board.
   b. Compression is a force where the wood fibers are elongated in line with the stress.

    c. Tension is a force where wood cells are squeezed out of proportion crosswise to the line of stress.

    d. Compression is greatest when lumber is quarter-sawed.

9. Cabinet pieces joined at right angles generally are placed in stress when used for their intended purpose. Where is the point of greatest stress?

    a. On the heel of a dado joint

    b. Tension on the joint and compression on the piece bearing the weight

    c. More so on a mortise and tenon than on a dowel joint

10. Which rule is *not* correctly stated regarding the use of curves?

    a. A curve in one direction has no straight lines in its composition

    b. Curves should be graceful and contain rhythm

    c. Turned curves should be attractive and somewhat flattened

    d. Curves should end at almost 90 degrees to the adjacent flat surface

ESSAYS

11. In 25 words, describe the differences that occur when staining oak and maple.

12. Describe a serious concern you would have if a lightweight framed door had a heavy glass panel.

13. Describe or make a list of the different classes of adornments. Include examples.

ANSWERS

1F, 2T, 3T, 4F, 5T, 6a, 7b, 8a, 9b, 10c

3

English Styled Furniture and Cabinets

This chapter is the first of several that provide information on cabinet-making and furniture making related to a specific country. There are objectives to meet in each chapter listed below the opening comments. The function of these objectives is to make the study on cabinetmaking in each country more significant. Further, each objective should create a goal for the reader that adds to understanding of the cabinetmakers of many years ago.

Generally, all chapters dealing with specific countries follow the pattern of first discussing information about cabinetmaking characteristics and history, then providing examples of cabinets, tables, and other pieces to illustrate how the characteristics of cabinets from Chapter 2 are employed and how each cabi-netmaker incorporated the country's unique design qualities into the work.

Objectives

1. To understand the names associated with English furniture from a chron-ological viewpoint.
2. To identify the characteristics of English furniture as well as the contri-bution of some of its most famous cabinetmakers and designers.
3. To understand the specific characteristics, materials, skills, and tech-niques craftsmen used to create English styled furniture.

3.1 CHRONOLOGY OF ENGLISH FURNITURE STYLES

The chronology illustrated in Table 3–1 provides an understanding of the changes in English furniture. Reviewing some of the data, we see that there were a variety of names associated with English furniture. Therefore, we are able to group specific periods, sovereigns, and craftsmen together. But notice that a great many periods existed before the famed English cabinetmakers became prominent, and that their influence covered only a short span of 40 years. Even so, their contributions were so significant that they changed the entire concepts of furniture making, not only in England but in Europe, Ireland, and later in the United States.

TABLE 3–1   CHRONOLOGY OF ENGLISH FURNITURE STYLES

Time	Period/Names	Reigns	Dates	Craftsman
Sixteenth Century				
1500–60	Elizabethean and Early Tudor	Henry VII, VIII, Edward VI, Mary		
1560–1603	Late Tudor	Elizabeth	Oak	
Seventeenth Century				
1600–50	Jacobean and Early Stuart	James I, Charles I		
1649–60	Puritan, Cromwellian	Commonwealth		
1660–88	Restoration, Carolean, Stuart, Late Jacobean	Charles II, James II		
1688–1702	William & Mary	William & Mary	Walnut	
Eighteenth Century				
1702–30	Queen Anne, Early Georgian	Anne (Last of Stuarts) George I (House of Brunswick)		
1730–1810	Georgian, Classic Revival	George II, III		Chippendale (1750–80) Adams Brothers (1750 –90) Hepplewhite (1770–1810) Sheraton (1791–1820)
Nineteenth Century			Mahogany	
1810–30	Regency, Great Revival, Empire	George III, IV		
1830–1901	Victorian, Gothic Revival	William IV, Victoria		
(1830–60)	(Early Victorian)			
(1860–80)	(Mid Victorian)			
(1880–1901)	(Late Victorian)			
Twentieth Century				

3.2 CHARACTERISTICS OF ENGLISH FURNITURE AND CONTRIBUTIONS OF SOME OF ITS MOST FAMOUS CABINETMAKERS AND DESIGNERS

English styles of furniture have for hundreds of years contained quality crafts-manship and design, although there has been a remarkable difference in both from 500 AD to the present. All work done under the heading of English styled cabinets and furniture was not done exclusively by the English. Throughout the years, cabinetmakers and woodcarvers migrated back and forth between the European continent, Ireland, England, and the early United States. They brought skills and techniques with them and took newly learned skills and tech-niques back. That is why some antiques are designated "French styled in Eng-lish," "Louis XV–Chippendale," "Louis XVI–Adams," "English furniture styled in Danish," and "German furniture styled in English." Chippendale, Sheraton, Hepplewhite, and the Adams brothers were the major known contributors to the breakthrough in furniture that provides the foundations for today's copies. Now let's examine the characteristics of cabinetry from the sixteenth century.

From examples of cabinets preserved in museums such as the Victoria and Albert in London, it is clear that cabinets as early as the Elizabethan and Tudor period (1500–1600) were hand made from solid wood, yet contained carvings and employed joinery. Boards were hand-hued from oak trees, al-lowed to air dry, and then dressed by hand to desired thicknesses. As one would expect, uniform thicknesses were close to but not as exacting as those we are capable of obtaining today. Styles included fluting, Doric and Corinthian crowns, hand-carved Gothic church ornamentation, and panel-and-frame con-struction. Hardware such as hinges, hasps, and handles were hammered from iron and brass. Hinges were sometimes butterfly style; and sometimes H or L types. Each surface mounted. Cabinets were very large and generally ornately carved. (See Figures 3–1, 3–2, and 3–3 in the next section.)

The Jacobean styles of cabinet range through the Stuart, Puritan, Crom-wellian, Restoration, and Carolean periods—roughly 80 years. (Refer to Table 3–1 for reigns.) This period remained mostly in the age of oak, but also marked the beginning of the age of walnut.

During this period significant style changes occurred. The early Jacobean styles were plain, straight-lined, and contained no ornaments. Cabinets gen-erally lacked the fine points. In addition, the pieces were rectangular, cubical, cumbersome, and solid. Extensive use of frame construction was used, as were turned legs.

Some of the pieces built during this time were press and court cupboards, chests, tables, sideboards, daybeds, trestle tables, and gate-leg tables.

But by the late Jacobean Restoration Carolean period, plainness gave way to exquisite cabinetry that included veneers, extensive carvings, turned legs, stretchers, marquetry, beautifully filigreed hardware, mortised hinges and drawers. Pieces included writing cabinets, tables, dresser-like cabinets, and variations of the gate-leg table, to mention a few.

During the William and Mary period (1688–1702), more exquisite cabinets were designed and built. Pieces generally were scaled down in size and details were added with the use of the "block front" style. Drop pulls with filigree backplates were used. Since this period was well within the walnut age, walnut was the principal wood used. Cabinet ends were almost always solid; rarely were panels used. Where a panel effect was needed, materials were inlaid in a solid side. Other styling characteristics included the trumpet-turned leg, crossed or X-shaped stretchers under tables, single- or double-hooded tops, ball or bun feet on table legs, beautifully shaped aprons and skirts, and, as mentioned earlier, large unbroken surfaces. Prominent pieces associated with the William and Mary period include the lowboy, the highboy, which is a chest of drawers on a frame, the secretary, and the card table.

English cabinet styling became more graceful with the introduction of Queen Anne furniture. It was the beginning of the Georgian period, too, and nearing the end of the walnut age. Several characteristics of cabinetry began at this time. One was the cabriole leg, sometimes plain, sometimes with shell carvings. It was double-curved and relatively plain. This was in keeping with the overall design characteristic of eliminating ornamentation. Tables were made without the use of stretchers or underbracing. A carry-over from William and Mary styling was the use of table aprons on many of the same types of furniture and cabinets. The range included the highboy, lowboy, hall table, drop-leaf table, sideboard, tea table, gate-leg table with turned legs, and corner cupboard. Most of the tables were styled with the cabriole leg. The crowns on highboys included broken pediments and bonnet tops.

As the Georgian period continued, the Classic Revival period began, which brought the famous designers and cabinetmakers. The first of these was Thomas Chippendale (1750–1780). Some of the designs credited to Chippendale were the modified cabriole leg with a ball at the bottom. As might be expected, no stretchers were used on tables having the cabriole leg. When Chippendale used straight legs on tables, they were carved on the outside. Stretchers on these tables were fret sawed or carved, or sometimes they were left straight. Chippendale was noted for his extensive use of carving and the absence of wood turning. He used the broken pediment frequently and almost always included rich designs. Highboys and tables designed by him generally had richly carved aprons.

Chippendale created many pieces similar to those in the William and Mary and Queen Anne periods. He also designed the chest of drawers with four drawers, card table, pie table, lazy susan, and secretary. Most of these designs were made in mahogany, since Chippendale did most of his work in the early age of mahogany.

The Adams brothers, who were architects, contributed to designs in furniture and cabinets. These brothers styled cabinets with rectangular features. On tables they used square, tapered, slender legs with no feet, and they too eliminated the stretchers. All of their designs were formal. Many included the egg and dart, the lyre, and relief and inlaying characteristics from early Greek architecture. They styled molding commonly found on buildings or in rooms of buildings. Since they lived in the mahogany age, most of their work was done in that kind of wood. Some of their best works include sideboards, bookcases, commodes, and cabinets on legs.

About twenty years after Chippendale and the Adams brothers entered the scene, George Hepplewhite gained prominence. His work was generally in the Classic Revival period in the mahogany age. Hepplewhite added several new ideas to cabinets and tables. For one thing, he modified the Adams' straight, tapered leg by including the spade foot. He also added reeding on some legs. His designs included much veneer on fronts, tops, sides, doors, and panels. He used the oval top on tables, which was new. He even painted ornaments on cabinet doors. Whereas the Adams brothers made plain architectural moldings, Hepplewhite designed beautiful sculptured moldings. Some of his most important designs include the card table, china cupboard, drop-leaf table, tambour secretary, flatop knee-hole desk, and sideboard.

Thomas Sheraton entered the scene as a recognized designer at about the time the Adams brothers were ending their era and Hepplewhite was nearing twenty years of prominence. Sheraton was also a designer of the mahogany age, a designer of the Classic Revival, Regency, Great Revival, and Georgian periods. Sheraton's designs were similar to Hepplewhite's in many respects. For example, he employed tapered legs, although many of his were turned. He also used the oval design on some tables and inlays. He also incorporated straight lines in pediments on his china cabinets. He was noted for designing tall cabinets that were beautifully proportioned according to major and minor masses. He like to incorporate fancy veneers wherever they added significance to the cabinet. Some of his prominent work included the chest of drawers, secretary, china cabinet, and Pembroke (drop-leaf) table.

Fine quality, beautifully styled furniture continued to be built throughout the Regency period (1810–1830) and well into the end of the nineteenth century. The sofa table leg arrangement continued and was modified for use on bookstands and other tables. Desks were much less ornate, but were generally veneered. Turnings were combined with flat pieces. Hardware, some of it styled by Chippendale and Sheraton, was used for decoration and for functional purposes. Most of the pieces were made from mahogany.

Victorian styled furniture spanned the reign of British queen Victoria. The greatest proliferation of furniture was produced during the Victorian era. Cabinetmakers borrowed from the past in a revival of Gothic, Elizabethan, Baroque, Louis XIV and XV, Rococo, Eastern, and Oriental styles. A great new bewildering combination of materials and styles were incorporated into pieces mass produced in factories and shops. Various woods were used and sometimes more than one type of wood was used in a single cabinet. Veneers mechanically applied with presses made those types of cabinets and furniture available to the average English household, whereas earlier custom-made cabinets were usually made only for the wealthy.

3.3 SPECIFIC CHARACTERISTICS, MATERIALS, SKILLS, AND TECHNIQUES USED TO CREATE ENGLISH STYLED FURNITURE

In this section specific examples of English styled furniture are illustrated. A short narrative which discusses the characteristics, materials, skills, and cabinetmaking techniques is provided with each picture. Since there were no standards of joinery for a large portion of the time represented by these cabinets, the suggestions regarding joinery are those currently used by cabinetmakers today.

The English schrank shown in Figure 3–1 was built around the year 1500. This cabinet has some design principles of mass and proportion that were discussed in the last chapter. The cabinet represents a very early version of a highboy. It is a primary vertical mass of three major equal masses. The lower one has an apron on each of the four sides that is tenoned into the leg. The

Figure 3–1 English schrank (circa 1500).

Figure 3-2 English bed (circa 1590).

legs are one piece from floor to cabinet top and are doubled reeded. The panels are probably set in grooves that run the full length of the leg. The cross members separating major masses are probably grooved, except where doors are used. There would be two solid wood shelves and a solid wood top. The carving in each face panel and door is, for the most part, all the way through the cabinet panel. Therefore, these could be done with a scroll saw first, then shaped with router or hand carving tool. The rosettes must be done with carver's chisels. The hinges were hammered wrought iron. The closest thing available today is the black simulated hinge with square-headed screws. We would probably use a light stain, wood filler, and oil rub finish.

The English bed shown in Figure 3-2 was built around 1593 from walnut. It is massive, but the actual bed as shown barely meets the size of a full size

Figure 3–3 Credenza (1610).

mattress and spring. As we can see, this unit is very complex in design and very detailed in character. All materials are solid walnut. Extensive use of large stock lumber was required to make this unit. The columns were turned and reeded. Crowns were carved and installed on top. The base was built up of a carved middle section, and then a top and base section (built-up, probably) were fastened. The bed back is a complex design of panel and frame, decorated with slender turned and reeded posts. It is a three-part mass of vertical primary design; the plain panel mass is bottom. A center mass is made of two minor horizontal masses. The third vertical top mass has extensive carving. The canopy is a complex design that uses moldings around the lower and upper areas. The middle sections are fluted. Although it is unlikely that anyone today would build a bed of this style, it does represent quality workmanship from very early in English history.

Figure 3–3 illustrates an English credenza of the Jacobean and Early Stuart (1610) period. It does provide us with several ideas of design and workmanship that express the principles discussed in Chapter 2. It is of the oak age, so we

60

can expect to make it from oak. Overall, it is a two major mass, vertical-primary mass design. The lower major mass is all panel design. Each end is a four minor mass of panels. The front construction shows two doors of four minor masses each. Look closely at the joint of the rightmost door and its horizontal divider. See the two circular dots; these are wood screws. This leads to a conclusion that the panels were designed with mortise-and-tenon joinery. From the position of the screws, we can further surmise that the molded surfaces were shaped from the single piece as we do today on colonial doors, for example. Other areas illustrate wood screws, thus providing definition of joinery. Notice the hardware on the doors. There are hammered H–L hinges on each.

A carved shell design begins the upper mass area. The upper mass is in stark contrast to the lower. Whereas the lower one is extremely plain, the upper is detailed ornately with hand carvings. Also notice that there are panels with arch design. These are unusual designs. The crown is complex, with molding along its bottom edge and larger crown molding at the top.

It is very unlikely that any one today would copy this design, since overall it is very inefficient and the mass would not fit very many rooms.

Now let's direct our attention to a very unique and functional seventeenth century piece of furniture of Jacobean and Early Stuart period shown in Figure 3–4. This unit is a storage cabinet, bench, and table. Overall it is a horizontal

Figure 3–4   Jacobean credenza (circa 1640).

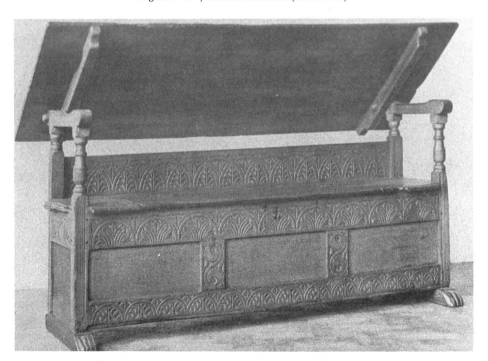

Figure 3–5 Walnut full-front writing desk with marquetry.

primary mass. The four turned and reeded uprights form the foundation for all other assemblies. Notice the use of wood nails/screws that lead us once again to the conclusion that mortise-and-tenon joinery was used. Hand carving includes the semicircle and fern in combination. The seat is solid oak, hinged on the rear for access to the storage compartment. The only support for the top are the two cross supports. The top is fastened to the arm rests of the bench with wood pegs.

Design and construction of cabinets began to change with the beginning of the walnut age. The walnut full-front writing cabinet with marquetry shown in Figure 3–5 is a beautiful example of the quality workmanship of the time. This cabinet was crafted during the Restoration, Carolean, Stuart, and late Jacobean period.

Many new features are present that need to be identified. Working from the floor up, notice the five partially turned, partially carved legs. These are separated by curved and straight stretchers. The two end and two front stretchers provide support for all five legs; the two rear legs are further supported by the rear stretcher. In later stylings the stretchers will be crisscrossed.

This is the first example that incorporates a drawer. The filigree knob in the center shows this. The drawer section is made with molding along the bottom as well as the top. The marquetry work combines rectangular, curved, and vegetation designs. The upper section of the writing table is probably an assembly. Look closely at the arrow point to see that there is a separate panel on top of the drawer section. The cabinet has four pieces; the sides anchor to the bottom panel, the top to the sides. There is one door which lowers down to become the writing surface (notice the pull knob at the top center). The marquetry theme of oval and vegetation with an integration of rectangular inlay is continued in this door. The crown assembly is made of a buildup of pieces, the lower one convex with inlaid marquetry. Several other pieces, square and curved, complete the crown.

It is very likely that when the door is in the down position there will be pigeonhole compartments. Cabinets of this quality were lacquered and hand rubbed.

Let's look at another writing desk, but from a later period (Figure 3–6). This desk with gate-leg frame was made during the Queen Anne, Early Georgian period in the early eighteenth century. The gate-leg base unit consists of six turned legs, straight stretchers, and an apron fitted between the upper parts of the legs.

The upper assembly is the writing cabinet. The door is inlaid with walnut, hinged to open, and serves as the writing surface. Small compartments are useful in the inside rear. The basic cabinet could easily be constructed with hardwood, but if walnut veneers were used, a cheaper wood such as poplar would be better. If veneers are to be used, the butt joint would make construction easier. The veneers would then cover the end wood. A piano hinge is probably the best choice for hinging the door. Since walnut is the basic wood used, an oil-rub finish produces a super-fine sheen and silk feel to the wood.

Figure 3–6 Walnut desk with gate leg frame (English, circa 1700).

Beauty continues to be the theme. The bachelor chest shown in Figure 3–7, designed and built by Drexel, illustrates a characteristic brought from the William and Mary period to the eighteenth century. This cabinet incorporates the block-front style. The cabinet is a primary vertical mass with three drawers, each one smaller than the one below it. There is a lot of work involved in the construction. Many curves are made in molded parts. The drawers have two blocked areas, one behind each draw pull. The center hardware is a lock plate. The sides are solid panels. Today we would use plywood. Drexel uses veneers. Separators are a part of the construction. They act as dust covers and drawer supports. This cabinet has a mahogany finish. The dust cover assemblies maintain the structure and shape of the cabinet. The ends and top unit are the whole cabinet. The back adds to racking resistance. To copy this design requires a shop with extensive tools such as shaper, router, bandsaw, and the tools necessary for veneering.

Queen Anne styling began early into the eighteenth century and along with it came the cabriole leg. This style of leg would be used for hundreds of years with various variations. The Queen Anne styled cabriole leg shown as part of the writing cabinet in Figure 3–8 is simply styled. It is devoid of carving and has no ball and claw. It does have the double curve. Notice that this writing

Figure 3–7 Bachelor chest from "Eighteenth Century Classics." (*Courtesy of Drexel Heritage Furnishings Inc., Drexel, North Carolina*)

Figure 3–8 Queen Anne walnut and oyster parquetry full-front writing cabinet (English, circa 1710).

table is similar to the one in Figure 3–5, but much less ornate. The lack of ornate marquetry and carvings is consistant with Queen Anne and Early Georgian. The construction of the cabinet consists of two assemblies, a drawer and a desk. There are two drawers with drop handles. The desk, with its drop writing table and compartmented drawer as well as pigeonholes, is a complex assembly. Partitions made from solid wood are grooved one into the other. From the appearance of the drawers, it seems as if veneer with grain of the opposite direction is applied to enhance the design.

The use of the cabriole leg began the trend of tables and cabinets without stretchers. The cabriole leg is anchored with screws and glue and sometimes blocks.

With the passing of Queen Anne of England, George I of the House of Brunswick began his reign. In this period styles changed somewhat, as Figure 3–9 shows. This walnut side table incorporates a heavily carved cabriole leg with double curve and ball and claw. These legs are set into solid side panels, where most strength is, and the front apron pieces, where less strength exists. The cabinet consists of a series of drawers separated by a horizontal dust cover and vertical dividers. Each drawer is veneered with contrasting edge veneer. The decorative carving of the lower center drawer represents a spray of feathers. More modern replicas of this table usually use the seashell design.

Figure 3–9 Sidetable in walnut
(Early Georgian, eighteenth century).

Except for the legs, the rest of the table is quite simple to construct. The surfaces are flat and veneered. Angles are all rectangular. There are no moldings.

With the age of mahogany, the designs and construction techniques reached new heights, since this was the time of the great English designers, Chippendale, Adams, Sheraton, and Hepplewhite. There are literally thousands of Chippendale styled cabinets, tables, and other pieces of furniture. Let's examine one mahogany secretary made by him. Figure 3–10 shows that this is a three major mass, vertical primary mass design. There are three different features, each of them a mass. The lower drawer mass incorporates solid veneered panels, dust cover separations between drawers mounted on a cut curved base. The drawers are face veneered and decorated with drop drawer pulls. The middle section, the secretary-desk, incorporates a drop-leaf writing surface which is supported by pull-out supports. Very thin (probably $\frac{5}{16}$ inch) dividers create pigeonholes. Small drawers complete the assembly. The third mass is shown as a china closet, but could easily be used to store books. The case can easily be made using dadoes in the sides that support the base, two shelves, and top. Facings are glued to the case, and flush doors finish the front. Moldings using cove and ogee patterns form the crown. The most difficult parts of the construction are the doors. There is a lot of fine partitioning of glass. The best technique to use is to make the partitioning so that the glass in one piece passes behind the wood. Mahogany stain and lacquer finish the cabinet.

The Adams brothers added many novel characteristics to their designs. Figure 3–11 is an example. This six-legged credenza shows a primary horizontal, three major mass unit. Six legs are cut out with a band saw, lightly rounded,

Figure 3-10 A Chippendale secretary (English, eighteenth century).

Figure 3-11 An Adams styled credenza (English circa 1750).

and grooved. A bead groove creates patterns that are filled. The end mass units are storage cabinets. Their sides and back are panels grooved into the legs. The bottom probably is dadoed into the panels. The curved door with its center pull is veneered and routed.

A dust cover assembly is the critical part of the middle mass unit. It must be strongly constructed and fastened securely to the end units. Further stability is added with the curved corner bracket panels beneath the dust cover. These construction techniques preclude the need for the top to provide support, thus eliminating stress on the top. The flat top with square edge and vertical veneer is fastened from its undersurface. The single drawer with two pulls and routing is further enhanced with edge veneer marquetry.

This credenza is a product of the Classic Revival period within the age of mahogany.

We have just seen the use of a slender leg in the credenza in Adams style. Now as we study an example of Hepplewhite styling, we see that even more slender legs are used. Figure 3–12 is the example. This side table was crafted by Drexel from its eighteenth century Classic series. The four legs begin square from the top, but once they extend beneath the apron they are tapered to the floor and end without feet. These are easily cut on a bandsaw or table saw. Once they are sanded, a fine routing is added to the outer surface only. The apron consists of four curved pieces that are veneered. Each piece should be tapered to fit into and against the legs, then doweled. The top is simple in design. Veneers are used along its edge and top. A satinwood border accents the veneered top. The cabinet is stained and lacquered.

Thomas Sheraton styling is illustrated by the nightstand by Drexel from its Eighteenth Century Classic series, shown in Figure 3–13. Notice that the lines are very similar to those of Adams and Hepplewhite. In this stand, the four legs are left square, without taper, but they are routed with a bead. The two small angle braces provide style more than support, since the upper cabinet section is sufficient to provide stability. Veneered side and back panels, are set into the grooved legs. The bottom probably is dadoed into the sides and back. A dust cover is needed to support the drawer and add more stability. The doors and drawer are banded with a narrow strip, rounded to provide style. Throughout the design, graceful rectangular forms are used. Even the band around the top is rectangular, but tapers down to the front. Filigree hardware decorates the drawer and doors. The finish is mahogany and lacquer.

With the advent of the nineteenth century, three furniture periods began. They were the Regency, the Great Revival, and the Empire. All were in the age of mahogany. The example of furniture selected to represent this period is a trestle bookstand in the Regency style made from mahogany, shown in Figure 3–14.

The roll-around bookstand is a principal vertical mass unit, with a major upper mass and minor trestle assembly. The upper mass employs a drawer unit and three shelves. Let's discuss the construction techniques used for this upper unit. The ends should be cut out on a bandsaw and sanded; the edges should

Figure 3–12 DemiLune console from "Eighteenth Century Classics." (*Courtesy of Drexel Heritage Furnishings Inc., Drexel, North Carolina*)

Figure 3–13 Nightstand from "Eighteenth Century Classics." (*Courtesy of Drexel Heritage Furnishings Inc., Drexel, North Carolina*)

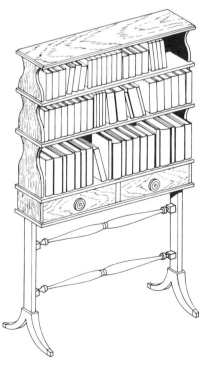

Figure 3–14 Trestle bookstand of the Regency period (English, circa 1810).

be slightly rounded. Shelves can be either doweled into the sides or blind dadoed into them. The edge of the shelves should be routed with an ogee curve. A small bead molding is used around the bottom of the drawer, extending to all four surfaces. The drawer should be made to fit within the sides, under the bottom shelf. The knobs are typical Regency styling. The back should be $\frac{1}{4}$-inch mahogany plywood, set into the sides, top, and bottom.

The trestle's lower mass is constructed with sofa table legs ending with metal caps and casters. These are two-piece units doweled and glued. The uprights are basically rectangular, but could be bowed slightly in the middle. Two identically turned stretchers provide stability and style. Notice that each stretcher has a square end. Each end should be made with a dowel that will ultimately be fitted into dowel holes in the uprights. Not shown is the horizontal member of the trestle that screws to the bottom of the upper unit.

After a thorough sanding, the cabinet needs to be stained with either a brown mahogany or red mahogany. Then the cabinet is lacquered to a high-gloss, polished finish.

Regency styling continued until almost the middle of the nineteenth century and then gave way to Victorian and Gothic Revival. The majority of furniture was made from mahogany. Some was finished satin, some high gloss.

The twentieth century saw a continuation of adaptations of earlier stylings until the advent of plywood and contemporary and modern styles. Furniture became very functional, often with stark, clean lines and frequently employing metal and glass or plastic.

A closing note: While my family and I lived in England, we toured many notable old buildings such as museums, pubs, churches, and hotels, and lived in a very old village outside of Huntingdon. We saw many examples of the furniture described in this chapter. World War II had a dramatic effect in that the English people both retained a measure of the old and experimented with new ideas and materials. The more modern styles of English cabinets are similar to those built in the United States.

REVIEW EXERCISES

1. The age of oak roughly lasted 150 years. (T/F)
2. The age of walnut included the William and Mary and Queen Anne styles. (T/F)
3. The major designers all were prominent during the walnut age. (T/F)
4. Earlier Jacabean styled cabinets were very ornate. (T/F)
5. The mortise-and-tenon joint was used as early as 1500 in England. (T/F)
6. The trumpet leg is associated with the William and Mary period. (T/F)
7. The Queen Anne table leg has a ball and claw. (T/F)
8. The famous cabinetmakers and designers produced work during the Georgian period. (T/F)

9. Sheraton built lighter furniture than Chippendale.   (T/F)

10. From the information provided in this chapter, when was a cabinet with a drawer first built?
   a. Circa 1500
   b. Circa 1580
   c. Circa 1640
   d. Circa 1700

11. Which illustration shows a Queen Anne desk with gate-leg frame?
   a. Figure 3–4
   b. Figure 3–5
   c. Figure 3–6
   d. Figure 3–7

ESSAYS

12. Explain in a few words how the cabriole leg changed the style of tables.

13. Make a matrix that shows the similarities and differences among the major English designers.

ANSWERS

1T, 2T, 3F, 4F, 5T, 6T, 7F, 8T, 9T, 10c, 11c

4

French Styled Furniture and Cabinets

The more one studies the styles of European furniture and cabinets, the smaller the arena appears. It's almost as if there was a large fraternity stretching from Greece to England. France's government and some of its people had their roots in the Roman Empire, yet later there were other influences from Spain, Germany, and England and the low countries. French craftsmen of furniture frequently based their styles on Greek and Roman classical figures, symbols, and designs, and modified them to the tastes and needs of the French royalty and gentry. Later the influence of the English designers became incorporated into the cabinetry and funiture of France. Nevertheless, the reader should not assume that the French merely copied the designs of others. This is not true. The individuality of French craftsmanship, especially during the reigns of Louis XV and XVI, was remarkable. Many of their styles were adopted by designers in Germany and the surrounding countries, and are some of the most desired today.

On a personal note, while my family and I lived in France we toured some of the chateaus and cathedrals and found many examples of the types of furniture described in this chapter. However, when we visited the homes of French families, we saw a wide variety of furniture. Their furniture was a lot like ours—a collage of old and newer twentieth century. Some was early 1900's, well worn, and several new pieces were modern veneered plywood furnishings, finished in heavy lacquers.

In this chapter we shall gain insight into the styles of French furniture and cabinets through several techniques: by taking a chronological approach, by studying the English designers who influenced the French, and finally by observing the construction techniques employed in several examples.

Objectives

1. To understand the characteristics of French styled furniture and cabinets as related to chronological viewpoints.
2. To identify the construction techniques and skills needed to create the furniture and cabinet styles.

4.1 CHARACTERISTICS OF FRENCH CABINETRY FROM A CHRONOLOGICAL VIEWPOINT

Much of the furniture of western civilization up through the mid-sixteenth century reflected the characteristics of classical styling which employed symmetrical shapes and forms. In France, however, with the rise of Houses of Bourbon and the reign of Henry IV, a new style evolved and swept through Europe. This style is called *Baroque*. Several references define the word *baroque* as a term that originated in Portugal and means an irregularly shaped pearl. This meaning is the essence of the Baroque style. In more modern terms, the style refers to the use of asymmetrical shapes and dimensions. In both a figurative and literal sense, it is indicative of movement. Recall from our discussions in Chapter 2 that the eye tends to follow the lines of a cabinet's trim, style, and design. This lesson is illustrative of the concept of Baroque, but the perception is extended even further. The asymmetrical proportions, characteristics, and materials of Baroque designs create power, boldness, and rich expression.

As shown in Table 4–1, the Baroque style lasted for a long time. Throughout its almost 200 years, the style itself changed. Early on, the styling was used on very large furniture—oversized by today's standards. These pieces included some asymmetrical styling, but many Greek and Roman classical characteristics remained. By the time of Louis XV, the style had moved away from the classic shapes and more towards the Baroque as the specific needs of royalty and court personnel caused a variety of characteristics to be designed and incorporated into furniture. We can see how this evolved by observing Figures 4–1, 4–2, 4–3, and 4–4.

The cabinet-on-stand shown in Figure 4–1 is an example of Louix XIII styling. Notice that many symmetrical proportions are evident. It is bulky and appears to have much mass. However, notice the extensive carving, turned segments, and flattened ball feet.

TABLE 4-1 CHRONOLOGY OF FRENCH PERIODS AND FURNITURE STYLES

Time	Periods/Names	Reigns/Governments	Styles
Sixteenth Century	House of Bourbon		
1589–1610		Henri IV (of Navarre)	
Seventeenth Century			
1610–1643		Louis XIII (le Juste)	Baroque (1550–1750)
1643–1715		Louis XIV (le Grande)	Louis XIV
Eighteenth Century			
1715–1774		Louix XV	Rococo (1720–75) Louix XV
1774–1792	First Republic	Louis XVI	Louis XVI
1792–1795		Convention	Directoire
1795–1799		Directory	
1799–1804		Consulate	
Nineteenth Century	First Empire		
1804–1814		Napoleon	Empire (1804–1815)
1814–1824	House of Bourbon—Restored	Louis XVIII	
1824–1830	House of Bourbon—Orleans	Charles X	
1836–1848	Second Republic	Louis-Phillippe	
1848–1848		Provisional Government	
1848–1852		Louis Napoleon	
1852–1870	Second Empire	Napoleon III	Empire (Renaissance, Revival, Louis XIV, XV, XVI, Rococo, Baroque)
1870–1871	Third Republic	Government of National Defense	
1871–1940		Various Presidents	

Regency (Early)

Regency (Late)

Neoclassic →

Figure 4–1 French Renaissance
schranks, Louis XIII (circa 1630).

In Figure 4–2, we see examples of Louix XIV Baroque style. There is more mixture and freedom in line and increased use of curves in the base and cap. The carvings are mostly asymmetrical. This schrank blends symmetry and asymmetry in the carving of irregular shapes.

Still within the Louis XIV reign but later, a greater emphasis of asymmetry is evident in the piece shown in Figure 4–3. This Baroque styled table is massive, and contains many curves, irregular carvings, and reliefs. The commode, with its round drawer fronts and curved legs, is a distinctly asymmetrically styled example.

Finally, the Louis XV table in Figure 4–4 shows the extent to which the Baroque style in France had moved into the movement. Some of the work done in this later period also shows more delicate styling and use of the cabriole leg.

Figure 4–2   French Baroque schrank, Louis XIV (circa 1680).

Figure 4–3 French Baroque table, Louis XIV (circa 1700).

Figure 4–4 French Rococo table, Louis XV (circa 1750).

Refer again to Table 4–1. Notice that during the eighteenth century and the reign of Louis XIV, the Baroque style began to give way to *Rococo*. Rococo, (from the French *rocaille,* meaning rockword) began in France. It is characterized by elaborate carvings and slender proportions. Others have described its characteristics as fanciful representations of rocks and seashells used extensively on tables, cabinets, cabriole legs, drawer fronts, trim, and aprons. All of the efforts in France were used to create delicate balance in the lines of a cabinet, table, or other piece of furniture. The Rococo style extended to about the end of the Regency period (the reign of Louix XVI).

History tells us that Louis XVI's reign ended in 1792 when he was overthrown and the First Republic was formed. While the new government was being formulated, no new furniture was being developed. It would appear that this was due to the French people's preoccupation with free citizenry and the sudden loss of a major market—the royalty. But in three short years (1795), a new government called the Directory took control, and with it came the style "Directoire." Furniture styled and made during the four years of this government bears its name. In all probability, the style was carried forward until Napolean's reign. Some pieces made in this style included gilding, fluting, tapered legs, stretchers on tables, and rococo carvings.

When Napoleon took the reins of power in France in 1804, he formed the "First Empire." He ruled for 11 years until his overthrow, when Louis XVIII of the House of Bourbon was restored to power. The style of French furniture has been called *Empire* and is associated with neoclassic style art. A major characteristic of the furniture was its massive dimensions.

Napoleon's designers were instrumental in furthering the Neoclassic style which had begun in the Directoire period. They adopted the characteristics of many Egyptian, Greek, and especially Roman antiques into their cabinets and furniture. Sweeping curves, symmetry, fluting and reeding, and other carvings of classical designs were incorporated into the Empire styles. These included acanthus foliage, animal-paw feet, birds such as the eagle, swags, brass overlays and inlays, and evoked feeling of imperialism.

Later, during the Second Empire (see Table 4–1), a revival of Baroque–Rococo styling began which lasted until the turn of the century. Louis XIV, XV, and XVI styled furniture was once again made by French as well as by cabinetmakers in other countries.

Now let us examine the styles of French cabinetry and furniture from another interesting viewpoint by showing the influence of English designers and cabinetmakers. Table 4–2 provides an illustration. Note the table is proportional. The center of the table is a calendar with a beginning date of 1715 and an ending date of 1820, covering a period of 105 years. On the left of the date line are the French periods during which significant styles of furniture were developed. These include Louix XV and XVI, the Directoire, and the Empire periods. On the right of the date line are the English designers who had influence over French styling: Chippendale, the Adams Brothers, Hepplewhite, and Sheraton.

TABLE 4–2 COMPARISON OF FRENCH PERIODS/STYLES TO ENGLISH DESIGNERS

French	Dates	English	Age
Louis XV	1715 1735 50 1755		Walnut
	70 1775 80 90	Chippendale Adams Brothers	Mahogany
Louis XVI	92	Hepplewhite	
Directoire	1795 99		
Empire	04 10 1815 1820	Sheraton	

Those cabinets and furniture pieces created during the later years of Louis XV's reign were, as you may recall, made in the Rococo style, yet some were influenced by both Chippendale and the Adams brothers. Therefore, a selected example of a Louis XV table, for example, could be dubbed "Louix XV–Chippendale" when, say, the table legs were fitted with a ball and claw. Likewise, a Louix XV cabinet or table that contained characteristics developed by the Adams brothers would be dubbed "Louis XV–Adams."

The same associations can be made for the remaining items in Table 4–2. Following are the possible combinations of names that French furniture and cabinets can have:

- Louis XV–Chippendale
- Louis XV–Adams
- Louis XVI–Hepplewhite
- Louis XVI–Adams
- Louis XVI–Chippendale
- Directoire–Hepplewhite
- Directoire–Sheraton
- Empire–Hepplewhite
- Empire–Sheraton

Figure 4–5 Hall chest from "Grand Villa." (*Courtesy of Drexel Heritage Furnishings Inc., Drexel, North Carolina*)

Note: These combinations are used to describe furniture in books about antiques, in antique shops, and in museums.

Let's conclude this section with several French-related terms that carry over to the furniture of the periods we have been discussing.

1. The "Bombé" is a style of chest from the late Baroque–Rococo period that also incorporates some Chippendale characteristics. It is characterized by bulging sides and front (Figure 4–5).

2. The "chiffonier," originally designed in France, was in fact a tall chest in which ladies kept odds and ends of needlework and fabric swatches. In later usage, personal garments and sometimes jewelry were kept in these cabinets. Sometimes the cabinets contained mirrors. In almost all cases the cabinets were heavily carved and contained many asymmetrical shapes.

The discussion just completed should provide a definite feeling of the character and nature of French styled furniture and cabinets. It should have established a framework of styles and the changes that have taken place over several hundred years. Now let us proceed to the next section, where we shall deal with the construction techniques used to create the French style.

4.2 CONSTRUCTION TECHNIQUES AND SKILLS NEEDED TO CREATE FRENCH STYLED FURNITURE

The several examples presented in this section are taken from Drexel Heritage Furniture's "Cabernet Classics" and "Grand Villa" collections. The designs are linked to the French Rococo period. As we shall see, the examples include deep moldings, gracefully curved cabriole legs, delicately carved rosettes and vinery, inlaid basket-weave parquetry, the use of pecan veneers and solids, and brass appointments. The finishing techniques include an aging process. The four pieces that have been selected for our discussion are a sofa table, lingerie chest, armoire, and hall chest.

Sofa Table

Figure 4–6 provides us with the visual dimensions and characteristics of the sofa table selected for our discussion. The table has overall dimensions of W60, D15, H26. Its basic parts include four cabriole legs, four apron pieces and a top, and associated reinforcing blocks.

    The piece has double-reverse curved legs, which can be cut on a bandsaw. A gentle rounding of the outer corner surface is made. A groove is routed into the inner surfaces of two sides of each leg and continues across the lower edge

Figure 4–6 Sofa table from "Cabernet Classics." (*Courtesy of Drexel Heritage Furnishings Inc., Drexel, North Carolina*)

of the apron. Three methods can be used to anchor the legs. One is to insert lag bolts/screws into each leg and then bolt the leg to the table. A second anchoring method would use dowels. Four dowels would be used to secure the leg to the two apron pieces. The third technique that could be used is the mortise and tenon. A tenon would be cut into the end of each apron. A corresponding mortise would be cut into the leg for each apron. Then the pieces would be inserted into each other during assembly.

Once the anchoring technique is decided on, the aprons can be cut. All the aprons should be styled with the same patterns included on the front and ends. Carefully note how the designers have followed the rules for curve and curve ending on the lower apron edges, as described in Chapter 2. This design is easily cut out on a band saw. A router with the same setting and bit as was used on the legs is used along the curved lower edge of the apron pieces.

Now the carving must be done. First, a pattern of the vinery with rosette in the center needs to be made on tracing paper. Then the pattern is transferred onto the apron. Finally, the leaves, vines, and rosette are carved into the wood.

Next the table top is made. Several techniques are possible. A veneer top can be made as follows. Use a $\frac{3}{4}$-inch-thick plywood base around which stock lumber is glued. This produces the overall size. Then this base is laminated with veneer. When dry, the shape of the perimeter is marked and cut. Finally, the edges are routed in an ogee pattern.

Sanding should be done to make all pieces smooth and lustrous. Then the table is assembled, stained, and finished.

Lingerie Chest

The seven-drawer lingerie chest shown in Figure 4–7 is a beautiful cabinet. Due to its detail, it is a complex project. Its dimensions are W22, D17, and H57, and it has jewelry trays in the top drawer. All seven drawers are identical in size and construction and consist of a basic drawer assembly of ornate panel-and-frame design, decorated with vinery. Drawer pulls are bronze, detailed in a rosette.

Overall, then, the cabinet consists primarily of a group of panel-and-frame assemblies: end assemblies, dust cover assemblies, and drawer front assemblies. In addition the assemblies there are a top designed much like the one for the sofa table shown earlier, an apron beneath the lowest drawer, and a back.

The simplest way to construct this cabinet would be to first make the end assemblies as a pair. The upright stiles need band-saw cutting on the bottom, a dado groove or rabbet for the panel, and reeding for style. Each crossmember rail must be cut and shaped according to the assembly technique used, dowel or mortise-and-tenon.

Next would be the task of making the dust cover panels or drawer separator assemblies. These would need to be fastened to the ends, probably with

Figure 4-7 Lingerie chest from "Cabernet Classics." (*Courtesy of Drexel Heritage Furnishings Inc., Drexel, North Carolina*)

dowels. During the assembly stage the apron piece, previously cut and molded, would be doweled as well. Then the top would be constructed and installed.

Seven drawer front assemblies need to be made from $\frac{3}{4}$-inch stock. The panel is probably glued directly to the frame or part of it may be rabbetted into the frame. In either event, the sides of the drawer would be dovetailed into the panel.

The back of the cabinet, probably $\frac{1}{4}$-inch plywood, must be inset into a rabbet in the top and both ends. Therefore, the dust cover panels must be recessed to allow for the back.

Careful sanding is done, then the drawer pulls and back plates are installed for fit. Before these are installed permanently, the cabinet needs staining and finishing.

Armoire

The armoire shown in Figure 4–8 is a large, ornate cabinet or wardrobe. Its dimensions are W47, D20, and H82. This one shown is from Drexel's "Cabernet Classics" collection. Looking at the inset with the doors ajar, we can observe two adjustable shelves, one fixed shelf, and four removable shirt partitions making seven open compartments. The two tray drawers beneath the lower shelf make up the upper section. The lower section has three tray drawers. All drawers roll on adjustable guides. The interior of the cabinet can be lighted by an interior lamp whose cord passes through the cabinet's back.

Technically, this is a very complex cabinet that requires a shop with a wide variety of capabilities as well as varied skills by the craftsman. Let's begin the analysis with the view of the closed cabinet. There are two ends made with frame-and-panel construction. These are not simple assemblies, since there are curves in the styles and molded shapes around the perimeter of each panel and in the stile. A dust cover assembly at the base stabilizes the base structure, as does the apron along the base. The complex curved top assembly requires a shop with the capability to produce curved plywood by laminating veneers. The solids can be cut from pieces glued together. The entire top assembly sets over and down onto the end assemblies. The piece across the front and top is curved to fit under the top assembly and, as can be seen by looking at the inset in Figure 4–8, is curved along its bottom surface as well. These lower curves correspond to the shape of the doors so that the doors overlap the piece by $\frac{3}{8}$ to $\frac{1}{2}$ inch.

There are two doors, but on one an astragal is fastened to it. This shows up in Figure 4–8, between the two closed doors. The astragal has routing designs in it, as shown in the figure.

The doors have a very complex panel-and-frame design. The sides and bottom are rectangular, but the top rail is curved, thus making each stile a different length. Since a dowel or mortise-and-tenon construction technique should be used to connect stiles to rails, this makes a very strong door frame. Notice the special cuts along the inner edges of the bottom and top rails, and the vinery and rosette carving in the middle rails.

Once assembled, the special molding, partially inset, serves two functions. First, it adds relief to the door giving the panel added depth. Second, the inner molding edge along with the door frame make a rabbet for the panel.

The panels are specially veneered with pecan that creates a crisscross pattern. This adds more style. Finally, the long mortise hinges and pull with back plate complete the French effect.

The five drawers should be made with the dovetail joint. The gap between drawers is to allow for ease of opening. Adjustable shelves need to be supported, so some technique of shelf support must be used.

The cabinet finishing process is a complex one. A great deal of sanding must be done. Stains and topcoats of oil or lacquer must be capable of preserving the woods and cabinet.

Figure 4–8 Armoire from "Cabernet Classics." (*Courtesy of Drexel Heritage Furnishings Inc., Drexel, North Carolina*)

Hall Chest

The hall chest shown in Figure 4–9, from Drexel's Grand Ville collection, is a version of French Bombé styling. This style, as you may recall, has a bulging profile on the ends as well as the front. This is the same cabinet used in Chapter 1 for another illustration. We discuss here the techniques and skills needed to make it.

This cabinet consists of panel-and-frame ends, horizontal rails across the front, dust covers for drawer protection, a top, and three drawers. Carving is

Figure 4-9 Hall chest from "Grand Villa." (*Courtesy of Drexel Heritage Furnishings Inc., Drexel, North Carolina*)

limited to the design in the center of the apron, and fluting is used in the top drawer front. The drawer fronts are flat.

The four stiles are complex pieces that require cutting on a band saw as well as carving on the foot. The three rails require a small routing to form a bead. The lower edge of the lowest rail requires several routing cuts after the initial shape is cut. A rabbet needs to be made to allow installation of the two panels. With all of this work done, the ends can be assembled. The bottom panel is curved, so it must be built up or molded in a heat chamber.

Next, three dust covers need to be made, each of which is a different dimension because of the Bombé design. These need to be installed into the end stiles, but not before the four horizontal front rail pieces are ready. When all parts are ready, they should be joined together with dowels.

Next a top assembly needs to be made from stock lumber and veneers. Its edges can be shaped with either a shaper or router (probably a shaper). When completed, it is set over the cabinet and glued and screwed to the reinforcing blocks. Although the drawer fronts may be flat or almost flat, their perimeter design of self-molding with router or shaper softens their connection to the rails and stiles. The shape of the drawer fronts conforms on the sides to the curves of the stiles. Drawer construction follows accepted form. All drawers slide on guides.

A nice style characteristic in the form of a half-curve molding separates the lower and upper sections of the cabinet. Antique bronze hardware completes the assembly.

Finishing on this cabinet is as described earlier for other French styled cabinets.

Summary

From the discussions about the technical aspects of designing and making French style cabinets and furniture, we can conclude that considerable skill and a wide variety of knowledge are needed. There is always a combination of materials. There is almost always a combination of angles and moldings. Yet in all cases, the rules of cabinetry that we studied in Chapter 2 are carried out with great precision.

REVIEW EXERCISES

1. Baroque styled furniture in France can be associated with the House of Bourbon. (T/F)
2. The period of "Early Regency" in France related to furniture in the Baroque, Rococo, and Directoire styles. (T/F)
3. Rococo is a style of furniture that originated in France. (T/F)
4. Some Louis XV furniture designs can include Sheraton features. (T/F)
5. A Directoire styled cabinet or table may include the influence of Hepplewhite's designs. (T/F)
6. Baroque styling:
   a. conformed religiously to Greek and Roman classical styles.
   b. was from a period where a break away from classical styles began.
7. The characteristic *not* found in Baroque furniture is:
   a. boldness.
   b. heavy proportions.
   c. asymmetry of design.
   d. tapered, fluted delicate features.
8. Empire styling included all but one of the following. Which is incorrect?
   a. Egyptian characteristics and features.
   b. Roman characteristics and features.
   c. Greek characteristics and features.
   d. German characteristics and features.
9. A Bombé styled cabinet from French design includes:
   a. tall slender proportions.
   b. writing surfaces as a drop leaf.
   c. bulging front and ends of a chest with drawers.
   d. gate leg design with at least five legs.

10. The cabriole leg used in French styled cabinets is mostly the:
  a. Queen Anne variety.
  b. Chippendale variety.
  c. A simple style with little or no carving.
  d. A single-curve design versus a double-curve design.

ESSAYS

11. In your own words, describe the techniques you would use to construct the lingerie chest shown in Figure 4–7.
12. Explain in a paragraph or two what makes building the doors for the armoire in Figure 4–8 so complicated.
13. If you had to build the Bombé style hall chest illustrated in Figure 4–9, describe how you would construct the end panel and leg assemblies.

ANSWERS

1T, 2F, 3T, 4F, 5T, 6b, 7d, 8d, 9c, 10b

5

German Styled Furniture and Cabinets

From my earliest days of recollection, I was, from time to time, in the presence of a master German furniture maker and woodcarver. His skills were absolutely superb. As if by magic, he could create a rosette or leaf and vine in a matter of minutes. Unfortunately for me, I did not live close enough to train under his guidance. His work is in thousands of homes in Germany and in the United States. As with many craftsmen, his training was done over a period of 15 years or more. Not only was training done with wood, but trainees often carved in stone and sometimes did bronze casting as well. What is interesting is that this concept of long apprenticeship dates back several hundred years. Although almost all German cabinetmakers were skilled in the techniques of the trade, their work differed dramatically due to the customs of the various peoples of Germany, and the influences that came into play during different periods in German history. In this chapter we explain why there are so many different styles of furniture and cabinets, study about the influences that brought them about, and examine the construction techniques used with German styled furniture.

Objectives

1. To identify the characteristics of German styled cabinets and furniture.
2. To examine several construction techniques and skills used in making German cabinets and furniture.

5.1 CHARACTERISTICS OF GERMAN FURNITURE AND CABINETS

Three conditions make it difficult to organize the study of German styled cabinets and furniture. First, today, as they did hundreds of years ago, northern Germans in the lowland lived by different standards and customs than the southern Germans in the high country. Second, the styles were dictated by the cultures and ruling classes. Third, the development of the country was not as smooth as, for example, England or France, due in part to the many ruling parties and duchies, the terrain, and the constant partitioning of the territory.

Many customs and cultures were developed on the personal initiative of German craftsmen, but to a great extent the influence of craftsmen from other countries caused styles to evolve. When the Roman Empire expanded north, the German people began to recognize and use classical, symmetrical styling brought by Roman craftsmen. Sometime later, the French, especially during the Louis XIV, XV, and XVI periods, influenced the craftsmen as well as the culture. Also especially significant was the influence of the famous English designers such as Chippendale, Sheraton, and the Adams brothers. As the architecture of the country changed, the furniture and cabinet styles changed as well. This was because many German architects were also cabinetmakers.

In the latter part of the fifteenth century, north German styling contained a lot of very detailed carving with overtones of religious influence. Figures of royalty and the church were carved into panels in doors. Great pains were taken to strictly adhere to symmetry. In addition, the Gothic arch cathedral design, which was the architectural design breakthrough of the era, was used extensively.

Miters were used on angles other than 90-degree corners. Although many cabinets were made with a base, seldom were bases solid as they are today. Instead, the cabinet-on-stand design was prevalent. Above all, the furniture and cabinets were oversized by today's standards. The sizes were similar to those found in England at the same time. In the mountains in the south of Germany, which was more or less under control of the Hapsburgs, cabinetmaking was very different. It was smaller in scale and included trestle design, fretwork, and extensive carvings of a natural motif. Here too the Gothic arch design was used in many pieces of the time. In the south, the design of cabinets was to create bases that were ornate and set on four legs with stretchers separating and securing them. Doors with panels were used extensively. In some cabinets the dovetail joint was used to anchor the sides to the ends, as well as the front to the end and base pieces. Overall, the workmanship was exquisite.

During the Renaissance (late sixteenth century), cabinets made in north Germany often were crafted with murals in wood. Whole scenes of towns were carved into the front of trunks and schranks. Buildings, people, and landscapes were carved in perfect relief and exquisite detail. For example, where we might use reeding on an outside style of a cabinet front, German craftsmen would carve the frontal view of a religious leader, a person of royalty, or a lovely woman. Cabinet crowns, although straight across rather than split-bonnet, were extremely ornate. Many had extensive carvings of a natural motif, such as flowers or animals of the forest, and elaborately carved moldings. One illustration of such exquisite workmanship is shown in Figure 5–1.

The Baroque period already discussed in earlier chapters existed in Germany as well. Cabinets were richly decorated with carvings and moldings. There were differences between northern and southern German craftsmen's styles. The north incorporated fewer examples of animals and human forms, whereas the southern craftsmen still used figures and vegetation in their work. Also evident in this period was the chest on stand. However, many of the stands had twisted-rope design legs. Stretchers kept the legs in proper alignment. Crowns still were level, but some cabinetmakers began to concentrate on the division of the crown into halves with a distinctive feature in the center. On at least one cabinet, a finial was used. As we have already learned, cabinets and tables built around 1700 were very, very heavy and oversized.

By the time of the Rococo period, following the Baroque period, designs changed considerably. Cabinets were made much smaller and were simpler in design, similar to those made in England and France. The Chippendale design of serpentine style chest of drawers and even a variation of the French Bombé style were made.

From early 1820 to the end of the nineteenth century, the styles became less and less ornate and much more functional. Hand carvings gave way to more and more machine work. Part of this may have been attributed to the decline of the House of Hapsburg and the overall changes in Germany as a country, but much of the cause lies with the cultural changes of the people. Between the end of the Rococo and the beginning of the Neoclassic period (1815–1845), the Biedermeier style became very prominent. The style was affordable to the middle class and expressive of their life style. Biedermeier styled furniture encompassed characteristics of Empire and Directoire styles. At its best, it softened the strictness and formality of Empire style, but was heavier than the Directoire styled pieces. It offered simplicity, durability, functionality, and a choice of lighter colored woods and finishes. Several characteristics also included the use of the wood's natural grain, contrasted with ebony, simple and modest inlay, and several design features later found in Danish modern. As with other styles, cabinetmakers began to experiment with the Biedermeier style, often with grotesque, surrealistic results. Such additions as serpents, more curves, and humanistic forms were added to pieces toward the end of the period.

A distinctive series of events caused the creation of some exquisite cabinets and furniture to be made. It occurred during the reigns of Louis I and II. Louis I, known as King Ludwig I, traveled extensively to Rome, where he observed style and character of architecture. He thus was instrumental in bring-

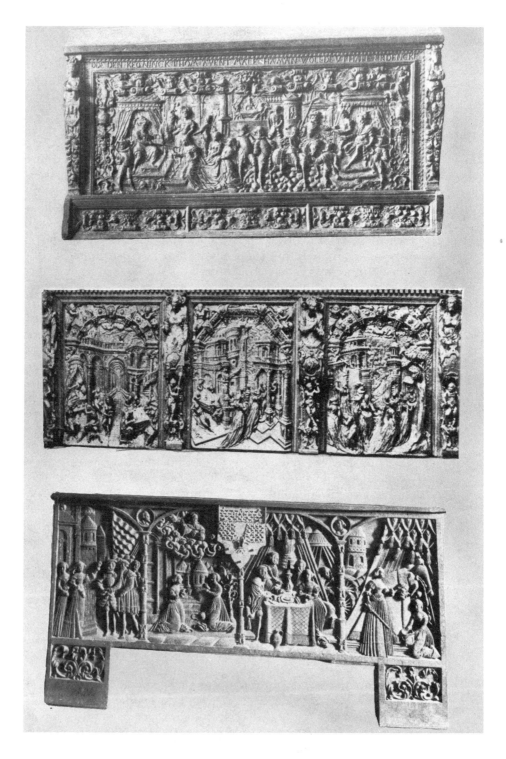

Figure 5–1 German trunk with a mural relief carving.

ing the ornate, classical style of architecture and furniture styles to Munich. Louis (Ludwig) II, also king of Bavaria, was responsible for the erection of a series of castles that embodied the finest craftsmanship of the time.

I have seen many of the ornate beds, dressers, schranks, tables, and many other cabinets firsthand. Most were inlaid with gold and some with mother-of-pearl. Almost all had high-gloss or dense, hand-rubbed satin finishes. It's difficult to express the breathtaking workmanship of these pieces. They were so complex and detailed that such a cabinet may have taken a year to make.

The wars of the twentieth century have done much to change the styles of German furniture. Particle core plywood is used extensively today. Cabinets are smaller in dimension and scale since stock materials are much thinner than in the past. However, even though the furniture and cabinets are made with different materials, modern machines, and modern styles, they are well made and are beautiful. They adhere to the design principles studied in Chapter 2.

In summary, the styles and characteristics of German cabinets and furniture followed many of the same periods as other European countries: Roman, Byzantine, Renaissance, Baroque, Rococo, Regency, Empire, and Biedermeier and Neoclassic. Although the precise styling and character was dictated by the desires and tastes of the different peoples of northern and southern Germany, in all cases the workmanship was excellent and endures even when viewed by today's standards.

5.2 CONSTRUCTION TECHNIQUES AND SKILLS USED IN MAKING GERMAN STYLED FURNITURE AND CABINETS

The first of several German styled cabinets and furniture pieces we shall examine is a scribe table that was created in Germany about 1790, shown in Figure 5–2. Since this table is rather large, it would be built if a person had a large bedroom or library, or it could be scaled down. As shown, it is massive in proportions, roughly, 60W, 24D, and 29H. It has three drawers built into the apron and two drawers built into the pigeonhole storage area. Notice the four-inch-thick legs, which add considerable emphasis to its massive appearance.

The technical construction should be considered as two separate phases, the table and the pigeonhole assembly. Let's begin with the table.

The four legs must be turned first, then hand carved. The simulated column from the Neoclassic period is evident in the foot and in the Corinthian or flame crown at the top of the turned part of each leg. The slightly curved carving on each leg is continued on the main section, giving a suggestion of smoke or fire rising. On the areas to be gilded, the carving is small. The apron around the table is made from solid stock and is very plain. The front apron is an assembly of smaller pieces, which create three openings for the drawers.

I would recommend that the lower rail across the front be made from one piece of five-quarter or eight-quarter stock, so that support is built into the table, thus reducing the chance of sag. All joints in the front frame should be

Figure 5–2 German styled scribe table.

doweled for added holding power. Since the drawers slide along the leg, no end pieces are made into the frame of the drawer opening. This means either a mortise-and-tenon joint or a doweled joint must be used to connect aprons to legs. My preference would be to use the mortise and tenon. A mortise would be made into two sides of each leg, then tenons would be made on each end of the apron pieces. After proper fitting, they should be separated, then glue applied to the mortise walls and the table assembled. This action may be done all at once or in two steps. If you have enough clamps, a one-step operation is fine. If you have a limited number of clamps, use the two-step process. First glue the legs to the end aprons, and later glue the front and back aprons to the legs.

Technically, there is a serious problem in gluing tables together, since there is a real tendency for racking or out-of-squareness. Racking occurs during the clamping operation. When a bar clamp is placed such that it is not exactly parallel to the adjacent line of the wood—in this case the apron—a parallelogram is created as the clamp is tightened. This causes the assembly to rack away from absolute true. When the four sides are finally glued with this rack included, only three legs at any one time will touch the floor. Considering the carving done on the legs on this table, the project would be a failure, so ensure that no racking occurs during clamping.

Out-of-squareness is the second problem. This happens in two ways. First, when the clamp squeezes the legs onto the apron, there is a tendency for the legs to either tile inward (usual) or outward due to the positioning of the clamp.

The best solution for this is to nail a spreader piece into the exact center of the bottom of each leg, then tighten the clamp while measuring the exact length from center to center of each leg. When both are precisely the same, a rectangle is formed. Next, a framing square is used to ensure that the angle is 90 degrees from center line to the top of the apron. The second misalignment also occurs when clamping, but this time the problem is that the leg tends to twist if the pressure of the clamp is not centered over the center line of the tenon. Look at Figure 5–3 for an example. In view (a), the clamp is aligned with its center force directly in line with the center line of the tenon. When the clamp is tightened, equal pressure is applied to each shoulder on the tenon. The result is a square aligned joint. In contrast, view (b) shows an inside twist. Because the center force on the clamp is too far into the inside, the inside shoulder is under

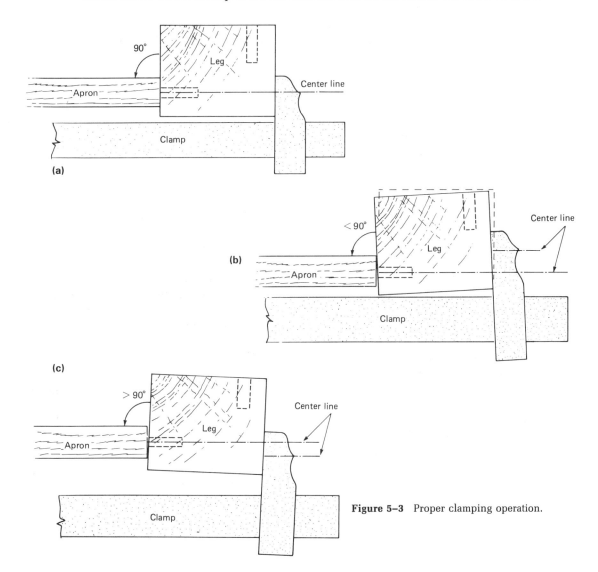

Figure 5–3 Proper clamping operation.

greater force than the outer one. The resultant imbalance creates an out-of-square relationship toward the inside. View (c) shows the opposite. If this is permitted to occur, there is no way that the fully assembled table can be made square. So 90-degree corners must be made during the clamping task—no margin for error is permitted.

This table top was made before the days of plywood. If you were to duplicate it, the top would need to be constructed of solid wood pieces glued together. Only by using this technique can warping be controlled. The band around the three sides of the table extends up about two inches. It has routing along its top edge and is scalloped on the ends, thus reducing the mass and sharpness of the corners. The top banding pieces should be screwed to the top from beneath the top. The top should be glued and screwed to the legs and aprons using bevel holes in both the legs and aprons. The use of bevel holes eliminates the need for glue/screw blocks.

Next, the drawer guides need to be made and installed. Today we would use metal guides, but when this piece was made wood guides were used. Modern metal guides limit the amount of drop to the drawer front to about $\frac{1}{4}$ to $\frac{3}{8}$ inch when the drawer is pulled open. Wood guides should hold to the same standards.

The drawers are set flush with the apron. Therefore, the drawer fronts should be made first to custom fit each drawer opening before the rest of the drawer is built.

Last, the table's corner ornaments need to be designed, cut, and installed. There should be two of these per leg for a total of eight. After the installation of the corner ornaments, the table is ready for final sanding and finishing.

Now let's discuss the construction of the pigeonhole unit which rests on top of the table. As you can judge from the figure, its length is roughly 2 feet shorter than the table. Its height is about 12 inches and its design is balanced. Its depth should be about 8 inches.

The entire design should be constructed with rabbet and dado joints. The end pieces should fit under the top and enclose the bottom, so there needs to be two dadoes for shelves/drawer supports and a rabbet for the bottom. The width of rabbet and dado must be equal to the thickness of the unit material used. Lumber $\frac{3}{4}$ inch think could be used, but would be a little heavy. However, given the mass of the table, it would probably look fine. The bottom needs dadoes for each of the four intermediate vertical partitions. The top must set down over all vertical members, ends, and partitions; therefore, end rabbets and dadoes must all be made the same depth. All vertical members need dadoes to permit shelf support. Finally, rabbets need to be made in the ends and top for inserting the back.

The unit should be assembled dry and held with clamps until all shelves are cut and fit. Once every piece is correct, the unit can be glued together. Next, the facing moldings, corner moldings, and decorative adornment which extends around three sides of the top need to be created and installed. Then the four drawers are made by using the same technique used with the table drawer. Finally, the handles are installed.

As you can guess from Figure 5–2, parts of this writing table are gilded. After the stain and top or final finishes are applied, apply the gilding to the legs, corner braces on the table and pigeonhole units, on the unit's facing, and on the adornment around the unit's top.

This completes the technical description of the writing table. It is an interesting project. As stated earlier, it is massive, but could be scaled down to better fit a small room.

The lamp table or nightstand shown in Figure 5–4 is of German design from the Biedermeier period around the 1830s. Our analysis of its construction techniques is a bit different than those in earlier chapters and for the table just covered. This cabinet requires a great deal of skill in applying veneer and using a router. Let's begin.

Four flattened ball feet need to be turned on a lathe. While making these, create a dowel about $\frac{1}{2}$ inch in diameter by 1 inch long as part of the foot. This eliminates the need for separate dowels and assures maximum strength and centering.

Figure 5–4 Lamp table or nightstand.

The base is a perfect square made from a frame, with reinforced corner blocks, and a flat surface raised about $\frac{1}{8}$ inch. A small molding trims the bottom edge. Once the frame and frame top are made, the piece needs to be veneered. Given the time that this cabinet was built (around 1839), the veneer used was probably mahogany. Once the veneer has been applied, the molding needs to be cut and glued in place. The feet are then attached by drilling a hole for each into the corner glue block. The foot should be flush with the outer corner of the base.

Next we would make the raised platform or step on the base. Since this piece is about $1\frac{1}{2}$ inches thick, a solid assembly is desirable. Notice that there is a cove grooved into each long side. Veneer needs to be applied to all exposed surfaces. Once this is done, the assembly should be set aside until later.

Now the two table-top supports need to be made. The base of these assemblies should be constructed from at least three pieces; more may be preferable. One rectangular piece should be used in the middle section. Two pieces wide enough to permit layout of the double "S" shapes are needed. A small brace piece, four $\frac{1}{4}$-inch dowels, a thin cap piece, and button add-ons complete the material requirements.

The lyre-shaped assembly is roughly 2 inches thick at the bottom to slightly over 1 inch thick at the top. What this means in terms of construction is that a band saw is used not only to cut the S curves, but also to taper the thickness.

Here is how you could create each lyre assembly. Lay out and cut the basic pieces that will form the main structure. Drill dowel holes and fit the pieces together without glue. Once fitted, lay out the shape with a pattern previously made on paper. Then separate the pieces and cut the taper on the inside of each upright. Working with a rectangular piece is much simpler than working with a curved one. If your band saw cannot open wide enough to cut away the wood, repeated passes on a joiner can accomplish the job. Once both pieces are tapered (make sure you have a pair for each assembly), reassemble all the materials, but this time use glue and clamps. Once the glue has dried, cut the shape according to your pattern, then sand all surfaces smooth. Use a drum sander for all curves and belt sander for the flat surface.

Next prepare the base piece for the dowels, which represent the chords of the lyre, and the top. Drill matching dowel holes. Add the edge routing to the lower piece so that it looks like a cap piece, and groove the upper piece to create a bead effect. Cut the dowels to the proper length and glue the assembly.

Now a combination of tasks must be done: some veneering, then routing, then more assembly. The veneer operation requires first that crosswise veneer be applied to the edges of the assembly. This is the only way that veneer will bend around the small arcs which have been cut with the band saw. Hot glue or a very good contact cement are the best choices for veneering. All edge veneers should be applied in one operation and allowed to dry. Once dry, they need to be trimmed flush. The surface veneer pieces are then applied. They too must be trimmed after the glue has dried. Next, a router bit is used to cut the flat groove along the perimeters, as shown in the figure. These will be gilded later. (An alternative that may be more appealing would be to paint gilding onto the finished assembly after staining has been done, thus eliminating the routing operation.)

Finally, the simulated chord unit must be installed. There is a slight bit of spreading possible at the upper end, but we can use this to our advantage. Metal pins, such as cutoff nails, can be installed in each side at about the point where the top piece of the chord assembly will fasten to the side. The pins probably should not project more than $\frac{1}{8}$ inch. If no flexibility is observed, then abandon the idea of using pins and rely solely on a glue band.

This completes the description of the supports. At this time the supports can either be set aside until later or can be mounted to the step of the base unit. If mounting is desired, then each support should be mounted with glue and two or three screws. Of course, the screws must be installed through the bottom of the step piece. Then the step piece can be glued. It must be screwed to the base from the underside of the base. Perfect alignment during these operations is an absolute must; no margin for error exists. This means that when the supports stand they are (1) in a truly parallel configuration, (2) 90 degrees from the cross section of the base and (3) an equal distance apart from top to bottom, measured vertically along the center line of each support.

Now let's build the top of the cabinet. It is a perfectly circular top whose sides (apron) are approximately 3 inches high. A close look at the figure reveals several significant details. The top piece overlaps the apron by about $\frac{1}{2}$ inch and its edge is without molding. Next, decorative carvings which gives the appearance of rectangles is made into or onto the apron. There are four of these. Two pieces of wood extend below the apron, each of which is the base for mounting the supports to the top.

About the only way to proceed with construction of the top assembly is to form the substrata of the apron. The wood used should be 1 to $1\frac{1}{4}$ inches thick. At least eight miter joints should be used to create the circle. Once the glue is dry, the octagon must be scribed with a circle and cut on the band saw, then sanded smooth enough to permit application of the veneer.

Next the veneer needs to be glued onto the apron. The grain should run lengthwise around the circumference of the apron. A single butt joint should be made where the two ends meet. Because of its large radius, there should be little problem bending the thin veneer. Clamps will be needed if liquid glue is used. The best type is the strap clamp since it (or they) will conform to a circle. If contact cement is used, the joint should be clamped to ensure a solid, firm bond, since this is the joint where the stress in the veneer is most likely to cause a rupture.

When the glue or cement has dried and cured, the excess veneer must be trimmed flush. Then the four rectangles need to be either routed or overlaid. (The method used for this operation must be the same as that used on the supports.)

Now the top must be made. A single piece of $\frac{3}{4}$-inch plywood should be used and cut into a circle whose diameter is 1 inch wider than the finished apron. The edge veneer needs to be applied first and trimmed, then the top veneer needs to be matched, applied, and trimmed. The top is mounted to the apron with glue and screws. The screw holes need to be made on a bevel into the thickest part of at least four of the eight pieces that made up the frame for the apron.

Two strips of wood are prepared next. These are about $1\frac{1}{2}$ inches wide by $\frac{1}{2}$ inch thick and long enough to be screwed to the underside of the top assembly. The edges should be rounded. Here's how they are used: First, each one,

Figure 5–5 China cabinet.

with its rounded side facing the floor, is centered over a lyre support assembly. One hole is drilled for a screw at each end through the piece and into the contacting point of the support. Then flat-head wood screws are installed. The task is repeated on the other support with the second strip of wood. Next, the top assembly is mounted to the strips. This is accomplished by placing the top veneered surface down, and then placing the support and base assemblies upside down onto the top assembly. Final positioning is done and four screws are used to unite the cabinet's top to its base.

A final touch to the design could include either a $\frac{1}{8}$-inch flat groove routing or gilding overlay onto the table top surface about 1 or $1\frac{1}{4}$ inches in from the outer edge.

The cabinet is now built and the finishing process begins. Sealers, stains, and lacquer are the proper materials to use on this cabinet. Satin-finish or high-gloss lacquer will produce the most beautiful finishes for this style cabinet.

As an alternative, you could make the cabinet with a 20-inch-diameter base, 22- to 24-inch-diameter top and about 27 inches high.

This ends our technical description of German styled cabinets and furniture. The skill and artistry evident in the early works of the craftsmen's skill remains today, as is seen in the china cabinet shown in Figure 5–5. This cabinet is fully collapsible for easy transportation and carries many of the early design features characteristic of German furniture, although it was built in the twentieth century.

REVIEW EXERCISES

1. German furniture styles were influenced by Rome, France, and England. (T/F)
2. In the later part of the fifteenth century, German styling contained many religious overtones. (T/F)
3. Unlike the furniture of other European countries, early German furniture was *not* oversized. (T/F)
4. A renaissance cabinet or chest made in northern Germany could contain a mural of a street scene. (T/F)
5. Baroque styled cabinets in the north and south were designed with the same subjects in the carvings. (T/F)
6. Germans included Chippendale characteristics in some of their chests of drawers. (T/F)
7. German styling significantly changed from ornate to functionally plain around 1820. (T/F)
8. What makes the table leg of the table shown in Figure 5–2 appear to be neoclassic?
   a. The carving of flame.
   b. The flame crown near the top of the leg.
   c. The simulated column part of the leg.
   d. Both b and c above.

ESSAYS

9. Describe the problem of *racking* when legs are glued to their apron pieces.
10. What advantage is there to using a bevel pilot screw hole to a wood block? Explain and use sketeches if necessary.
11. Why is the veneer on the edges of the "lyre" assembly of the stand in Figure 5–4 crosswise? Explain in technical terms and description.

ANSWERS

1T, 2T, 3F, 4T, 5F, 6T, 7T, 8d

6

Belgian Styled Furniture and Cabinets

The furniture styles of Belgium, like those of many other European countries, are rooted in the classical and earlier periods. In this chapter we shall see how one of Belgium's largest furniture manufacturers has set modern styles, yet at the same time carried forward many of the early design concepts and traditions. In the first section of this chapter we observe how the proportionally massive characteristics of earlier styles have been retained, although they have been scaled down somewhat. This chapter is also interesting from the point of view of the wide variety of styles, shapes, and functions illustrated. In the second part of the chapter we discuss the construction techniques employed in many of the cabinets.

Objectives

1. To gain awareness of the characteristics and styles of cabinets and furniture constructed by Karel Mintjens of Belgium.
2. To understand the cabinetmaking skills, materials, and techniques used in making Belgian styled cabinets and furniture.

6.1 CHARACTERISTICS OF BELGIAN STYLED FURNITURE AND CABINETS

All of the illustrations used in this section have been provided by Karel Mintjens, N. V., of Westmalle, Belgium, or its American outlet in Leesburg, Virginia. This company testifies that they are Europe's largest manufacturer of traditional oak furniture.[1] The company specializes in modular units and stand-alone pieces such as tables, chairs, and frames for cushioned furniture. Since many pieces are not large but are very specialized, we can learn quite a bit from studying them. As do most well organized manufacturers, Karel Mintjens' plant has large scaled machines and kiln-dries the lumber it imports.

We shall examine three modular systems as well as several groups and a few individual pieces in order to meet our first objective.

The "1.2.3 Program," shown in one configuration in Figure 6–1(a), consists of a variety of base units 30W, 20D, 23H, and upper units 30W, $15\frac{3}{4}$D or 20D, $27\frac{3}{4}$H or $55\frac{1}{2}$H. At this time, take a good, close look at the modular units in Figure 6–1 before proceeding with the discussion.

This group is designed in accordance with many of the design principles learned in Chapter 2. The units with doors are horizontally balanced. The drawer unit of three drawers is vertically balanced, with each drawer of equal size. The single door unit and open shelf is a drop-down door that when open reveals a bar. The lower music center unit is an unbalanced design, with the vertical section smaller than the horizontal one. Also notice the application of the principle of ending the curve at a right angle. The base units are all finished with an add-on baseboard. The raised panels in the doors actually are not raised at all—the routing of the pattern creates this illusion. Look at the wood grain pattern in the door for evidence. These doors are solid oak. The glazed doors, in contrast, are the usual stile-and-rail design made by using either the mortise-and-tenon or doweled technique.

Before continuing with other characteristics of this group, let's digress to the coffee table in Figure 6–1(a). This piece illustrates an example of mass, a characteristic of the preclassical period. The legs are large, and so is the banding connecting the legs. Also notice the four turnings. This technique was used extensively hundreds of years ago.

Figures 6–1(b) and (c) add more to our understanding of the characteristics used by Karel Mintjens. In view (b), one upper glass door unit of $55\frac{1}{2}$ inches is used. Notice the partitioning in the doors is coincident with the shelves and also subdivides the glass area. We can also see two $55\frac{1}{2}$-inch base units, one housing stereo components and the other a TV cabinet with rollaway door. The illustration also shows an upper corner cabinet. In view (c) only one more thing is added—the base corner unit. The rest of the pieces are another variation of the stackable units.

[1]U.S. Branch Office: Karel Mintjens Furniture International, P.O. Box 1440, Leesburg, Va 22075.

(a)

(b)

(c)

Figure 6–1 Modular units from 1.2.3 Program. (*Courtesy of Karel Mintjens, Westmalle, Belgium, and Leesburg, Virginia*)

An additional feature used in this modular group that is not present in the units shown in Figure 6–1 but which can be seen in Figure 6–2 is the use of carved panels in several doors. Each one of the carvings illustrates a pictorial scene, a technique reminiscent of the very early work done for royalty.

Now let's shift our attention to another modular group from Karel Mintjens, "Super KM," shown in Figure 6–3. There are several design characteristics that differ from the 1.2.3 Program group.

1. The head rail design on the doors is different. This unit uses a more gentle ogee shape.
2. The solid doors have inset oak panels versus the routed design in 1.2.3 Program.
3. The base has recesses on each piece, whereas it was overlayed on the 1.2.3 Program.
4. The apron pieces on each open cabinet differ in that they have more curvature.

In the "Combi 571" group shown in Figure 6–4 we see another characteristic, the curved door and cabinet. The door is of the stile-and-rail design, with partitioning for small glass panels.

Figure 6–2   1.2.3 Program. (*Courtesy of Karel Mintjens, Westmalle, Belgium, and Leesburg, Virginia*)

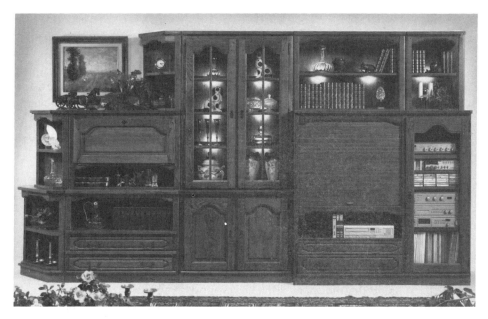

Figure 6–3 Super KM, Combi group 591. (*Courtesy of Karel Mintjens, West-malle, Belgium, and Leesburg, Virginia*)

Figure 6–4 Super KM, Combi group 571. (*Courtesy of Karel Mintjens, West-malle, Belgium, and Leesburg, Virginia*)

The Combi groups shown in Figures 6–5 and 6–6 are the third group of modular unit styles from Karel Mintjens. The overall dimensions of the units in this group are the same as the others, yet they appear more massive. Several characteristics account for this.

1. The head rails of the doors are distinctly more massive.
2. The door hinges are bold and add to the mass.
3. The deep recessed base with protruding feet adds considerably to the illusion of mass.
4. The plain drawer fronts increase mass appearance.
5. A single gently curved apron is used on all open cabinets.
6. Interior corner units are included, as shown in Figure 6–6.

Setting aside the modular concept, we now examine several examples of more traditional Belgian styled furniture and cabinets from the "Juliana" and other groups by Karel Mintjens. In these groups, as with the others, the design characteristics of vertical and horizontal mass are employed with great care. Let's observe the grouping shown in "Juliana 280," shown in Figure 6–7.

The bar cabinet on the left illustrates a three-mass unit in primary vertical mass design: the base, the lower drawer section, and the major upper mass section. The carved raised inset panels depict hunting scenes and game animals. The legs are turned and the apron is sculptured only in the front.

Figure 6–5 Combi group 869. (*Courtesy of Karel Mintjens, Westmalle, Belgium, and Leesburg, Virginia*)

Figure 6–6 Combi group 873. (*Courtesy of Karel Mintjens, Westmalle, Belgium, and Leesburg, Virginia*)

Figure 6–7 Juliana 280. (*Courtesy of Karel Mintjens, Westmalle, Belgium, and Leesburg, Virginia*)

The long sideboard is taller than the bar and uses the primary horizontal equal design principle, with accent on the glazed panel doors.

The table of trestle design and chair are designated "Cromwell." The table can be disassembled. Notice that the design of the table and chair legs resembles the hind legs of large animals. Overall, the design of the table is basic in that very little, if any, extensive cabinet joinery is needed.

Now let's examine another group called "Annemarie" by Karel Mintjens, shown in Figure 6–8. The sideboard is a primary horizontal design mass unit with three masses. The smaller one is a drawer unit sandwiched between the two larger ones. Looking closely at the cabinet detail, we can see the fluting between mass units. Below and above the fluting are some carvings. The doors are stile-and-rail with flat inset panels surrounded by raised molding.

The "Showcase" is a three-piece horizontal mass unit. Each mass is of equal proportions, so the distinctly different designed doors and inset drawers create a balance.

The "Windsor" styled table and chair are characteristic of the style. The table and chair are slender in scale, yet employ the turned legs and flared-back chair customarily incorporated in this type of chair.

To give you further examples of Belgian styled furniture, Figures 6–9 through 6–13 are provided. The pieces shown in Figures 6–9 and 6–10 are distinctly for the kitchen. Figure 6–11 shows a den unit. Figures 6–12 and 6–13 show dining room groups. Each group illustrates distinctive and unique characteristics which are adaptations of design principles discussed earlier in this chapter.

Figure 6–8 Ammemarie. (*Courtesy of Karel Mintjens, Westmalle, Belgium, and Leesburg, Virginia*)

Figure 6–9 Kitchen group. (*Courtesy of Karel Mintjens, Westmalle, Belgium, and Lees-burg, Virginia*)

Figure 6–10 Kitchen group. (*Courtesy of Karel Mintjens, Westmalle, Belgium, and Leesburg, Virginia*)

Figure 6–11 Den group. (*Courtesy of Karel Mintjens, Westmalle, Belgium, and Leesburg, Virginia*)

Figure 6–12 Dining room group. (*Courtesy of Karel Mintjens, Westmalle, Belgium, and Leesburg, Virginia*)

Figure 6–13   Dining room group "Carl." (*Courtesy of Karel Mintjens, Westmalle, Belgium, and Leesburg, Virginia*)

6.2 CABINETMAKING SKILLS, MATERIALS, AND TECHNIQUES USED IN MANUFACTURING OF BELGIAN STYLED FURNITURE AND CABINETS

In this section of the chapter we identify the skills and techniques used in making Belgian styled furniture. We shall refer to various illustrations shown earlier in this chapter. While studying this material, the reader should relate the detailed descriptions about constructing the pieces to his or her own skills and knowledge. Alternate construction techniques will be given where they exist.

The single type of lumber used in these cabinets is oak, so one's choice is limited to white, red, or black oak. One or more types of oak are available in various parts of the country from lumberyards, builders' supply houses, and specialty shops. In my part of the country, red oak is readily available, but other types are not. If you were to build cabinets using the styles created by Karel Mintjens for your personal use, you would only require a single source. If, however, you were to substitute oak plywood for built-up panels, then a source of plywood would also be needed.

Before using oak to construct any cabinets, it must be dried to less than 15 percent moisture content. The moisture content of most oak purchased from lumberyards and other sources is either 15 percent kiln dried or 19 percent air dried. Air dried wood is not dry enough for cabinetmaking. Since the wood stock containing the moisture is usually flat-sawed, the wood may contain stress and tension. With 19 percent moisture, it may split after it has been cut to needed lengths due to the further drying that takes place in the dry house or shop. The release of tension and stress from splitting may also create warping and twisting. The wood therefore should be allowed to dry further before use. Since air drying is probably the technique most of us can do cheaply, we opt for it. The simplest way is to place the wood somewhere where it is dry and hot. For those with heated basements, the warmth over the long winter will do a good job, and by the following spring the wood should be ready for use. The attic is a good place to store wood for drying from early spring through the summer to fall in the more northern climates, and year round in southern and western climates. The best option is to purchase kiln dried wood.

We shall begin our design analysis with the cabinets shown in Figure 6–14, which is the same as Figure 6–1(a). Panels of oak $\frac{3}{4}$ inch thick must be prepared to create the basic parts of each cabinet shown. Oak should be cut and planed to matching edges, then glued, clamped, and allowed to dry for a day or more. A better way to do this is to precut the lumber to lengths $\frac{1}{2}$ inch longer than needed. Then the pieces should be ripped 2 to 4 inches wide, alternated end for end or alternately flipped over, glued, and clamped. Using smaller pieces should make clamping easier and should also provide a measure for controlling squareness and flatness. All panels for base units need to be $20\frac{1}{2}$ inches wide to allow for dressing to 20 inches. Some upper units will need panels 20 inches wide when dressed; others will need $15\frac{3}{4}$ inches wide pieces when dressed.

The construction technique easiest to use to make the basic cabinet is the dado. The bottom and shelf panels can be easily dadoed into the side panels. Dadoes made in the underside of the top at each end will securely anchor the top as well as maintain squareness. This technique ensures a simple, efficient structure. It is easy to do, easy to glue, and is very strong.

The construction technique for installing the cabinet back material of $\frac{1}{4}$-inch oak or substitute plywood should be the rabbet. Rabbets should be made in the top, sides, and bottom to allow inset of the back. The shelf should have been made $\frac{1}{4}$ inch narrower than the bottom to allow room for the back.

The construction technique for facings is the butt joint. Four pieces are needed for open-shelf cabinets, five for cabinets with two doors. Facings are about $1\frac{1}{2}$ inches wide, slightly wider ($2\frac{1}{2}$ inches) for the base and narrower ($\frac{3}{4}$ inch) for the bottom of the upper units. Finally, the overlay baseboard is cut, trimmed, and glued onto the facing pieces.

Doors are solid oak, made from ripped pieces glued into panels. Once fitted with either no inset or $\frac{3}{8}$ inch inset for hinges, the router is used to create the raised-panel effect.

Each glazed door is made with two stiles, two rails, and partition strips. If done on a shaper, special bits are used for the stiles and companion bits are used for the ends of the rails. If a shaper is not available, mortise-and-tenon or

Figure 6–14 Modular units from 1.2.3 Program. (*Courtesy of Karel Mintjens, West-malle, Belgium, and Leesburg, Virginia*)

doweling techniques can be used to join the stiles and rails and connect the partition strips.

The open cabinets have an apron with two router-curved segments that must be made before being placed on the cabinet front.

The drawer unit can be constructed with the dado design, with shelves used in place of dust covers. The drawer fronts are routed to create the design. Drawer sides and backs should be made of $\frac{1}{2}$-inch oak. The bottom should be made of $\frac{1}{4}$-inch-thick oak or plywood.

So far we have established the fundamental design concepts. Some finer construction techniques must also be planned and carried out. First, the overall top width is, as we have stated, 20 inches. As seen in the side view in Figure 6–15, there is sufficient overhang of the top to account for both facings and doors. Hence, panels can be made of different widths to save costly lumber. This technique, therefore, creates an unbroken top surface, and allows for a slight rounding of the edges of the top across the front. Both upper and lower cabinets follow this design principle.

The coffee table shown in Figure 6–1(a) is of an interesting design that can be constructed using the doweling technique. Each leg is a two-piece as-

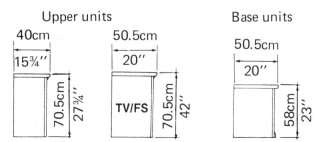

Figure 6–15   Side view of cabinet construction.

sembly, a curved part with another one below it. This technique allows for easy turning of the lower section on the lathe. The turned spindles can be fashioned with dowel ends, which makes assembly simpler. The banding is easily done with the router. The top is made from solid oak, about $1\frac{1}{4}$ inches thick. Observe the cleat under the top. There are two of these. Each one is glued and screwed to the leg units and then glued and screwed to the top.

A survey of cabinet dimensions is as follows:

1. Base units $37\frac{3}{4}$ or $20\frac{1}{4}$W × 20D × 23H.
2. Upper units $37\frac{3}{4}$ or $20\frac{1}{4}$W × 15 or 20D × $27\frac{3}{4}$ or $55\frac{1}{2}$H.

Now let's look again at Figure 6–7. The construction technique used on the bar and sideboard is the dado. But there is more.

The base unit should be constructed separately and glued and screwed to the minor mass unit containing the drawers. Legs can be turned with little problem. Aprons are straight except for the front, which is laid out with a series of French curves.

The minor mass is a basic cabinet that is wider and deeper than the major mass above it. Two drawers complete the unit. Persons not adept at carving can substitute plain drawer fronts or buy carved ones from specialty shops and glue them in place.

The upper unit consists of a bar and storage unit. The drop-down door acts as a serving and drink-mixing shelf. The two doors make for easy access to the storage unit section.

Notice the shaping on the edges of the top and horizontal mass divider segments. This is done with either a shaper or router. The work should be done before assembly is started.

The "Cromwell" styled trestle table and chair are easily constructed since joints are shiplap and overlap types.

Where the legs cross, a shiplap joint is used. Then a reinforcing gusset is applied to the outside. A slot is made through this joint through which to pass the lower support end. Finally, a wedge locks the support in place.

Four apron pieces connect the top and legs. Shaping of the legs is easily done with a band saw, followed with a router.

The chair is equally simple to construct. Four leg pieces, two back pieces, and the cross pieces are simple to make. The seat can be solid wood or framed and webbed. The legs and back supports should be fastened and the chair stained and finished before padding and covering the seat.

Finishing techniques require a paste wood filler to eliminate the irregular surface condition found in most oak. Stain and a tough finish are then applied. A polyurethane finish is appropriate for surfaces which are likely to come in contact with water and alcoholic beverages and which are subject to abrasion. Other surfaces can be lacquered.

Hardware should be dark-finished bronze that does not stand out very much. The wood grains and design details should be the most dominant characteristics, not the hardware.

There are other styles of Belgian furniture that follow very old-fashioned, traditional, and classical lines. The pieces illustrated here are of the more modern types, yet, as we have seen, many old characteristics can be used.

REVIEW EXERCISES

1. The units in the 1.2.3 Program are all designed with the balanced horizontal mass characteristics. (T/F)
2. In the 1.2.3 Program, the doors are panel-and-frame. (T/F)
3. A design feature of the cabinets shown in Figure 6–1(b) is that the horizontal mutins are positioned in front of fixed shelves. (T/F)
4. A carved panel within a door is a technique found in very early periods in European cabinetmaking. (T/F)
5. The "Combi" group of cabinets is basically designed with more delicate proportions and thus has an overall lighter mass. (T/F)
6. In Figure 6–7, the bar cabinet on the left illustrates:
   a. a two-mass unit in primary vertical design.
   b. a three-mass unit in primary horizontal design.
   c. a major upper mass section and two minor masses.
   d. a pair of major masses and a minor base mass.
7. The sideboard shown in Figure 6–8 is a primary horizontal mass unit with:
   a. an unequal, unbalanced design.
   b. two major masses separated by a minor mass.
   c. an equal balance design.
   d. doors that are made with raised panels.
8. Which is *not* a typical characteristic of a Windsor chair?
   a. Slender scaled pieces.
   b. Turned legs.
   c. Straight back.
   d. Curved shoulder piece.

9. Oak suitable for making Belgian styled cabinets must contain:
   a. 19 percent moisture.
   b. 15 percent moisture (kiln dried).
   c. 10 percent moisture.
   d. 5 percent or less moisture.
10. To manufacture a hardwood oak panel for cabinet sides, tops, and shelves, the panel must be made from $\frac{3}{4}$-inch-thick oak with pieces:
   a. 1 to 3 inches wide.
   b. 2 to 4 inches wide.
   c. 3 to 7 inches wide.
   d. 4 to 9 inches wide.

ESSAYS

11. In 25 words or less, explain why the butt joint should be used for cabinet facings.
12. Explain why the apron on the open cabinets (Figure 6–14) needs to be routed *before* being glued in place.
13. Explain why the leg on the coffee table (Figure 6–15) is made in two pieces.

ANSWERS

1F, 2F, 3T, 4T, 5F, 6c, 7b, 8c, 9d, 10b

7

Danish Styled Furniture and Cabinets

Today, people associate "Danish Modern" with the style of cabinets most frequently used by the Danish people. We devote most of this chapter to this style, since in today's market it is the only Danish style available. However, this was not always the case. In fact, for hundreds of years, from the fourteenth century until the twentieth, cabinets built by Danish craftsmen carried the detail, style, and large proportions of most European furnishings. These combined many of the principles discussed earlier in this book. For example, veneer was used for banding and inlays. Carvings not only included fruit, but full reliefs of noblemen and warriors, Doric and Corinthian column crowns in miniature, and dentils. Trestle tables were used, but unlike those made by early Americans, they contained extensive fretwork carvings throughout the leg units and apron.

Objectives

1. To examine the variety of Danish cabinet designs.
2. To understand the construction techniques used by Danish cabinetmakers.

7.1 VARIETY IN DANISH CABINET DESIGNS

The designs of the furniture and cabinets you will see in this chapter represent the latest collections from a leading manufacturer. Hundevad & Company of Ulfborg, Denmark, is one of thirty today who create quality cabinets, some tailored for the American market. This company is a member of the Danish Furnituremaker's Quality Control organization. Various aspects of the design, construction, and finish of these cabinets have been performed with direct input from the Teknologisk Institute in Copenhagen.

Let's examine some of the cabinets that these craftsmen have created. The "HU-UNIT System Series 8320" by Hundevad is comprised of blockboard, veneered cabinets that serve many general and special purposes. Figure 7–1 illustrates three individual units that are uniquely joined to appear as one continuous cabinet, subdivided into three masses. In the next section we discuss the construction techniques.

In Figure 7–1, each section consists of two ends and a back as well as many shelves. Although it does not appear so, these units can be taken apart and reassembled.

In Figures 7–2 and 7–3 we observe first simplicity of design and a variety of sizes. The bookcases are very basic. There are no obstructions to the full use of each shelf. In Figure 7–3 we see the inclusion of drawers that require no pulls, as well as vertical dividers. These cabinets have no doors. However, doors can be added, as shown in Figure 7–4.

Figure 7–1 HU-UNIT SYSTEM 8320, three sections. (*Courtesy Hundevad & Co., Ulfborg, Denmark*)

Figure 7–2   HU-UNIT bookshelves, cases. (*Courtesy Hundevad & Co, Ulfborg, Denmark*)

Figure 7–3   HU-UNIT, general purpose, plus vertical dividers. (*Courtesy Hundevad & Co., Ulfborg, Denmark*)

Figure 7–4   HU cabinet with doors. (*Courtesy Hundevad & Co., Ulfborg, Denmark*)

Now let's examine the "HU Bedroom Series 8200," by Hundevad & Company, shown in Figures 7–5 through 7–8. Each is a set of stand-alone cabinets and bed created in a contemporary style. Figure 7–5 and 7–6 are the same, except that one shows the cabinets without the doors. Two heights are used, $33\frac{1}{2}$ inches and $51\frac{1}{4}$ inches.

We need to observe several more significant characteristics of this style cabinet. All the surfaces are veneered with teak wood. These include the edges, drawers, and both surfaces of shelves. No handles or other projections are present, so that the clean, unbroken appearance is maintained.

Figure 7–5   HU Bedroom Series 8200. (*Courtesy Hundevad & Co., Ulfborg, Denmark*)

Figure 7–6   HU Bedroom Series 8200. (*Courtesy Hundevad & Co., Ulfborg, Denmark*)

Figure 7–7 HU Bedroom Series 8200. (*Courtesy Hundevad & Co., Ulfborg, Denmark*)

Figure 7–8 HU Bedroom Series 8200. (*Courtesy Hundevad & Co., Ulfborg, Denmark*)

7.2 CONSTRUCTION TECHNIQUES USED IN MANUFACTURING DANISH STYLED FURNITURE AND CABINETS

To duplicate the techniques of construction that the Hundevad Company craftsmen use would require an extensively outfitted shop. For example, Hundevad uses a seven-step process just to prepare each panel. The process, called "blockboard," is shown in Figure 7–9 and involves the following steps:

1. The core of the blockboard is kiln-dried solid pine or fir.
2. The pine or fir is cut and dressed into strips.
3. The strips are turned 90 degrees and are glued to form a solid board.
4. The laminated board is sanded to the exact thickness desired.
5. Strong abacki veneer is glued to the board under high pressure.
6. After allowing the board to relax for 8 to 10 days, it is again sanded into the correct thickness.
7. Finally, an exquisite teak veneer is glued to the board, which is now ready to be made into HU-UNITS.

Since few enterpreneurs and hobbyist cabinetmakers have equipment to create the board as shown in Figure 7–9, we must resort to other means. Several options are available to those with limited shops.

First, we can order from a supply house teak-veneered plywood in full sheets, and teak veneer to edge the cut pieces. For most needs, this solution for obtaining boards for cabinet sides, tops, and shelves is appropriate. Quarter-inch-thick plywood can be obtained for use as backs and drawer bottoms.

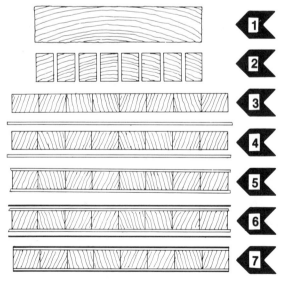

Figure 7–9 Blockboard. (*Courtesy Hundevad & Co., Ulfborg, Denmark*)

Second, we can buy teak wood, at considerable cost, to make drawer fronts, sides, and backs as well as joiner pieces.

A third, rather expensive, technique that would more closely preserve the integrity of the style would be to buy plywood such as fir and large quantities of teak veneer that has been sliced from a log rather than peeled. With these materials and contact cement or glue in hand, the serious work can begin. Let's assume that we already have completed the design and layout phases and are ready to cut and prepare the pieces. We would first cut the panels from plywood to finished width and length or slightly larger. Then we would cut and fit wood-grain matched veneer pieces to fit each side of each panel. Then the veneer would be glued one side at a time. If contact cement is used, it should be applied with a roller to both surfaces, allowed to become tacky, and then the two glued surfaces placed in contact. The tricky part is to apply the veneer without creating air pockets. Use of a wood roller aids in the application of the veneer. Once the veneer has dried, it can be trimmed and surface sanded. Now we have a piece with the grain pattern exactly as we need it.

If, for example, carpenters' glue is used, it must be applied at a uniform thickness, covering the entire surface. The veneer already matched and glued at its joint is then laid onto the glued plywood surface, positioned, and rolled with a wood roller. Following this, the other side can be prepared and veneered as well. Then the board must be sandwiched between other pieces of plywood and securely clamped until the glue has dried.

Given that we started with $\frac{3}{4}$-inch plywood, the veneered piece is now slightly thicker, roughly $\frac{1}{6}$ of an inch thicker.

Another technique we must use during planning and construction concerns hanging the doors. Since no hardware shows, we must use blind hinges. These are relatively simple to install. Directions come in every package. An alternate technique is to use a sliding door. Plastic tracks should be used. They are available from builders' supply houses in several different styles.

Since compartments are made to house drawers, drawer guides are not needed.

Now let's discuss the remainder of techniques we can use during the planning, design, and cutout phases. First, two options should be considered for joining the shelves and sides. One way is to use dowels, the other is to use dado joints. If dowels are used, their placement must be exact. This is a tedious and exacting task. Holes need to be made with a Forstner[1] type bit to preclude off-centered dowel holes. Special care must be used when drilling the holes so that they do not come through the outer surface. A stopper on the bit, properly placed, ensures that this does not happen. If a drill press is used, its depth gauge must be accurately set.

A second consideration with doweling is that both holes must be slightly deeper than the dowel is long. This small space is needed for excess glue and any sawdust that may be freed when the dowel is inserted.

---

[1]Forstner is a trade name for a type of drill bit especially made for use with wood.

Commercial hardwood dowels should always be used, especially in this application. These dowels are less apt to sheer, and thus will support shelf loads better. The glue bond between the shelf edge and cabinet side will, of course, also contribute to strength of the cabinet, but because the joint is basically flush, the holding strength is not adequate in and of itself.

If dadoes are used for joining shelves to sides and partitions to shelves, it is important to first determine during the design phase when the teak edge veneer is to be applied. Why is this so? Simple!

1. Dadoes may extend from edge to edge if the shelves are flush with the front edge, in which case the edge veneer is applied after assembling the cabinet (Figure 7–10). The vertical edge veneer must be unbroken throughout its length. This would not be possible if the veneer were applied before the dado cut is made through the piece. Hence, we need to make the decision in the design phase.

2. Assuming the same requirement for side and shelf to be flush, the design phase decision could be to apply the edge veneer before dadoing. This decision is correct, since we intend to use a *blind dado*. The blind dado is made from the rear edge to within an inch of the front edge. The critical part of this joining technique is to make each dado uniformly deep. Some cabinetmakers prefer to use a router, while others prefer dado blades in a radial arm saw. Router guides must be very accurately positioned if routing is done. The router does eliminate one problem created with dado blades. The dado's depth is uniform, whereas the sloping saw edge must be chiseled clean to the depth of the dado. Finally, the shelf must be accurately notched to fit against the cabinet side where it extends from the dado to the cabinet front edge.

3. We assumed in item 2 above that the dado was made to a width equal to the thickness of the shelf. But our design phase could also have dictated a $\frac{1}{2}$-inch-wide dado versus the full shelf thickness. In this case, not only would the leading edge be fitted to the cabinet side, but a rabbet would have to be made along the entire edge of the shelf.

4. The decisions discussed in items 2 and 3 must be made if the shelf is recessed from the edge of the cabinet side.

Drawers may be made from poplar or plywood. Veneer should be applied to the outside of the sides after the drawer is assembled. This is important to remember, since the veneer must reach all the way out to the drawer front. Edge veneers should also be applied after the drawer is assembled.

Finishing the cabinet is not very difficult. Rubbing on teak oil will produce a fine finish. This finish is very soft and needs repeated coatings periodically. However, adding lacquer to the teak oil finish will make the finish harder and retard the aging process as well as the darkening that usually takes place.

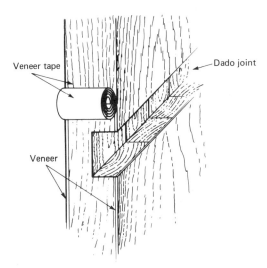

Figure 7–10 Dado joints.

Although there is a lot of skill needed to make quality Danish styled cabinets, the squareness of the style limits the number of different types of joinery required. Tools need to be sharp and accurately aligned. Design concepts need to be well thought out. Probably the most difficult task is the veneering. However, there is a great deal of pleasure to be derived from building cabinets of this style.

REVIEW EXERCISES

1. Early Danish furniture was very similar to German styles. (T/F)
2. HU-UNIT cabinets are made of blockboard and veneers. (T/F)
3. Full use of a bookshelf in Danish modern is restricted by the shelf support cleating used. (T/F)
4. The principle wood used to veneer Danish modern cabinets is maple. (T/F)
5. Almost all Danish modern cabinets and furniture have no hardware pulls or handles. (T/F)
6. When veneering with contact cement, both sides to be joined must have a coating of cement. (T/F)
7. The type of hinge used in Danish modern cabinets is:
   a. blind.
   b. loosepin.
   c. $\frac{3}{8}$" offset.
   d. full offset.

8. The most common joint used in the Danish modern style is:
   a. butt.
   b. dowel.
   c. miter.
   d. mortise and tenon.

9. The second most common joint used in the Danish modern style is the:
   a. dado.
   b. miter.
   c. dovetail.
   d. keyed lap.

ESSAYS

10. Explain in a paragraph or two how you would cut the pieces for the bookcase shown in Figure 7–3.

11. Explain or list the sequence you would use to assemble the pieces for the bookcase in Figure 7–3.

ANSWERS

1T, 2T, 3F, 4F, 5T, 6T, 7a, 8b, 9a

8

Spanish Styled Furniture and Cabinets

Over the centuries, the Spanish people have had more than their share of influences from other nationalities. For a time there was the Greek influence, followed by the Corinthian influence, and then the Roman occupation of Spain. The Moors occupied the country for over 300 years, and they also influenced the culture and its furniture and cabinet styles.

With the rise of power of Ferdinand of Aragon and Isabella of Castile the reign of royalty began, which lasted almost 500 years. Rulers from Ferdinand and Isabella through the Spanish line of the Hapsburgs accounted for much of the furniture and cabinet styles of the Spanish Renaissance, through the Baroque period, and beyond.

In this chapter we identify characteristics of Spanish furniture and cabinets, and then examine some construction techniques used in making Spanish styled furniture.

Objectives

1. To identify some characteristics of Spanish styled furniture and cabinets.
2. To understand some of the construction techniques and materials used in Spanish furniture and cabinetmaking.

8.1 CHARACTERISTICS OF SPANISH STYLED FURNITURE AND CABINETS

We pick up this study from about the 1500s, during the Spanish High Renaissance era, which lasted roughly 100 years. During the last 30 to 40 years of the period, Spanish style was heavily influenced by an architect named Juan de Herrera during the reign of Philip II.

When Philip III took the throne from Philip II, the Baroque period began in Spain. Another architect, Jose Churriguerra, influenced much of the furniture styles during the reigns of Philip III and Philip IV.

Spanish cabinetmakers generally are not credited with many original design concepts. Some critics consider their work to be inferior to that of English, French, German, and Italian craftsmen in originality and quality. Perhaps so, but Spanish workmanship was very good and included complex technical construction techniques.

As with much of the pieces made during the 1500s, Spanish furniture and cabinets were portable, oversized and heavy. Much was made from oak boards with panels carved and inset. The carvings generally had symmetry of design and frequently depicted heraldry of the royal houses. Due in part to the early Greek and later Roman influences, Gothic cathedral carvings also were used to decorate chests and schranks. Rosettes were used in this time frame as well.

Several anchoring techniques were employed, including the use of metal or leather straps on corners and the use of the handmade dovetail joint.

By the 1600s, cabinet and furniture designs took on a more proportional appearance. This means more use of moldings, especially the rope pattern. Vertical and horizontal masses were carefully considered. Carvings, although excellent, became less overbearing and bold. Wood turnings were used more frequently too. These included turned-foot sections on cabinet legs and the use of the twisted-rope design on table legs. Table aprons were carved with vinery. Tables generally were made with stretchers. Cabinets were decorated with plant-ons that added character. They also contained two different types of hinges—the strap hinge, where the long part was exposed on the door and the other half was hidden in a mortise, and the full mortise hinge. Cabinet locks were used extensively, and many of the door and drawer pulls were the "teardrop" variety. Cabinet crowns were generally flat, but frequently were either built up from molding or plain. Where molding was used, an early form of the bed molding or Roman ogee can be found. Also during this period, much emphasis was placed on the use of rectangular design. Some were vertical, others horizontal, but often a cabinet front consisted of both, which made for an unusual arrangement.

The "Vargueno," a cabinet with a drop-leaf writing surface, was founded during the 1600s.

By the 1700s, more and more attention to balance and form was evident. There also was a distinct trend toward smaller cabinets with flattened ball feet.

Figure 8–1 Spanish Renaissance cabinet (circa 1700s).

Carvings as well as marquetry were fashionable on drawer fronts. Hinges were smaller and were hidden. Inlay was used on flat surface doors. Figure 8–1 shows a beautiful cabinet from this period.

There was still the Hapsburg influence in some of the cabinets. For instance, some contained full relief carvings of human figures, as was done in Southern Germany and Austria.

The 1700s was also a time for the drop-leaf desk. With the desk writing surface down and flat, a mass of small pocket drawers filled the background. Each drawer front was carved with a variety of designs, ranging from architectural scenes to a design closely resembling abacus circles on a dowel, which reveals the influence of Islamic artistic tradition and is a beautiful example of symmetry. Handles on these cabinets and others employed the "teardrop" pull.

Of course, with the Baroque style the twisted-rope carving was employed on beds, chairs, tables, and just about everything else. Filigree carvings were also used on cabinets, chests, and headboards. Throughout this period, turnings of all types were used in addition to the twisted-rope design. Stretchers on tables even included lathe-created turnings.

8.2 CONSTRUCTION TECHNIQUES AND MATERIALS USED IN SPANISH STYLED FURNITURE AND CABINETS

In this section we examine three examples of modern furniture and cabinets that incorporate some Spanish characteristics. Here our study focuses on the construction techniques and materials used. All three cabinets were originally built by Drexel Furniture. The first is an armoire from Drexel's "Sandia" collection, the second is a door chest from Drexel's "Velero" Spanish Baroque series, and the third is a bookcase from Drexel's "Esperanto" series.

The armoire in Figure 8–2 is a four-door cabinet which has five drawers and six pigeonhole shelf spaces. Its dimensions are 40W, $19\frac{1}{2}$D, and 76H. To access the four lower drawers, one must open both lower doors. To access the open shelves and top drawer, one must open both upper doors (see inset to figure). Throughout the following discussions, descriptions always refer to this figure.

The overall design is primarily vertical, with two major masses, a lower one and an upper one. The lower mass is slightly higher than the upper. Each major mass is divided lengthwise to form two doors; each door mass has six minor masses or panels. Notice that in each lower door the bottom panels are taller than the middle and upper ones, and that the upper ones are larger than the middle ones. Notice that the panels on each upper door are a mirror image of the lower doors. The largest panels are on the very top.

Technically, the cabinet is not difficult to construct. The ends, top, bottom, and shelves/dividers can all be cut the same width. The shelves and dividers can be trimmed later to allow for the thickness of the back. Dado joints should be made into the sides to support the shelves and drawer dividers. A rabbet should be made in the back edge to allow the back to be inset. The bottom dado on the sides should be made high enough to allow part of it to be exposed above the top of the base trim. This ensures that the bottom drawer will glide smoothly outward.

Next, facings need to be cut and glued on to the assembled case. The first pieces to install are the middle ones, since these wrap around the sides from

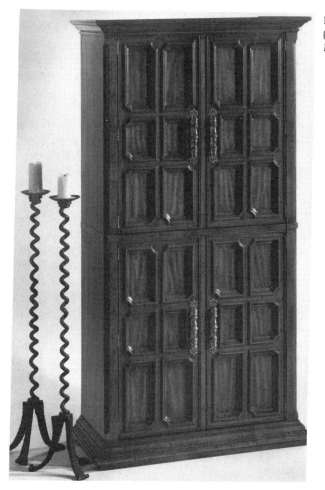

Figure 8–2 Armoire from "Sandia." (*Courtesy of Drexel Heritage Furnishings Inc., Drexel, North Carolina*)

the front. Actually two different types of pieces are needed. The wide one goes along the front from the case outward about $\frac{1}{2}$ inch further than the stile thickness. The two side pieces are only about $\frac{1}{2}$-inch thick, so that a uniform thickness exists to divide the upper and lower sections. The stiles should be installed next and should extend from the middle to the top and middle to the bottom. Finally, the rails, one top and one bottom, are fit between the stiles and glued. Before gluing them, however, the routing must be done on both the inner and outer edges.

If $\frac{3}{4}$-inch plywood is used for shelving and dividers, then at this time it would be a good idea to apply edge-veneer tape, trim it, and sand it.

The next step involves making the moldings for both the crown and base. These are combinations of ogee, Roman ogee, and cove. If shop equipment is a limitation, these moldings can be made using the build-up technique. The moldings are installed on the front and ends, but not the back. The top molding is flush with the top. The bottom molding is raised off the floor $\frac{3}{4}$ inch. The cabinet is now ready for final sanding prior to staining and finishing.

All five drawers are of uniform width, length, and depth. This makes mass production easy. None of the drawers has a pull; rather, the drawer fronts are kept low enough to permit one's fingers to slide between the divider and the front. The sides and back, however, could be made the same width as between dividers, minus a $\frac{1}{4}$-inch allowance. The drawer front should be dovetailed into the sides and the back should be dadoed into the sides. The bottom needs to be inserted into grooves in the sides and front and should be nailed to the back.

Probably the most difficult part of this job is constructing the doors. Carefully look at the design characteristics of these doors in terms of work to be done. Each door is essentially made of three parts: a thin plywood veneer back material, a frame, and molding. The sum of the thickness of the plywood panel and frame must not exceed the thickness of the cabinet framing materials, since the doors are inset and operate with mortise hinges. If the thickness of the door exceeded the thickness of the stile, the door would bind against the shelf edge and would not close.

The amount of frame material revealed after the molding has been installed should be uniform and about $1\frac{1}{2}$ inches. This consideration is altered by one of two decisions: first, to cut the molding flush with the framing, or second, to rabbet the molding so it can be set down and over the framing. One or the other of these decisions must be made, since each causes the width of the frame material to be different.

The next consideration, also involving the frame, is the short angle molding that is in every panel except those next to the handle. Each panel has two angle moldings. The ones shown are curved, but they could be made without curves or eliminated entirely and the style would still be representative of Spanish Baroque. The molding must be mitered to fit and must project beyond the frame by $\frac{3}{8}$ to $\frac{1}{2}$ inch.

Several important parts of the job were omitted above so that they could be discussed here. If you know that $\frac{1}{4}$-inch plywood is the thinnest available, then the framing material may need to be planed. The other alternative is to use thicker cabinet stiles, which, of course, changes the trim discussed earlier. The framing materials need to be doweled and glued so that when the back plywood is glued on the doors, the strength of the door does not rely solely on the plywood's strength. If the frame is dressed to $\frac{1}{2}$-inch thickness, four $\frac{3}{16}$-inch dowels should be used on each side where the hinges are to be fastened, and four more on the pull side. All other joints can be butt types. The plywood panel will have end wood showing on all edges of the door, which if visible would present an objectionable appearance. Several techniques may be used to minimize this situation. First the plywood can be cut with a planer saw blade, so that no tearing will occur. Next, the edges need to be sanded with very fine (180 grit) paper, and then a seal or wash coat of shellac or lacquer needs to be applied before any staining is done. A second method requires the use of veneer tape around all four edges of the assembled door to completely hide the plywood's edge. However, allowances must be made when sizing the door within the openings. The third technique is to use a paint or heavy-bodied stain of the same color as the stained door and cabinet.

When the doors are completed, they need to be fit and hung with mortise hinges. I prefer to use the loose-pin type, because of the ease of working with them.

From the description above, we can conclude that overall this is a complex project. Considerable design skills are needed to make everything proper. Considerable materials and an extensive workshop are required to complete the construction phase. Finally, a good spray outfit is needed to apply the lacquer once the stain has been applied, dried, and sanded.

Our next example is a door chest from Drexel's "Velero" collection (Figure 8–3). It embodies deep carvings, massive and heavy hardware, and the partitioning design found in many Spanish cabinets. The choice of woods are pe-

Figure 8–3 Door chest from "Velero." (*Courtesy of Drexel Heritage Furnishings Inc., Drexel, North Carolina*)

can hardwood and pecan veneers. The dimensions are 42W, 20D, and $56\frac{1}{4}$H. It is a primarily vertical unit consisting of two unequal mass sections, with the larger on top. The lower section is a horizontal mass with four horizontally oriented minor masses, the drawers. The upper mass, although taller vertically than the width, has a mixture of minor horizontal masses created by partitioning the doors. This gives a unique blend to the integration of two types of mass units. Moldings adorn the top, separate the sections, and decorate the base.

We shall begin the technical description with the base cabinet. The sides need to be dadoed to the bottom, drawer divider, and lower shelf of the upper section. Adjustable shelves should be used in the upper section area but, if need be, fixed shelves could be installed, in which case dadoes need to be made for them. The sides also need to be rabbetted for insetting the back. Two blind dadoes need to be made into the top so that it sets down $\frac{1}{8}$ inch onto the sides. A rabbet needs to be made between the dadoes to allow inset of the back. The shelves and divider need to be affixed to the side. Next the top needs to be glued on and the back needs to be installed. Once these are done, the cabinet facings and moldings can be made.

The stiles should extend from the floor to the underside of the top, where it extends several inches out. The rails fit between the stiles at the top, between sections (flush with the shelf), between drawers, and across the base. Each one is different, so that a certain amount is exposed and the rest is covered with molding. For example, the molding under the top is only $\frac{3}{4}$ inches down, whereas the molding in the midsection is about $1\frac{3}{4}$ inches and the bottom base molding is about 2 inches wide. Once the facings have been installed by using the butt joint, they must be sanded.

The top's edge must be routed with a $\frac{1}{4}$-inch round bit on the top side and underside either before or after assembly. If solid-core plywood is used, the routing will look very nice. If regular plywood is used, the plies will show and the effect will be less than desirable, so the moldings should be made as add-ons to the top. Then cut and install the molding under the top (use an ogee or Roman ogee). The center molding should be built up when shop tools are limited. It may be made from two or three pieces. Once made, it should be cut and installed with glue. The base is also molding, and it too may be built up. There is one other part of the base. A piece of $1 \times 1\frac{1}{4}$ or similar size molding could be added at the floor level, with its corners mitered. This would add a dimension of stability as well as provide additional support for the base molding. The basic cabinet should now be finished. Next, the doors and drawers need to be constructed.

The drawers and doors are to be designed with a $\frac{3}{8}$-inch inset (overlap). The doors require an inset rabbet on the hinge side and top, and the drawers need it on all four edges. The depth (thickness) of the doors can range up to $1\frac{3}{8}$ inches, depending upon the thickness of the trim (facings) and the amount projecting outward over the trim. Because they must look finished on the inside, a solid panel of plywood could be used to provide the veneered smoothness required. The facing surface of the plywood would be the front, as shown in the figure. Then a molded frame needs to be made from solid stock, mitered on all corners to fit, and glued to the back. Additionally, support material must be added beneath the pull handles. Once the doors are built, the rabbet needs to be made and other fitting also must be done.

Whereas the Drexel Company probably has shapers large enough to make the molding for the door frames, most of us do not. To achieve the same design, we could shape the outer piece and then make a quarter-cove molding for the inner molding.

Four basic drawers and then four drawer fronts need to be made. As you can see in Figure 8–3, they are framed like the doors, but there are several differences. The frames are not as deep as those on the doors, and each drawer front has a carved add-on unit. The procedure for making the front is the same as that for making the door. The drawer front extends over the cabinet facings $\frac{3}{8}$ inch, but no rabbet is needed. The back panel is from the same thin plywood as was used for the doors. The carved add-ons may be handmade or purchased from one of several specialty shops that carry a variety of these made from wood and cast epoxy with wood grain features.

Once the fronts are made, they need to be fastened to the basic drawer with glue and screws. This completes the construction phase.

The finishing phase is next. When it is done, the result should be a cabinet with a high satin look and a rich brown color. Distressing can be done as a final step.

Our final example shown in Figure 8–4, is a bookcase from Drexel's "Esperanto®" series, which is 36W, 14D, and 77H. This cabinet was selected because it includes several unique design and construction features which should add to our understanding.

The basic cabinet is a simple box construction with dadoed shelves and inset back. However, observe the shape of the shelves—each is elliptically curved and routed. The routing creates an illusion of a thinner shelf and is a very effective technique for reducing bulk. Also notice that the cut of the ellipse does *not* extend to the trim. These shelves must be completed before assembling the cabinet.

The frame is very simple. No miters are used. The butt joint is appropriate, since there is very little stress on any joints. The mullion is grooved slightly to carry over the theme of the doors below. Overall, the stiles of the facings are really narrow, in the range of $1\frac{1}{2}$ to $1\frac{3}{4}$ inches wide. Also notice that a rabbet is included throughout the height of the open shelf space. The top and bottom rails are wider than the stiles, but the center rail is the same width as the stiles. Flattened ball feet are used to finish off the base.

Two identical panels are needed to complete the cabinet top. Each one is made of five pieces of hardwood with a plywood veneer back. Notice several things about their construction. First, all joints are butt joints. The curved pieces are cut on a band saw. The curves end on a sharp, 90-degree angle, which, as

Figure 8–4 Bookcases from "Esperanto." (*Courtesy of Drexel Heritage Furnishings Inc., Drexel, North Carolina*)

you should recall from Chapter 2, is proper. The leading edges are routed with a round bit. In addition, a small routing is made into the two closed-in pockets. This work may need to be done before the plywood back is applied. Once these units are made, they need to be sanded thoroughly, then fit into the frame and glued.

The doors are unique and are built up onto a plywood back. They are hung with hidden hinges on the top and bottom corners. There is no hardware, so a finger pull needs to be made. Each door has four panels separated by a half-width stile on the outsides and three full-width, grooved stiles separating the panels. The half-stile at the center needs to be routed for a finger pull. Its position is critical and should not extend into the area preserved for the add-on. Each panel is decorated with three overlay assemblies. Each one contains a small rosette-type carving and a small routing in its exposed end. All three pieces are different widths. Also notice that the grain runs horizontally, whereas in the other components it runs vertically. The only materials needed to assemble the doors are glue and clamps. A note of caution needs to be made here: No glue must be allowed to set on the veneer surface of the plywood where stain and finish are to be applied. Once the glue has dried, fitting and hanging are done.

The cabinet is complete. Drexel finished the interior in green and stained the rest of the cabinet. You could stain the entire cabinet and still adhere to Spanish styling.

In this chapter we have learned that certain characteristics of cabinet styles are Spanish and that they were used throughout a relatively long period of time. They came about by the desires and customs of the Spanish people and those who occupied the country for many generations. We also learned that many characteristics were related to styles found in other European and Mediterranean countries. Overall, the furniture style is a bold one, with many subdivisions of small pockets. In contrast to the many subdivisions, the hardware used was heavy, ornate, and bold. As with much furniture of the time, only the wealthy and royalty could afford it and it needed to be transportable.

REVIEW EXERCISES

1. Spanish styled furniture may contain Greek and Roman characteristics. (T/F)
2. Spanish styled furniture still retains the influence of the Moorish people. (T/F)
3. Of all the European countries, Spain did *not* experience Baroque influences. (T/F)
4. Many of the portable cabinets made in early Spain included inset carved panels. (T/F)
5. Cathedral carvings in the 1500s were not mixed with rosettes. (T/F)
6. The twisted-rope design in Spanish cabinets was first used in the _____ century.
   a. 15th
   b. 16th
   c. 17th
   d. 18th
7. When looking at a 1600s Spanish cabinet or table, which characteristic will *not* be found?
   a. Twisted rope design
   b. Teardrop drawer pulls
   c. Highrise bonnets
   d. Vinery

8. From the period 1500 to 1700, which design characteristic became more evident?
   a. Inclusion of vinery
   b. Attention to balance and form
   c. Panel-and-frame construction
   d. Tables with stretchers

ESSAYS

9. Prepare a list of the pieces required to build the armoire cabinet shown in Figure 8–2.

10. Explain why the bottom shelf dado in the sides of the armoire in Figure 8–2 should be made to allow part of the bottom shelf to show.

11. Why does the technical description of the door chest in Figure 8–3 include blind dadoes in the top? Explain.

12. Explain in a paragraph or two the assembly sequence for the doors used in the *bookcase* (Figure 8–4).

ANSWERS

1T, 2T, 3F, 4T, 5F, 6c, 7c, 8b

9

Italian Styled Furniture and Cabinets

Throughout the ages of Western civilization, the Romans and Italians have played a significant role in the cultures of everyone they contacted. Their influence was also felt in the designs of furniture and cabinets in many ways and in a variety of applications. As we have already noted from earlier chapters, the Romans occupied much of Europe and even parts of England. Their stay was long and thus their influence was a strong one. We can recall from history that Romans controlled the ruling parties in Spain and Europe, especially those lands north of Italy. Since the Romans were extensive travelers, many of their ideas in architecture and furniture were reflections of the styles of the Greeks and Egyptians. They did, of course, make adaptations.

The periods of change in Italian styled furniture and cabinets are the same as those of the European scene that we have been studying. Therefore, we can reflect that certain trends already identified in earlier chapters were prevalent in Italy as well. There were the Gothic styles in the twelfth century, which gave way to the Greco-Roman forms by the fourteenth century, then to the Baroque style, and later to the Neoclassic style and the modern trends of today.

In this chapter we carry on the theme of earlier chapters and examine the characteristics of Roman and Italian furniture and cabinets, and then discuss the construction of an example of a piece of Italian styled furniture.

Objectives

1. To understand the characteristics of Roman and Italian styled furniture and cabinets.

2. To gain knowledge of the technical construction techniques used to make an Italian styled cabinet or furniture.

9.1 CHARACTERISTICS OF ROMAN AND ITALIAN STYLED FURNITURE AND CABINETS

Since Italy was the central area of the Roman Empire when Greece and Egypt also were prominent as cultural centers, a great variety of furniture and cabinets were made and used. Even before the birth of Christ, Roman furniture and cabinets incorporated heads of animals, cabriole or animal legs, inlaid materials, some lathe-turned wood, and marquetry. Fittings such as hinges and handles were made from cast bronze. Other pulls were fashioned from imported ivory.

Noblemen, churchmen, and businessmen all were able to afford the finer cabinets and furniture until the fall of the Roman Empire. For the next 500 years, the skills and artistry once a part of the Roman empire were lost. The furniture constructed was mainly rudimentary pieces that could be fashioned from crude tools.

In the middle of the nineth century (850 AD), a revival began during which Romanesque furniture was created. Even with the limited technology, some chests, although crude and heavy, did contain carvings of floral motifs and vines. The principal wood used was oak, since it was abundant and could be carved fairly well.

Shortly thereafter, the Gothic or classical period began, during which architects created furniture based upon their designs developed for churches. As we already identified in the other studies of European countries, Italy's craftsmen incorporated rectilinear concepts of design. These included pillars, rounded and painted arches, and buttresses. These characteristics were carved into doors, panels and the like, sometimes in deep relief, other times as filigree carved entirely through the panel. Since this was a primary design characteristic, little if any inlaid work was done. However, decorative motifs were used on the most ornate cabinets, chests, and tables. It was also during the twelfth century that the walnut age began in Italy, and walnut supplanted oak as the primary wood used in construction of furnishings.

By the turn of the fifteenth century, the Italian Renaissance began in the city of Florence. Once again, stability in the form of government and social conduct created an environment where craftsmen gained experience and knowledge because their craft was in demand. During this period of almost 200 years, there was considerable cultural exchange with Greece and the Eastern cultures, so that Roman furniture reflected the designs and characteristics of these areas. For example, stars and crescents were carved into cabinets. Scroll-work was used on tables, chests, and cabinets. Gilding started again, as did the inlay of bone, shell, and precious metals. In addition, arabesque influences were used that included intertwined flowers and foliage, and sometimes geometrical designs either carved into or painted on the wood.

The period was one of significant growth for the craftsmen, and they frequently became known as artists. What also aided them was the fact that the wood could be milled, sawed and lathe turned. This permitted the construction of cabinets and furniture that were lighter and more complex in design, with a wider variety of joinery. Still, the craftsmen tended to use a simplicity of outline when decorating their cabinets with adornments. This concept is still prevalent in the Italian furnishings of today.

As you may recall from our earlier discussions, the Baroque style began in Italy around 1580, and later spread through all of Europe. As we have said, Baroque was a period and style where designers and cabinetmakers threw out the traditions of the past and relaxed their concern with form. In fact, they did everything to hide form. Cabinets and furniture became extremely ornate, and designs were distorted with twisted scrollwork and massive carvings. Pediments which up to this time were almost indistinguishable became large, often overwhelming the cabinet iself. Veneering again was used as were inlays. Counters and cabinet tops of marble were fashionable. Gilding was used extensively.

Italians as well as other Europeans broke away from the Baroque style after almost 200 years, when the interum Rococo style became fashionable, especially in France. But what really caused the shift in Italian styling and created the Neoclassic period was the discovery of the ruins of Pompeii around the mid-1700s. This revival of the classics caused much cabinetry and furniture to be fashioned in the strong vertical and horizontal lines which characterize the Italian styles of furniture today. Legs on tables and stands, for example, were made slender, square, and tapered. Many had carefully placed grooves and reeding. Cabinets were outfitted with the bases of columns from ancient Rome and Greek architecture. Simple carvings and add-ons, including the urn, oak leaf, palm, and lyre were used. This uncluttered look prevails today.

Now let's examine two cabinets of modern manufacture that incorporate Italian and Roman characteristics.

9.2 CONSTRUCTION TECHNIQUES USED IN MANUFACTURING ITALIAN STYLED FURNITURE AND CABINETS

In this section we will examine the technical construction techniques used to create two cabinets which were designed and built by the Drexel Heritage Company. The first is a serving commode made several years ago in Italy. The other is an end table from a newer collection called "Grand Palais." Our goal here is the same as in earlier chapters—we need to understand the technical construction aspects of these cabinets if we are to attempt to make them or teach others how to design and make them.

The serving commode is shown in Figure 9–1. Its dimensions are 45W, 19D, and $35\frac{1}{4}$H. It is a primary horizontal design consisting of two horizontal major masses, the shelf section behind three doors, and the drawer section. There is also a minor mass base unit and top. The major masses are irregular or nonconforming in that the larger one has three doors whereas the smaller one has only two drawers. Within each mass, though, there is harmony.

This will be a difficult cabinet to construct for persons who have limited machining capabilities, as without them it is difficult to replicate the curved section that rises vertically at each outer corner. We shall look at a possible way of making these pieces, but if appropriate materials are not available in your shop, an alternative is to retain the angle but eliminate the curvature, and go for a straight piece with either reeding or fluting.

The best materials to use for this cabinet would be lumber core veneered plywood, $\frac{1}{4}$-inch veneered plywood for door panels and solid stock lumber for trims, moldings, and frames of doors and drawers.

We should approach the construction as follows: First, make the basic cabinet and top, then the base, then the drawers and drawer fronts, and finally the doors.

Using a working drawing or plan, the bottom of the cabinet should be laid out, including its curved sections. Then a model of the curve needs to be made

Figure 9–1 Server from "Marchesa." (*Courtesy of Drexel Heritage Furnishings Inc., Drexel, North Carolina*)

from scrap plywood to act as a forming block for the pieces that will make up the curved sections. This means that a series of small pieces of solid stock need to be cut about 3 feet long and then tapered and beveled so that when glued they form an arc. Once dried, they need to be sanded and shaped into a smooth arc. To do this may require the creation of a planer blade or scraper which conforms to the exact arc needed. Once the pieces are ready, veneer must be applied to both surfaces, inside and outside. Contact cement would be a good bonding agent for this job.

Next, the end pieces need to be cut and dadoed for the bottom shelf dust cover below the drawers and rabbetted for the back. The inside shelf is adjustable, so no dadoes are needed for it. However, pilot holes can be drilled for shelf supports while the pieces are unassembled. Then each end and curved piece needs to be mated with a butt joint and glued. Before gluing, though, the curved piece should be dadoed to receive the bottom shelf and dust cover. The final cutting of bottom shelf and dust cover is made next. Then the ends, bottom, dust cover, and back should be glued and allowed to dry.

The cabinet framing for doors and drawers is done next. Look closely at the figure. Notice that there is a molding separating the lower and upper major masses. Although simple in shape and style, it must be added. One method of creating the frame and trim is to do them separately. Construct a frame of solid stock with full-length stiles of 1-inch width, with rails above the drawers, below the drawers, and across the bottom. Cut two additional stiles 1 inch wide to separate the doors, and finally cut to fit with butt joints. When fitted, the stiles should be either glued as an assembly outside of the cabinet or glued in place within the cabinet.

With the frames for the drawers and doors in place and sanded, the top should be made and installed. Since, as was suggested, lumber core plywood is used for the large panels of the cabinet, a single piece 45 inches wide by 19 inches deep needs to be cut. This piece extends over the ends and front of the cabinet. It has two curved areas that conform to curved side panels. Then the edge is molded with either a router or a shaper.

Next, the top must be fastened to the cabinet. As usual, one of the several methods may be selected that best fits the local conditions, i.e., shop or craftsman capabilities or design considerations. The first method does not require extensive machine operations. The cabinet top is laid upside down on a workbench or across a pair of sawhorses. Care must be taken to protect the top from scratches, so a blanket or pad should be placed between the cabinet top and workbench top. Next the cabinet is placed *upside down* on the cabinet top and positioned as it will be when permanently attached. With the use of a pencil, a scribe is made on the underside of the top. This line is made by reaching into the area first through one drawer and then the next. The idea is to make an outline in pencil that conforms to the exact dimensions of the interior of the cabinet. Once this is accomplished, the cabinet is removed, and the underside of the top should show a continuous outline of the back, ends, and front of the cabinet.

Our next task is to prepare $\frac{3}{4} \times \frac{3}{4}$-inch strips of softwood that will act as glue blocks. These should be hand cut to fit against the line toward the center of the cabinet top. They need to be glued and screwed in place.

Several pilot holes need to be made in the pieces just fastened to the underside of the top where the cabinet ends will butt against them. Pilot holes do not need to be made for the back, since brads can easily be nailed into the strip from outside the back panel, through the back panel and into the strip. Nor do any need to be made into the front strip, since it would be impossible to install the screws anyway.

With this work accomplished, the cabinet can be glued and fastened to the top. Glue needs to be applied to the outside face of the $\frac{3}{4}$-inch strips and onto the cabinet top not to exceed $\frac{3}{4}$ inch in width starting from the strip. Once the cabinet is in place, screws need to be installed on the ends through the pilot holes made earlier. Clamps need to be used along the front, and several brads need to be nailed through the back.

A second, more difficult method of securing the top includes the making of a dado about $\frac{1}{4}$ inch deep that conforms to the shape of the cabinet. The process begins the same way, but only two lines are made on the underside of the top, one inside and one outside. Then a router with a dado bit is used to make the dado between the lines. Glue blocks are next fastened to the inner edge of the dado on the ends only. Next, the dado groove is glued and the cabinet is set in place. Screws secure the ends. Clamps secure the top to the frame across the front and nails secure the back to the top. (*Note:* In our first installation, the clamps were secured from glue strip to cabinet front. None were used on the top.)

The base is an add-on feature. This means that it is added over the basic cabinet. It is made from five pieces, routed along the top edge with a Roman ogee pattern, and screwed from the inside through the ends and cabinet facings. Then a $\frac{1}{4}$- to $\frac{3}{8}$-inch molding is cut and installed as shown in the figure. Notice that it is curved to conform to the cutout in front and that it curls back on itself. Miters are used on the exterior corners. The wood strips used in the curved sections may need to be steamed to permit bending. All pieces must be glued.

Pieces of the same dimensions need to be made to separate the two mass sections. They too must be glued in place.

This completes the cabinet assembly. Next, the drawer fronts and doors need to be made. Their design is similar. Three-quarter to 1-inch stock should be used and molded with a Roman ogee pattern. A $\frac{1}{4}$-inch-wide by $\frac{3}{8}$-inch-deep groove should be made close to the inside edge of the molded stock to receive the $\frac{1}{4}$-inch thick plywood veneered panel. The 45-degree miter is the only cut needed on each door. A butt joint is used, but may be reinforced with 90-degree-angle dowels, one to each corner. As each door and drawer front is assembled, its panel is inserted before the fourth side is glued in place.

Once these assemblies are dry, they should be sanded thoroughly. Then the doors need to be fit and hung, and the drawer fronts need to be attached to the basic drawer unit.

This completes the technical description of this cabinet. Finishing processes must be done next. Obviously, this is a complex cabinet to build, yet it should be an interesting and enjoyable project to undertake.

Our second example of Italian or Roman styled cabinets, the end table from Drexel Heritage's "Grand Palais" collection, is shown in Figure 9–2. This is styled in the Neoclassic spirit, which incorporates mixing of hardwood walnut and rosewood and corner posts trimmed with gilt flame motifs.[1] The table's dimensions are 26W, 16D and 25H. It has a walnut veneer top and shelves, rosewood veneer apron and base, and gold and ebony accents on the posts.

Figure 9–2   End table from "Grand Palais." (*Courtesy of Drexel Heritage Furnishings Inc., Drexel, North Carolina*)

[1]Description from Drexel, "Grand Palais," page 5.

First, lumber core plywood should be used on this table, to make cutting and molding the top shelf and bottom easier. The top must conform to the cabinet width and depth. Then its corners must be trimmed off as shown, creating about a 2 to $2\frac{1}{2}$-inch flat surface. Next, a routing needs to be made to create the appearance of a veneered top. For the underside of the top an apron needs to be made which is about 2 inches wide and is held slightly back of the top's outer edges. The rosewood veneer when applied will make up the difference. Finally, a $\frac{1}{4}$-inch trim with a beaded edge is applied using miter joints and glue. The bead should protrude its full width. Blocking must be added at the corners to receive the four posts.

The base needs to be made next. This consists of the bottom shelf whose edge has been molded and an apron with rosewood applied, plus blocking at the corners.

Next, the four posts need to be turned then carved. Carefully note the bellows area near the foot of the post. Also note the banding above and below each area to be gilded and the flair at the top of the post. We have here a representation of a Roman column and capital. Hand-carving of the flame pattern is done where gilding will be added. The posts should end with $\frac{3}{4}$-inch self-dowels about 1 inch long, thus avoiding the need for separate dowels and creating increased strength.

The middle shelf needs to be cut smaller than the top or bottom, since the dimensions are one-half the thickness of the post to the span between the posts. Its connecting point with the post is an arc with the same diameter as the post at that point. A dowel in each post and shelf at the contact point will provide the support needed.

Assembly is very simple and quick. Insert the post into the four holes previously drilled in the base. Insert the dowels into the posts and install the middle shelf. Then align the top over the posts and insert them into their previously drilled holes. Clamp and check for squareness. With this gluing and clamping action, the entire end table is assembled.

Final sanding should be done once the glue is fully set. Then the finishing needs to be done. Since most cabinets are stained and top-coated, this step requires considerably more effort. Since there are two different veneers, walnut and rosewood, no single stain could produce the desired finishing colors. If you opted for this natural effect, then natural-colored sealer and top coatings should be used. A sequence such as the following might be used successfully:

1. Apply a wash coat of lacquer or shellac to seal the surfaces, then sand.
2. Apply the ebony stain above and below the carved areas to be gilded.
3. Apply the final lacquer coating everywhere except the top if the top is to have an alcohol and water-resistant finish. Otherwise, finish the entire cabinet with final coating.
4. Apply the gilding by hand. Gold-leaf paint should be used.

5. If required, mask the entire cabinet, then spray a polyethylene-type varnish.

6. Rub and polish the cabinet. Follow with a light coat of wax.

From the technical descriptions in this chapter, you should have gained knowledge about the characteristics common in Italian and Roman styling of cabinets and furniture. Although a technical description of a table that included square tapered legs with reeding or fluting was not provided, remember that this style is predominant in Italian styled furniture.

REVIEW EXERCISES

1. In the days before the dark ages, Italian cabinets contained design characteristics of inlaid materials and extensive carving. (T/F)

2. Even though the dark ages lasted almost 500 years, most of the cabinetmaking skills and knowledge remained unchanged throughout. (T/F)

3. The principal wood used for Italian furniture around 1050 was oak. (T/F)

4. Italian craftsmen styled much classical period furniture and cabinets according to architectural designs used in religious buildings. (T/F)

5. The age of walnut began in Italy during the thirteenth century. (T/F)

6. In which century did the Renaissance begin in Italy?
   a. 1100s
   b. 1200s
   c. 1400s
   d. 1500s

7. During which period was wood saw-milled and lathe-turned?
   a. Classical
   b. Renaissance
   c. Baroque
   d. Neoclassic

8. Which style was begun after the discovery of the ruins of Pompeii?
   a. Renaissance
   b. Baroque
   c. Rococo
   d. Neoclassic

9. Which period/style of cabinet or furniture still has a significant impact on twentieth-century Italian cabinets and furniture?
   a. Classical
   b. Baroque
   c. Rococo
   d. Neoclassic

ESSAYS

10. With reference to the commode in Figure 9–1, explain how to make the long vertical curved pieces and how they fit into the front and ends.

11. Explain how you would fasten the commode top to the cabinet sides, front and back.

12. Explain how you would apply gilding to a cabinet such as the commode.

13. Why is the stand in Figure 9–2 so easy to assemble? Explain.

ANSWERS

1T, 2F, 3T, 4T, 5F, 6d, 7b, 8d, 9d

PART 2
Technology: Present and Past

10

Cabinet Woods

The most expensive cabinets are made with high-quality woods in the forms of lumber, veneers, and plywood. Of course, high-quality woods command the highest prices, but they provide beauty, richness, and durability in cabinets and furniture. The extended life of such pieces is an asset that justifies the expense of top-grade materials.

In this chapter we present the various aspects of lumber, veneer, and plywood that are vital for all cabinetmakers to understand. The subjects we discuss include the differences between softwood and hardwood, their specific properties, their imperfections and moisture content, the processes used to prepare them for cabinetmaking and other topics as well.

Objective

1. To increase the understanding of wood's properties in order to build better cabinets and furniture.

10.1 TYPES OF WOODS

Softwood

The softwood tree is defined as a conifer or evergreen that has needles or scale-like leaves and bears its seeds in cones. Figure 10–1 illustrates a softwood tree.

Hardwood

The hardwood tree is defined as a deciduous tree that has broad leaves that shed annually and very hard heartwood. The leaves of the numerous hardwoods assume many shapes and sizes, but usually follow a set pattern of pale green at birth, darkening green at maturity, and yellows, reds, and browns before dying and falling to the ground. Their seeds are contained in pods, cone-like fruit, or nuts, and are carried to the ground in many ways. The examples in Figures 10–2 and 10–3 illustrate the characteristics of many hardwoods.

Figure 10–1 Southern pine needles, cones, and bark.

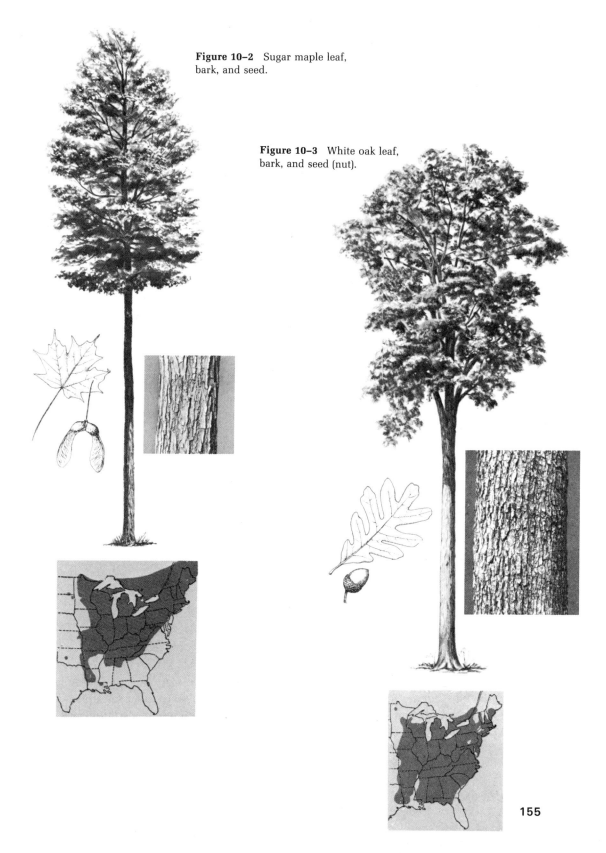

Figure 10–2 Sugar maple leaf, bark, and seed.

Figure 10–3 White oak leaf, bark, and seed (nut).

155

10.2 MOISTURE CONTENT OF WOOD AND DRYING METHODS

The moisture content of freshly cut wood will vary depending upon the season of the year and the climatic conditions prior to cutting the tree. For cabinet-making, one should always buy kiln-dried wood. Kiln-dried means that the wood has been placed in a drying oven until its moisture content is reduced to 15 percent. In contrast, green or air-dried lumber contains 19 percent moisture or more. When kiln-dried hardwood or softwood is used for projects, very little shrinkage occurs. However, if green lumber is used, considerable shrinkage takes place. If, for instance, you precut stock pieces with 19 percent or more moisture content to a length of 24 inches, store them in a hot, dry place, and allow several days to elapse before using the pieces, they might then measure $23\frac{15}{16}$ inches long. Their widths might also shrink. With kiln-dried lumber, this shrinkage is minute and sometimes nonexistent.

If the stock has a stamp "KD" on its surface, it is kiln-dried. If it does not, there is no way you can tell what the moisture content of the wood is, no matter what the lumberyard salesperson says.

Hence, it is a good idea when using stock lumber to precut the lumber to lengths slightly longer (1 inch or so) than needed, store them in a dry place, and let shrinkage and further drying occur before use.

Unseasoned lumber may contain 100 percent moisture content, but seasoned lumber may contain as little as 5 percent moisture. The various ratings that we will examine specify maximum limits of moisture.

Air-Drying Technique

A large percentage of boards and lumber are air-dried in the southwestern United States because of the high temperature and low humidity level there. The stacking techniques employed (Figure 10–4) allow hot, dry air to circulate around each piece and evaporate the moisture within the wood to a moisture content of 19 percent. The stamp on a piece of wood dried by the air method is "A-DRY."

Kiln-Drying Techniques

Figure 10–5 shows a stack of boards being rolled into a kiln for drying. After the kiln's doors are sealed, steam is used to create heat which circulates about the pieces in the stack. After one or more days, the moisture content has been reduced to 15 percent, and the pile of wood is removed from the kiln. The pieces in the pile are then stamped "KD" for kiln-dried.

Figure 10–4   Air-drying method. (*Courtesy of Western Wood Products Association*)

Figure 10–5   Kiln-drying lumber. (*Courtesy of Western Wood Products Association*)

10.3 BLEMISHES AND GRAINS

Warping and Twisting

Green lumber presents a real problem during drying: warping, twisting, and splitting may occur, as shown in Figure 10–6. These problems occur because flat-sawed lumber has surfaces where the grain on one side of a board has more annual rings than on the other side. The different drying rates of the cells result in uneven shrinking of the wood surfaces, so that they warp and twist. Warps are any deviation from a true or planed surface. They include the bow, crook, cup, and twist. Improper cutting or seasoning of lumber causes one or more types of warps. Twists are similar to wringing a towel dry of its water. (See Chapter 2 for more details.)

Buying kiln-dried lumber reduces this problem. Furthermore, if you store the stock until further drying is completed, you can recut and resurface it to eliminate the warping or twisting that may have occurred. If you cannot eliminate either problem, do not use the stock at all, since the imperfections will cause improper fitting of pieces and unsquare cabinets.

Knots

A knot is a hard place in a tree where a stem or branch grows. It appears as a contrastingly darker-colored cross section on a piece of cut lumber. The various names assigned to knots are round, oval, spike, pin, sound, unsound, pith, hollow, firm, light, intergrown, watertight, encased, loose, fixed, clustered, and star-checked. Several kinds of knots are shown in Figure 10–7.

Shakes

A shake is a lengthwise separation of wood that usually occurs between or through the rings of annual growth. Shakes usually occur in a tree as a result of heavy winds that exerted severe strain on the cells and caused them to part, or water freezing in the wood cells, which also causes tearing of the cells.

Splits

A split is a separation of the wood due to the tearing apart of its wood cells. This usually occurs from internal pressure within the tree or piece of lumber. Figure 10–8 shows several examples of splits.

Checks

A check is a separation of the woods normally occurring across or through the rings of annual growth, usually as a result of seasoning, as shown in Figure 10–8.

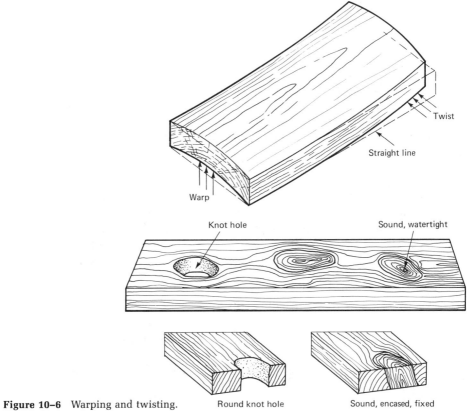

Twist

Straight line

Warp

Knot hole

Sound, watertight

Figure 10–6 Warping and twisting.

Round knot hole

Sound, encased, fixed

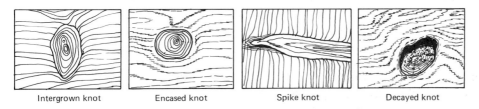

Intergrown knot

Encased knot

Spike knot

Decayed knot

Figure 10–7 Knots.

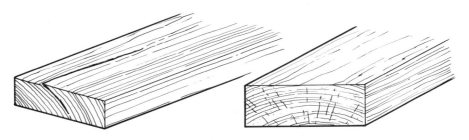

Figure 10–8 Splits and checks in lumber.

Decay

Decay is disintegration of the wood cells due to the action of wood-destroying fungi or bacteria. Decay is also known as dote, rot, and unsound wood. It may be heart-center decay, white specks caused by the fungus *Fomes pini*, honeycomb pockets, or peck (channeled or pitted areas or pockets).

Stains

Stained wood is one that has a marked variation from natural color. Stains usually are patchy and form irregular patterns.

All of the preceding characteristics may be found in any tree to varying degrees. The fewer, the better; however, the degree of their presence determines the quality of lumber, veneers, and other products derived from the tree.

10.4 WOOD GRAIN AND HOW TO USE IT

Both softwood and hardwood lumber can be cut from trees in several different ways. Each produces different grain patterns that are useful in cabinetmaking. We need to know these so that we can select the proper stock for a particular job.

Flat-Grain Sawing Method

Figure 10–9 shows typical boards that have been sawed from a log using the flat-grain sawing technique. Several distinctive features clearly identify this type of grain. First, by looking at the grain (annual rings) on the board's end, you can observe the slight arc of the rings. In some cases, as Figure 10–9(b) shows, the arcs are incomplete. This type of pattern indicates that the board, although flat-cut, is cut very near the center of the tree or from heartwood. Second, looking at the top surface you will probably see both a fairly wide section with no annual rings and, toward the edges, smaller spacings between rings. Third, turning the board over, you should see a reverse pattern of the top and also closer annual rings.

Care of wood to prevent warping was discussed earlier; however, it is important to understand that because of the different spacing of annual rings caused by flat cutting, the surfaces tend to dry at different rates.

Edge-Grain Sawing Method

Edge grain is that grain which is seen by looking at the edge of a board (Figure 10–10). Generally, the best edge grains are those in which an annual ring can be traced from one end of the board to the other and remains on or within $\frac{1}{8}$ inch of the same surface, and the grains are closely spaced and evenly distributed.

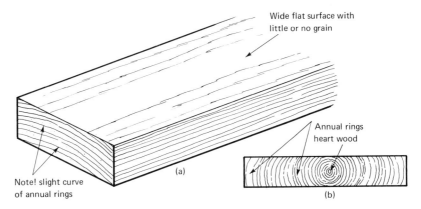

Figure 10-9   Flat-grain board.

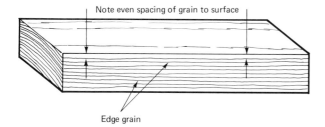

Figure 10-10   Edge grain of a board.

In some woods, such as oak and maple lumber, the edge grain may resemble flat grain on the top surface, because the board was cut near the heartwood. In cabinetmaking, such lumber may present some problems in dressing the edges.

Quarter-Sawed Method

The third sawing method, as Figure 10–11 shows, is quarter sawing. This type of cutting is commonly done on oak which is to be used for flooring or for some furniture pieces. Its characteristic is generally uniform spacing of annual rings on the surface, so that shrinkage, warping, and other curing problems are minimized.

Matching Grain of Veneer

One of the most useful properties of wood in furniture making is the grain of the wood. This single feature is used by master craftsmen to create many effects. Designs in table tops and diverse, harmonious patterns in cabinet surfaces are created by utilizing the grains of the wood. Since it is the outer surface grain that is seen, a process called veneering is used (Figure 10–12). This process requires that thin sheets or strips of wood veneer be laid, arranged, fitted,

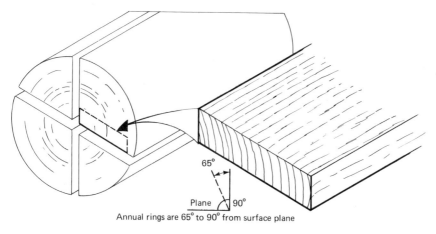

65°

Plane ⊾ 90°

Annual rings are 65° to 90° from surface plane

Figure 10–11   Quarter-sawed grain.

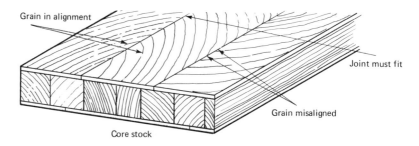

Grain in alignment

Joint must fit

Grain misaligned

Core stock

Figure 10–12   Veneer grain alignment.

and glued to a substrate. Figures 10–13 and 10–14 show two examples of veneered surfaces. The table top shows veneer cut to fit like wedges of a pie. The
cabinet front shows veneer running up and down.

Plywood is a good example of a veneered laminate. The cross-sectional
view shown in Figure 10–15 illustrates the cores and outer veneered surfaces.
The grain on the veneered plywood, lumber-core, or particle-board surface always runs lengthwise. Careful examination of the surface of a sheet reveals
that joints are made in the surface veneers. Cabinet-grade (AA) plywood requires that very good veneers be used. They may or may not be matched, but
they will be uniform in color.

Balance Obtained with the Use of Grain

Cabinetmakers can create various moods by careful selection of wood and veneer. Illustrated in Figure 10–16 are the effects of (1) grain parallel or horizontal
to the top surface, (2) grain with a balanced look, (3) grain with an unbalanced

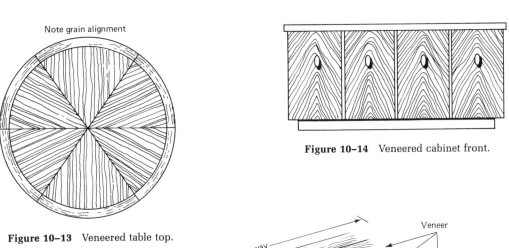

Note grain alignment

Figure 10-13 Veneered table top.

Figure 10-14 Veneered cabinet front.

Veneer

8 ft way

Laminations of wood stock

Note: laminations are cross aligned to provide strength

Figure 10-15 Veneered plywood.

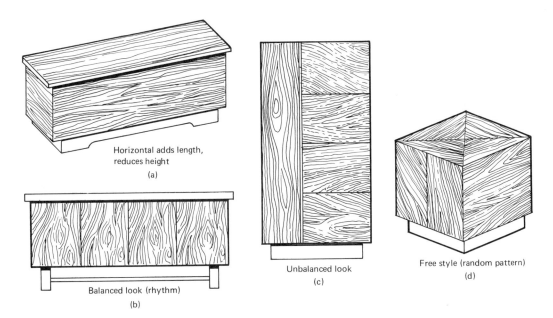

Horizontal adds length,
reduces height
(a)

Balanced look (rhythm)
(b)

Unbalanced look
(c)

Free style (random pattern)
(d)

Figure 10-16 Balance created with wood grain pattens.

appearance, and (4) a free-style or contemporary pattern. All four patterns can be created by careful planning and arrangement of wood stock.

10.5 GRADING OF CABINET WOODS

Softwoods

Many grades of lumber are assigned to softwood. In this book we are only interested in the types commonly used in cabinetmaking, so these are the ones listed in Table 10–1. A short narrative describes each grade.

TABLE 10–1   GRADES AND DESCRIPTIONS OF SOFTWOOD LUMBER

Grade	Description
Select B or better C or better	The finest woods taken from near the outer portion of the tree; contains no heartwood; knots and other imperfections are nonexistent or are spaced at wide lengths.
No. 1 No. 2	These woods have a larger percentage of flaws—knots, splits, checks, bark, and heartwood—although excellent stock 8 feet and longer frequently can be found.
No. 3 Utility	The poorest of all lumber, not used for surfaces to be finished. It contains many knots and checks, some twisting and warping, pitch, $\frac{1}{4}$-inch slope of grain, and stained wood. May be used for bracing and under supports.

Hardwoods

Hardwoods are graded differently from softwoods, but they are graded on a similar basis—their appearance. The grader observes the cut board or veneer and using his or her expert eye makes a judgment call as to the grade by the kinds and amount of blemishes in the board. Table 10–2 lists the grades of hardwood lumber and veneer.

TABLE 10–2   HARDWOOD AND HARDWOOD VENEER GRADES AND CHARACTERISTICS

PART A. Hardwood Grades Grade	General description
Firsts	Clearest, best quality hardwood, free of defects.
Seconds	The quality of each grade below *firsts* is considered
Selects	by including knots, pith, warp, wane, stain, splits, checks
No. 1 Common	holes and others, as well as their locations based on the
No. 2 Common	faults per specific length, size or percentage in the grade
Sound wormy	assigned. In lot sales of 1000 bd ft, more than one percentage
No. 3A Common	can be included (i.e. 80% No. 2 Common, 20% No. Selects).
No. 3B Common	Poorest quality of acceptable hardwood.

PART B. Grades of plywood*

Use these symbols when you specify plywood.

Veneer grades	Description
N	Intended for natural-finish, smooth-surface veneer. Select all heartwood or all sapwood. Free of open defects including knots, knotholes, pitch pockets, open splits, other open defects and stain. Outstanding choice for cabinets. Combinations of surfaces (Front and Back) may be N-N, N-A, N-B, N-C, and N-D.
A	Smooth, paintable. Not more than 18 neatly made repairs. Veneer is firm, smoothly cut, and free of knots, pitch pockets, open splits, and other open defects. Veneer is suitable for staining. Excellent choice for cabinet work. Combinations of surfaces may be A-A, A-B, A-C, A-D.
B	Solid surface. Shims, circular repair plugs, tight knots, sander skips, slight open splits, vertical holes, and horizontal tunnels are permitted. May be suitable for staining in some exposed areas of use where, for example, knotty characteristics are desirable. Excellent for interior uses in cabinets.
C (plugged)	Improved C veneer with splits limited to $\frac{1}{8}$-in. width and knot holes and borer holes limited to $\frac{1}{4} \times \frac{1}{2}$ in. Admits some broken grain. Synthetic repairs permitted. More sander skips permitted than grade B. Regular C veneer has greater defects. This veneer is not suitable for exterior uses in cabinetmaking. Some pieces may be useful for interior purposes and cabinet backs. Where plywood drawer bottoms are used, the underside may be C grade veneer.
D	Not suitable for cabinetmaking. All defects are permitted within greater latitude than for C grade. Knots and knot holes to $2\frac{1}{2}$ in. across. Limited splits, stitching, voids, wane, and white pockets are permitted.
Speciality Grade (SP)	This is a veneer that is specifically selected for a special purpose, i.e. burl or crotch grain veneer.

*Data from American Plywood Association U.S. *Product Standard PS 1–83* and APA Product Guide, *Sanded Plywood.* Also includes professional comments from the author.

In summary, hardwood and softwood lumber and veneers are used extensively in cabinetry, in moldings, other trims, and laminated applications. Grades are titled differently, but the characteristics inherently found in wood are used to define the grade.

10.6 SIZING OF WOODS

Softwood Sizes

Sizes of common stock that are cut for framing and millwork are important to cabinetmakers as well. The following information is the basis for cutting lumber from a tree and affects the availability of stock.

When cut, a 2 × 4 measures a full 2 inches by 4 inches. Other framing members, such as 2 × 6s, 2 × 10s, and nominal 1-inch boards all are generally cut to their full dimensions. The factors that affect their final sizes are the planing techniques and, as we learned earlier, the methods of seasoning. Therefore, lumber is ordered in nominal dimensions, which are the full-cut width and thickness of a piece of wood before final sizing and seasoning.

After planing, or "dressing to size" as it is customarily stated, and dried to a specified moisture content not to exceed 19 percent, a piece of lumber is at an actual size. Let us examine several different sizes using data from Table 10–3. First, notice that two listings are under the "Nominal Dimensions" heading. The left figure states the nominal thicknesses in quarters. For example, a nominal 1-inch board is called a four-quarter board. Another example is the five-quarter stock, which refers to boards with nominal $1\frac{1}{4}$-inch thickness. What would a nominal 2-inch, say, a 2 × 4, be called? It is cut from nominal eight-quarter stock. By now it should be clear that the quarter represents a quarter of 1-inch thickness.

TABLE 10–3 NOMINAL VERSUS ACTUAL LUMBER SIZES

Nominal dimensions Quarters	Inches	Surface thickness	Nominal width	Surface width
3/4	$\frac{3}{4}$ in.	$\frac{5}{8}$ in.	2 in.	$1\frac{1}{2}$ in.
4/4	1 in.	$\frac{3}{4}$ in.	3 in.	$2\frac{1}{2}$ in.
5/4	$1\frac{1}{4}$ in.	$1\frac{5}{32}$ in.	4 in.	$3\frac{1}{2}$ in.
6/4	$1\frac{1}{2}$ in.	$1\frac{13}{32}$ in.	5 in.	$4\frac{1}{2}$ in.
7/4	$1\frac{3}{4}$ in.	$1\frac{19}{32}$ in.	6 in.	$5\frac{1}{2}$ in.
8/4	2 in.	$1\frac{13}{16}$ in.	7 in.	$6\frac{1}{2}$ in.
9/4	$2\frac{1}{4}$ in.	$2\frac{3}{32}$ in.	8 in. and wider $\frac{3}{4}$ in. off nominal	
10/4	$2\frac{1}{2}$ in.	$2\frac{3}{8}$ in.		
11/4	$2\frac{3}{4}$ in.	$2\frac{9}{16}$ in.		
12/4	3 in.	$2\frac{3}{4}$ in.		
16/4	4 in.	$3\frac{3}{4}$ in.		

A recent trend by the lumber manufacturers has been to reduce the thickness of structural lumber $\frac{3}{32}$ inch beginning with $\frac{5}{4}$-inch-thick pieces and thicker. This means that a $\frac{5}{4}$-inch board actually measures $1\frac{5}{32}$ inches thick and a 2-inch board measures $1\frac{1}{2}$ inches.

If boards are surfaced before drying (S-GRN), they usually are dressed $\frac{1}{32}$ inch thicker than actual measurements so that their final thickness after drying is proper. If they are surfaced after drying, they are dressed to their actual sizes.

There are numerous dimensions of boards, structural lumber, timbers, and beams, and those used in built-up members. Recognizing their sizes is important when they are called for in specifications, blueprints, technical data, and tabular listings.

a. *Boards*. Boards are usually limited to nominal 1-inch thickness, but range in width from nominal 2-inch to 12-inch. Therefore, they are 1 × 2, 1 × 3, 1 × 4, 1 × 5, 1 × 6, 1 × 7, 1 × 8, 1 × 10, and 1 × 12. Five-quarter stock may be either boards or lumber.

b. *Lumber*. Lumber is usually expressed as 2 to 4 inches thick and up to 12 inches wide. Sometimes the design of cabinets and especially tables requires the use of lumber.

Several notations are used to denote the surfacing of boards, structural lumber, and even beams and timbers. If a piece of lumber, for instance, is dressed on its flat sides, it is labelled S2S, denoting "surfaced two sides." If it is also dressed for width, then S4S labelling is used, meaning "surfaced four sides."

Hardwood Sizes

Hardwood pieces cut from the tree are most frequently cut for a desired thickness at the sawmill and then dried. They are surfaced either before or after drying, but less frequently edge-cut or surfaced. Therefore, it is customary to see these pieces as S2S (surfaced two sides). Furthermore, cutting to standard and nonstandard widths is done; if dressed, the pieces would be S4S (surfaced four sides).

Rough-cut thicknesses are as thin as $\frac{3}{8}$ inch and range up to 4 inches thick. Rough widths are equal to the diameter of the tree unless quarter-sawed.

The surfacing (planing) operation reduces the thickness accordingly, and if the surfacing is done on the edges, the pieces are uniform in width as well as thickness. Table 10–4 lists some representative examples of rough and surfaced dressed hardwood standards.

TABLE 10–4   ROUGH AND SURFACED HARDWOOD DIMENSIONS

Rough (in.)	Dressed S2S (in.)	Rough (in.)	Dressed S2S (in.)
3/8	3/16	$1\frac{1}{4}$	$1\frac{1}{8}$
1/2	5/16	$1\frac{1}{2}$	$1\frac{3}{8}$
5/8	7/16	2	$1\frac{13}{16}$
3/4	9/16	$2\frac{1}{2}$	$2\frac{10}{16}$
1	13/16	2	$2\frac{3}{4}$
		4	$3\frac{3}{4}$

Because of hardwood's scarcity, nominal 1-inch and 2-inch stock is acceptable in much shorter lengths than for softwood. Depending on the grade and species, stock may be as small as 3 feet in length by 4 inches wide. As a rule, though, pieces are cut in longer lengths and then later recut to eliminate objectionable defects.

10.7 SPECIES OF WOOD[1]

There are many species of wood that we can describe in detail. Since this book is basically a study of European cabinetmaking, only woods likely to have been used or still in use for cabinet construction are listed. Having these references handy will make the job of planning for their use more complete. Three considerations are provided about each type of wood: its properties, its uses, and its description.

Rock Elm

Properties.   Rock elm (Figure 10–17) is a heavy wood, averaging 44 pounds a cubic foot. The wood is classified as hard, with a specific gravity of 0.57. It is stronger, harder, and stiffer than any of the other commercial elms. With the exception of hickory and dogwood, rock elm has higher shock resistance than any other American hardwood.

Although rock elm undergoes large shrinkage when drying, it tends to shrink somewhat less than the other commercial elms. As with all the elms, care must be taken to prevent warp during seasoning. Rock elm is somewhat difficult to work with, either with hand or machine tools, and the heartwood has low to moderate resistance to decay. However, all the commercial elms have excellent bending qualities.

Uses.   Elm lumber is used principally for containers and furniture. In some cases, the different species of elm are employed indiscriminately, but when hardness or shock resistance is required to a high degree, rock elm is preferred. Considerable quantities are used in the manufacture of furniture, especially the bent parts of chairs.

Description.   Heartwood is brown to dark brown, sometimes with shades of red. Summerwood pores are arranged in concentric wavy lines that appear lighter than the background wood. The springwood pores in rock elm are visible only upon magnification.

---

[1]The material in this section is reprinted from *Wood . . . Colors and Kinds,* Agriculture Handbook 101, Forest Service, U.S. Department of Agriculture (Washington, D.C.: Government Printing Office, 1956).

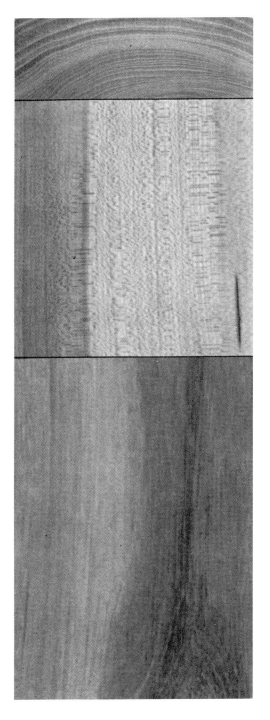

Figure 10–17 Rock elm.

Black Walnut

Properties.   Black walnut (Figure 10–18) is classified as a heavy wood, averaging 38 pounds per cubic foot. The wood is hard, with a specific gravity of 0.51, is strong and stiff, and has good stock resistance.

Even under conditions favorable to decay, black walnut heartwood is one of our most durable woods. It can be satisfactorily kiln-dried or air-dried, and holds its shape well after seasoning. Black walnut works easily with hand tools and has excellent machining properties. The wood finishes beautifully, with a handsome grain pattern. It takes and holds paints and stains exceptionally well, can be readily polished, and can be satisfactorily glued.

Uses.   The outstanding use of black walnut is for furniture. Large amounts are also used for gunstocks and interior finish. In the furniture industry, it is used either as solid wood cut from lumber or as veneer and plywood. It also is extremely popular for interior finish wherever striking effects are desired. The wood of black walnut is particularly suitable for gunstocks because of its ability to retain its shape after seasoning, its fine machining properties, and its uniformity of texture.

Description.   Heartwood is chocolate brown and occasionally has darker, sometimes purplish, streaks. Unless bleached or otherwise modified, black walnut is not easily confused with any other species. Pores are barely visible on the end grain, but are quite easily seen as darker streaks or grooves on longitudinal surfaces. Arrangement of pores is similar to that in the hickory and persimmon, but the pores are smaller in size.

Black Cherry

Properties.   Black cherry (Figure 10–18) is a moderately heavy wood with an average weight of 35 pounds per cubic foot. The wood is also moderately hard, with a specific gravity of 0.47. Stiff and strong, it ranks high in resistance to shock.

Although it has moderately large shrinkage, black cherry stays in place well after seasoning and is comparatively free from checking and warping. It has moderate resistance to decay. The wood is difficult to work with hand tools, but ranks high in bending strength. It can be glued satisfactorily with moderate care.

Uses.   Nearly all the black cherry cut is sawed into lumber for various products. Much goes into furniture. Other uses include burial caskets, woodenware and novelties, patterns and flasks for metalworking, and finish woodwork in buildings.

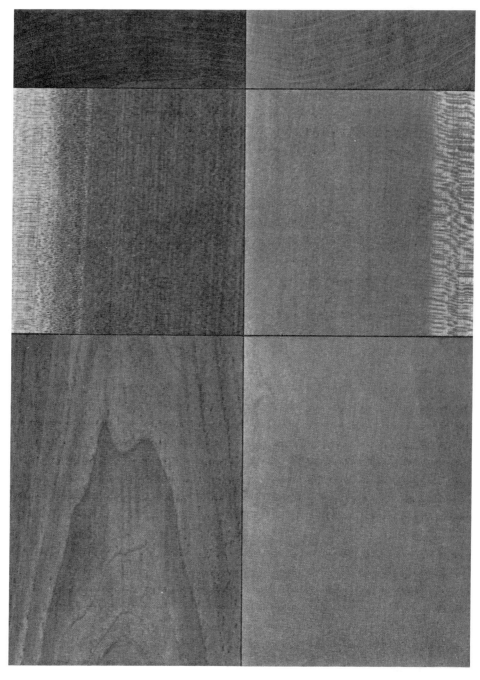

Figure 10–18 (a) Black walnut, (b) Black cherry.

Description.   Black cherry, which is not easily confused with other spe-cies because of its distinctive color, has light to dark reddish-brown heartwood. Although individual pores are not easily visible to the naked eye because they are diffuse, their pattern is sometimes distinctive. On end-grain surfaces, the pores may appear to form lines that parallel the growth rings, while on plane-sawed surfaces, they may appear to follow the outline of the growth-ring boundary, but in fact, parenchymal tissues produce the green-to-green bound-ary colors of the ring.

The wood rays of cherry are barely visible on end-grain surfaces and tend to produce a distinctive flake pattern on true quartersawed surfaces. They are higher along the grain than those of walnut and hence show more promi-nently on quartersawed surfaces.

White Ash

Properties.   White ash (Figure 10–19) is a heavy wood with an average weight of 42 pounds per cubic foot. Ranked as a hardwood, it has a specific gravity of 0.55. It is strong and stiff and has good shock resistance.

The wood of white ash is noted for its excellent bending qualities. In ease of working, tendency to split, and ability to hold nails and screws, it has mod-erately high rank. White ash lumber can be rapidly and satisfactorily kiln-dried, and it holds its shape well, even under the action of water. The wood remains smooth under continual rubbing but is low in decay resistance.

Uses.   The use of white ash that dwarfs all others is its utilization for handles. The wood is used in the manufacture of furniture, where it is especilly valuable for the bent parts of chairs. It is available as a veneer or plywood, and because of its contrasting grain between spring growth and dormant season it produces a bold pattern. It takes stain well and finishes very much like oak.

Description.   White ash heartwood is brown to dark brown, sometimes with a reddish tint. As in black ash, the zone of large pores is visible and usually sharply defined. The white dots or lines that indicate summerwood pores are usually more prominent in white ash than in black ash. The small wood rays are generally visible only on quartersawed surfaces.

White ash is sometimes confused with hickory, but the two species are readily distinguishable. The zone of large pores is more distinctive in ash than in hickory. Also, the summerwood zone in ash shows white dots or lines that are visible to the unaided eye, but in hickory these dots or lines are visible only upon magnification.

White Oak

Properties.   The white oaks (Figure 10–20) are heavy woods, averaging 47 pounds per cubic foot, and are very hard, with a specific gravity ranging

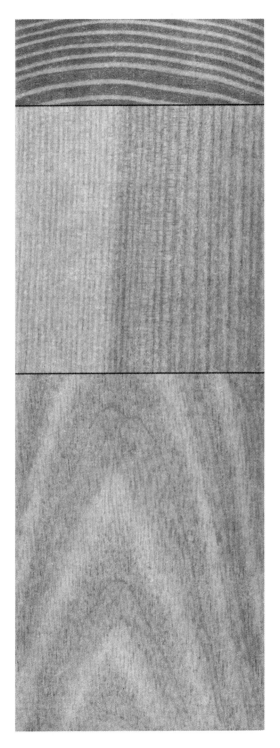

Figure 10–19 White ash.

from 0.57 in chestnut oak to 0.81 in live oak. Led by live oak, they rank high in strength properties.

The wood of the white oaks is subject to large shrinkage and seasoning must be done carefully to avoid checking and warping. Pores of the heartwood, with the exception of chestnut oak, are usually plugged with tyloses, a frothlike growth that makes the wood impervious to liquids. The heartwood itself is comparatively decay resistant, generally more so than that of the red oaks. White oaks are above average for all machining operations except shaping.

Uses.   Most white oak is made into lumber for flooring, furniture, casks general millwork, and boxes and crates. White as well as red oak is also used as veneer and may be purchased as either veneer or plywood.

Description.   Heartwood is grayish brown. The outlines of the larger pores are indistinct, except in chestnut oak, which has open pores with distinct outlines. On smooth-cut, end-grain surfaces, the summerwood pores are not distinct as individuals. Wood rays are generally higher than in red oak, the larger ones ranging from $\frac{1}{2}$ to 5 inches in height along the grain. As in red oak, rays appear lighter in color than the background wood on end-grain surfaces, and darker than the background wood on side-grain surfaces.

Red Oak

Properties.   The red oaks (Figure 10–20) are similar in many properties to the white oaks. A major difference is that red oak, because it lacks tyloses in its pores, is extremely permeable (porous). A heavy wood, it averages 44 pounds per cubic foot and the average specific gravity of the more important species ranges from 0.52 to 0.60. The wood is hard, stiff, and has high shock resistance.

Red oak undergoes considerable shrinkage while drying, and seasoning must be done carefully to avoid checking and warping. It is well above average for all machining operations except shaping, and the heartwood ranks low to moderate in decay resistance.

Uses.   Most of the red oak cut in this country is converted into flooring, furniture, millwork, boxes and crates, caskets and coffins, agricultural implements, and woodenware. Considerable quantities are used for veneering purposes and, as was mentioned in the uses of white oak, red oak plywood is abundantly available. The hardness and wearing qualities of red oak have made it an important cabinet wood.

Description.   Heartwood is grayish brown with a more or less distinctive reddish tint. Pores are commonly open, and the outlines of the larger pores are distinct. On smoothly cut end-grain surfaces, the summerwood pores can be

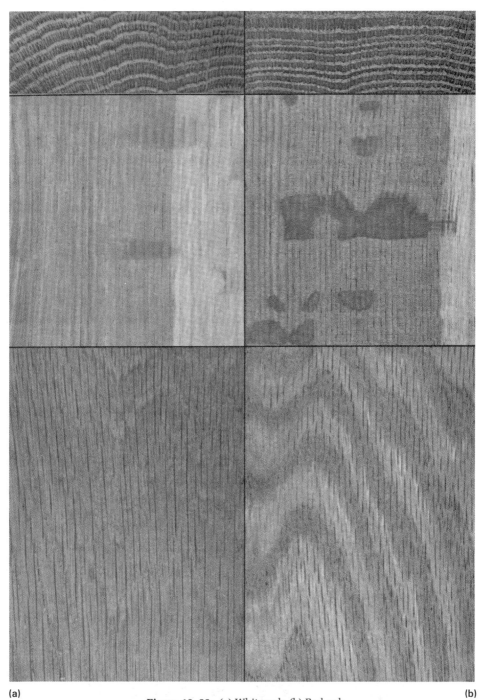

Figure 10-20 (a) White oak, (b) Red oak.

seen as individuals and readily counted when examined with a hand lens. Wood rays are commonly $\frac{1}{4}$ to 1 inch high along the grain. On end-grain surfaces, rays appear as lines crossing the growth rings.

10.8 PLYWOOD

Manufacturing Methods

Several different manufacturing methods are used in the construction of plywood including the layered veneer core, lumber core, particleboard core, and hardboard core.

Veneer core plywood is made by a process of setting or placing layers of veneers one on top of the other with an alternate layer's grain running at right angles. In essence, the pieces of veneer are fed through clippers that cut the ribbon of veneer into usable pieces and eliminate those with unrepairable defects. These are then dried to a 5 percent moisture content. Small defects are removed and patches are inserted in their place. Next, sheets are glued and sandwiched together in one continuous operation (Figure 10–21). The sandwiches are loaded into racks of a hot press, where heat in the range of 230 to 315 degrees and pressure in the range of 175 to 200 psi are applied.

Figure 10–21 Sorting plys by grade in the making of plywood. (*Courtesy of American Plywood Association*)

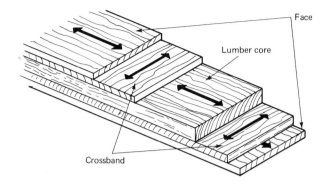

Figure 10–22   Lumber core plywood.

Figure 10–23   Particleboard or hardboard core plywood.

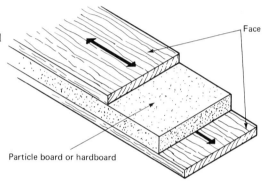

Sizing and sanding operations follow the gluing operation. After the plywood panels have been dried, the plywood is ripped by parallel saws to standard or custom widths and then trimmed for length. They are then fed through drum-sanding machines, where touch sanding, smooth sanding, and face and back panel sanding are done in one operation. The panels of unfinished plywood are now ready for use or further manufacturing.

Lumber core is plywood made with a core of small strips of lumber carefully aligned throughout the length of the sheet. Pieces of wood are cut to uniform widths and thicknesses (such as $\frac{3}{8}$ in. $\times$ 1 in.), and are edge-glued and aligned parallel.

Two layers of veneer, one cross band and one parallel to the lumber core, are applied to each side of the lumber (see Figure 10–22). Drying, cutting, and sanding operations are the same as for veneer core plywood.

Particleboard or hardboard core plywood is made with full width and length particleboard or hardboard cores sandwiched between layers of wood veneers. In the manufacture of this plywood, a single face veneer is glued to the core of particleboard and one or more layers of veneer may be applied to a hardboard core. Figure 10–23 illustrates this construction. Again as explained before, the dried panels are cut to size and sanded as needed.

Appearance Grades for Veneers

The *appearance grade* of the veneer used on the face and back of a sheet of plywood is assigned a letter or number under the U.S. Department of Commerce product standard specifications outlined in PS 51-71 for hardwood and decorative plywood and PS 1-66 for softwood plywoods. In descending order of quality, they are as shown in Table 10–5. For example, a sheet of plywood suitably selected for natural finishing would carry a grade stamp of A-A or A-2 for hardwood and N-A, A-A, or A-B for softwood.

TABLE 10–5   APPEARANCE GRADES FOR VENEERS

Quality	Hardwood grade	Softwood grade	Remarks
Premium	A	N	No defects
Good	1	A	Minor defects: color, pin holes, spots, pin knots
Sound	2	B	Matching grain not required, knots, patches, dote*
Utility	3	C	Splits, dote, knots, lays, patches
Backing	4	D	Almost anything goes: large knots, splits, dote, patches, rough cut marks

1. Composed from Product Standards PS-51-71 and PS 1-83, U.S. Department of Commerce.

*Note: Dote is a form of incipient decay which makes wood dull, lifeless, and lacking in strength.

Sizes and Thicknesses of Plywood

Most combinations of width, length, and thickness of plywood and paneling are available. The commonest size panels are 4 × 7 ft. (48 × 84 in.) and 4 × 8 feet (48 × 96 in.). Other sizes range from 4 × 4 ft. to 4 × 16 ft. and custom widths are also available.

Thicknesses of plywood and paneling range from $\frac{1}{8}$ in. to $1\frac{1}{8}$ in. Hardwood plywoods range from $\frac{1}{8}$ in. to $\frac{3}{4}$ in. ($\frac{1}{8}, \frac{5}{32}, \frac{1}{4}, \frac{3}{8}, \frac{1}{2}, \frac{5}{8}$, and $\frac{3}{4}$ in.). Softwood plywoods range in thicknesses of $\frac{1}{4}$ in. to $1\frac{1}{8}$ in. ($\frac{1}{4}, \frac{5}{16}, \frac{3}{8}, \frac{1}{2}, \frac{5}{8}, \frac{3}{4}, \frac{25}{32}, \frac{7}{8}$, 1, and $1\frac{1}{8}$ in.).

Veneer Patterns

Face veneers may be rotary peeled, plane- or quartersawed from a flitch or half-round, and sawed to produce various patterns of grain. Becuse of this variety of veneer grain patterns, numerous matches may be made of face veneers.

- The *book match* is a technique where alternating veneer sheets are turned like leaves in a book or opening a folded road map and are arranged on

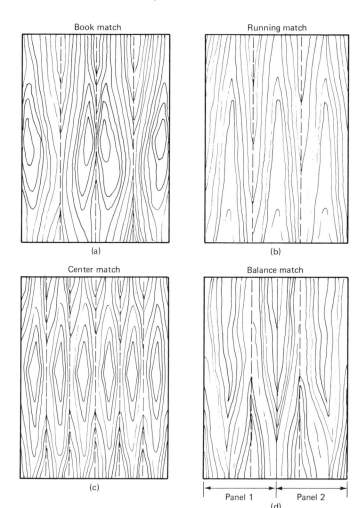

Book match
(a)

Running match
(b)

Center match
(c)

Balance match

Panel 1 | Panel 2
(d)

Figure 10–24 Plywood veneer patterns.

a panel accordingly. Figure 10–24(a) shows this match method and several others that are defined below.

- The *running match* [Figure 10–24(b)] is a technique where each panel is arranged from as many veneer sheets as necessry for a specified panel width. If a portion of a veneer is left over, it becomes the start of the next panel.

- The *center match* [Figure 10–24(c)] is a technique using an even number of sheets of veneer approximately equal in width and arranged so that a veneer joint occurs in the center of the panel.

- The *balance match* [Figure 10–24(d)] is a technique where either all odd or even veneer sheets are clipped to an equal width for balanced arrangement within each panel.

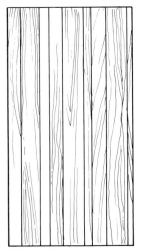

Figure 10–25 Random or no-match plywood veneer.

- The *random* or no-match technique shown in Figure 10–25 is one where as many pieces of veneer as necessary are aligned across the panel. This technique is used on V-groove paneling, and each random piece is found between grooves.

Quality cabinets are made from plywood with hardwood and softwood veneers and various cores. These plywoods are graded as cabinet grade according to the quality of surface veneers, as was listed in Table 10–5. Each side of a plywood panel can have a different grade of veneer, for example, grade AB. Workmanship used in their construction may be the same as is used in the cheaper cabinets or better where higher quality is desired. Special features are usually included, which of course add to the quality, versatility, and price.

REVIEW EXERCISES

1. Hardwood is obtained from conifers or trees that have needles. (T/F)
2. Kiln-dried lumber has a moisture content that does *not* exceed 15 percent. (T/F)
3. Warping or twisting is a condition of wood caused by uneven drying and shrinking. (T/F)
4. Flat-grain sawed boards will warp less than quartersawed boards. (T/F)
5. Cabinet-grade plywood should have A-A rated surface veneers. (T/F)
6. Which cabinet-grade softwoods are the best quality?
   a. No. 1
   b. No. 2
   c. B or better
   d. Select

7. Which cabinet-grade hardwood is the best quality?
    a. Firsts
    b. Selects
    c. No. 1 common
    d. Sound wormy

8. In nominal versus actual lumber sizes, if a piece of wood is nominally $\frac{8}{4}$ (8 quarters), its surfaced thickness would be:
    a. $1\frac{1}{4}$ inches
    b. $1\frac{13}{16}$ inches
    c. $2\frac{3}{32}$ inches
    d. $2\frac{3}{8}$ inches

9. Plywood made with alternating layers of veneer running in the same direction is called:
    a. Veneer core
    b. Lumber core
    c. Particleboard
    d. Laminated core

10. What is the name given to plywood that has pieces of veneer applied to its surface similar to a road map being opened?
    a. Running match
    b. Center match
    c. Balance match
    d. Bookmatch

ESSAY

11. In your own way, prepare a chart of the woods covered in this chapter showing their adaptability to cabinets or furniture described in Chapters 3 through 9.

ANSWERS

1F, 2T, 3T, 4F, 5T, 6d, 7a, 8b, 9a, 10d

11

Basic Drawing for Furniture and Cabinets

In this chapter we discuss several tools that are needed for cabinetmaking. First, several ways of making drawings are shown and explained, then a variety of illustrations representing styles and features of European cabinets and furniture is provided. After studying this chapter, you should have no trouble deciding what drawing tools to buy and generally when to use them.

Objectives

1. Identify the characteristics of various types of drawings that make them useful to cabinetmakers.
2. Select the drafting tools and techniques of drawing that meet a need for a cabinet drawing.

11.1 TYPES OF DRAWINGS SUITABLE FOR CABINETMAKERS

There are five types of drawings suitable for cabinetmakers: informal sketches, working drawings, cabinet drawings, isometric drawings, and perspective drawings. Each addresses a specific need of the cabinetmaker.

The sketch is used to communicate with a prospective owner. It shows the owner what the cabinetmaker believes the owner would like to have built. An experienced cabinetmaker usually uses notepaper or bond paper to make a variety of views of the cabinet, then adds details such as lengths, widths, depths, trim, hardware, special characteristics, internal structure, and so on until the owner is satisfied that proper communications have been achieved.

The cabinetmaker may then return to his or her shop and create more refined drawings from which the cabinet will be made. A *working drawing* entails three or more separate views—the front, end or side, and top view—plus any number of detail drawings. However, important as these sketches are to the cabinetmaker, they may not communicate to the owner the things most important to him or her. Therefore, one of the three other types of drawing must be done by the cabinetmaker. One type, called the *cabinet drawing*, is very desirable, since the front view is without distortion. Every line and dimension is accurate. The projection is made at a 45-degree angle and the cabinet depth is reduced to one-half its actual depth. Another view he or she could select is the isometric one, where the front and one end are raised 30 degrees above the horizontal plane. All dimensions are true. A third variety would be the perspective kind, where there is considerable distortion. The drawing would be made with one or usually two vanishing points (VP) and a horizontal plane.

The last three types just mentioned have good purpose for conveying concepts, but provide little information required by the cabinetmaker. Therefore, once the project is agreed upon, the cabinetmaker will almost always use either the sketch or working drawings.

Sketches

Figure 11–1 shows a sketch of a project. It contains all of the required elements of a sketch. These are the basis for this section.

The first consideration to make is to select the viewpoint to be sketched. Will it be a frontal view, end, top, oblique, cabinet, or perspective? Will it be conceptual, which is to say, an attempt to convey an impression? Or will it be a factual one that contains many, if not all, details and specifications? The answer to each of these questions will at one time or another be yes, so let's get on with some basic rules for making sketches.

RULE 1. *Sketches must be made proportional to the actual dimensions of the cabinet.* All cabinetmakers have either a natural or learned ability to describe cabinets or stock in proportions. If, for example, a cabinet is to be a primary horizontal mass, the sketch will have horizontal dimensions longer than the vertical ones. If drawers in a cabinet are graduated from deepset on the bottom to shallowest on the top, the sketch will show the dimensional differences. Rule 1 requires the ability to use proportional sketching from the largest to the smallest character of a cabinet.

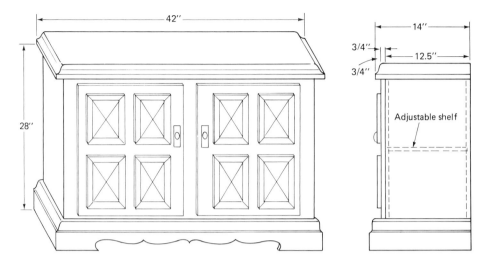

Figure 11–1   Sketch.

RULE 2. *Select the appropriate materials to make sketches.* Several types of paper can be used, which include plain bond, plain graph, and isometric graph. Pencils used should be light and medium soft so that erasures are possible. Once light lines and curves have been applied to the sketch, emphasis can be added by darkening specific ones as needed.

RULE 3. *Wherever possible, use the proper type of line, curve, and notation in the sketch.* Figure 11–2 shows a variety of lines, curves and notations used in sketching. These must be appropriately selected and used. Construction, object, hidden, dimension or extension with arrowheads, center lines, and others must convey their special meaning. When making these lines, curves, and notations, the pencil stroke for right-handed and left-handed cabinetmakers may differ. Customarily, though, lines are made left to right, top to bottom, right oblique downward and left oblique upward. Short strokes are later filled in with longer, darker ones. Lines parallel to the edge of the paper can be traced with one finger held along the paper's edge while sliding the pencil along the paper. Circles, arcs, and ellipses drawn freehand are made with short lines. Usually a series of short reference marks are made around a central point to act as radii from the center. The trained eye can approximate the length very well. Next the points are connected with short strokes of the pencil. When the drawing is complete, the lines are darkened.

RULE 4. *Begin the sketch with the largest dimensional parts first, then add internal details.* Making the overall parameters first causes the remaining detail to be proportionalized within a specific boundary. Subdivisions are made with penciled tick marks until the correct number are obtained, then lines are drawn along the tick marks.

RULE 5. *Use shading to bring out detail otherwise hidden.* In cabinetmaking, shading is done two different ways. The first way is to simulate the wood

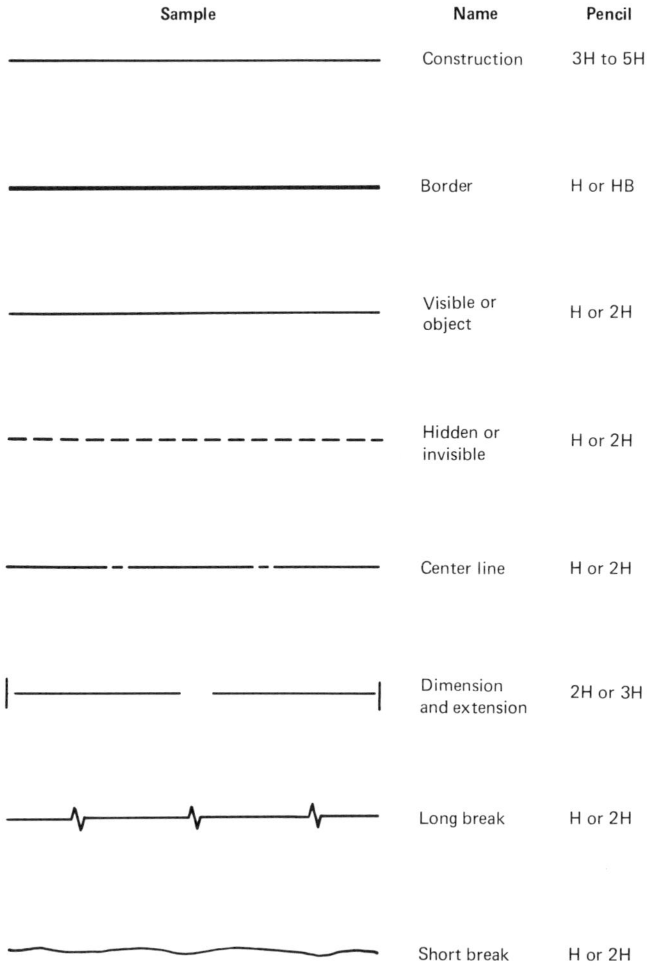

Sample	Name	Pencil
────────────────	Construction	3H to 5H
────────────────	Border	H or HB
────────────────	Visible or object	H or 2H
─ ─ ─ ─ ─ ─ ─ ─ ─	Hidden or invisible	H or 2H
──── ─ ──── ─ ────	Center line	H or 2H
├──────── ────────┤	Dimension and extension	2H or 3H
──⋀──⋀──⋀──	Long break	H or 2H
∿∿∿∿∿∿∿	Short break	H or 2H

Figure 11–2 Lines, curves, and notations.

grain patterns of the various pieces used in the cabinet. By simulating grain in the sketch, the owner sees how the effects of grain change the cabinet's appearance. The use of grain also conveys the method by which doors, stiles, and rails are made. Sometimes mitered corners are used; at other times, mortise-and-tenon joints are used. Shading also shows the connections or joinery used for facings and trim. Another use for shading is to show the owner points in the cabinet which are in relief to each other.

Working Drawings

A common name for a working drawing or set of working drawings is a blueprint. If we were building a house, we would need a set of working drawings, or blueprints, to provide details about the house. Some pages would show the floor plan (top view), others would show the elevations (front, ends, and back), and still others would show details (cross sections, hidden detail). Although the same views and detail drawings are needed for cabinetmaking, since cabinets are not as complex, all of them can be included in one or two pages, as shown in Figure 11–3.

What will you need to make a working drawing? The most comfortable way to construct a working drawing is to have a drafting table that is equipped with a sliding T-square. You also need several different sized right-angle triangles, templates for circles and ellipses, several French curves, pencils and, most important, an architect's ruler. In the United States, the ruler would probably be marked in inches. In Europe and other parts of the world, it would be based on the metric system.

Once you have these tools, you can begin to produce a set of drawings necessary to construct a cabinet. Although in the next section we study the technique of scaling with the use of an architect's scale, we first must understand the need to scale on a working drawing. Even though a working drawing shows the length and other dimensions of every piece of the cabinet, it is only through the use of the scale that the pieces as drawn reflect their proportion to the whole project. Recall that a cabinet is either a primary horizontal or primary vertical mass. This should be absolutely clear to anyone who reads or uses the working drawing.

Figure 11–3   Working drawing.

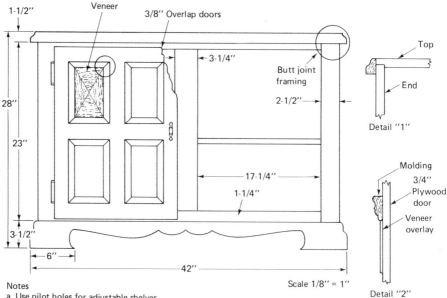

Notes
a. Use pilot holes for adjustable shelves
b. Dado bottom into end
c. Rabbet back into cabinet

Economy of drawing can be used when making working drawings where, for example, more than one side is to be drawn. Since the ends are in relationship to the front view, a single reference line drawn across the paper suffices for all three views: the left side, front, and right side. Using this technique permits fewer measurements. For example, only one dimensional measurement needs to be made for cabinet height.

If a top view is also needed, it could be placed above the front view of the cabinet. This shows relationship and also decreases the number of dimensions required, thus simplifying the drawing.

Remember that the working drawing must be very accurately drawn and all dimensions must be accurate. This drawing or set of drawings will be used in the shop to guide the construction effort. Hidden details could be overlooked if just the front view were drawn or if too many hidden lines were included; therefore, it is better to add one or more detailed drawings that show these views more clearly. Detail drawings can be made using the scale originally chosen, but more often than not the scale is larger to permit easier reading.

Once all the data are included in the drawing(s), the lines must be darkened and excess guide lines or marks should be erased. Avoid clutter on the drawing(s).

Cabinet Drawings

A cabinet drawing is less common than an oblique drawing. The visual representation of a cabinet drawn using this technique is generally viewed from above for cabinets that rest on the floor and from below for cabinets set on a wall.

The distinctive characteristics of this type of drawing follow. Figure 11–4 shows these rules applied to a cabinet drawing.

1. The frontal view is complete, as it is on a working drawing. All lines are horizontal and vertical; there is no distortion.
2. The oblique angle to project the end and top or bottom is always 45 degrees.
3. The projection of the cabinet end and top or bottom is always one-half the actual dimension of the end and top or bottom.
4. The true dimension is always shown on the oblique lines, even though they are drawn half length.

A cabinet drawing is a favorite type with cabinetmakers, simple because it is easy to draw with a drafting table and tools and equally simple to sketch. The owner is most frequently interested in the details of the face of the cabinet, not its plain sides. Once the face is drawn, extending oblique lines at 45 degrees merely completes the impression of a mass unit.

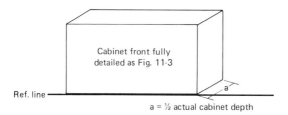

Ref. line

a = ½ actual cabinet depth

Figure 11–4   Cabinet drawing.

Isometric Drawings

There may, on occasion, be a need for an isometric drawing. This is one where one corner of a cabinet or piece of furniture appears closer than the rest. The isometric drawing uses angles of 30, 60, 90, and 120 degrees. Figure 11–5 shows some of the rules for isometric drawings. The first step is to always draw a horizontal reference line from which all other lines will project. The following rules are based on this premise.

1. All vertical lines are 90 degrees from the horizontal reference.
2. All isometric lines are 30 degrees from the horizontal reference.
3. Three sides are always shown.
4. Once all isometric lines are drawn, non-isometric lines and circles can be added.

Non-isometric lines are those that require angles other than the basic isometric ones. These may show slopes, as on a drop-leaf desk lid, for example. A perfect circle will become an ellipse in an isometric drawing because of the parallelogram created. To do this is a relatively simple task. Look at Figure 11–5(c) as we describe the task.

Figure 11–5   Isometric drawing.

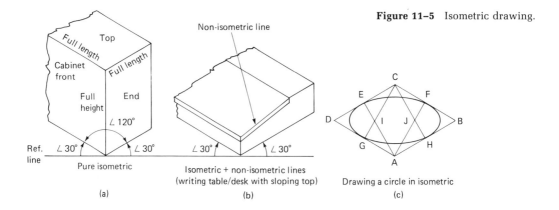

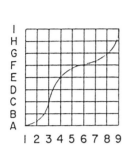
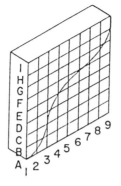

Figure 11–6 Isometric drawing of a French curve.

First, each side needs to be divided in half (points E, F, G, and H in the figure). Next draw light construction lines connecting points A to E, A to F, C to G, and C to H. Adjust a compass to connect points A to E. Draw two arcs, one from E to F with point A as the reference, and one G to H with point C as the reference. Next, adjust the compass for the radius I, the intersect point, to E. Then scribe two more arcs, one from E to G with I as the intersect point, and the other from F to H with J as the intersect point. Finally, erase the construction lines.

In Figure 11–6 we show a simple method to create a true isometric representation of an irregular French curve. The concept is to first use a square grid, such as is provided on graph paper. On the paper, draw the view of the curve, then number the grid left to right and bottom to top until the entire curve is covered. Next, prepare a similar grid in isometic lines with the same number of segments. Transfer the curve segment by segment to the isometric grid, using the numerous intersect points as references. When finished, erase the construction lines in the grid.

Dimensions in isometric are full dimensions. There is no shortening as in cabinet drawings. Dimension lines are always parallel to the object lines. Further, extension and dimension lines should be placed outside the object as they are drawn on working drawings. As a practical working tool there would be no use to a cabinetmaker to prepare the isometric drawing.

Perspective Drawings

The perspective drawing is pretty to look at and would be important in a promotional bulletin or advertisement, but it is of no use in a shop and cannot be done freehand very well. Even though overall proportions are used in making the drawing, they are distorted because of the vanishing points employed.

When drawing cabinets, two vanishing points are usually used. These are at extended edges of the drafting surface. They may be in any one of several positions, all of which are shown in Figure 11–7.

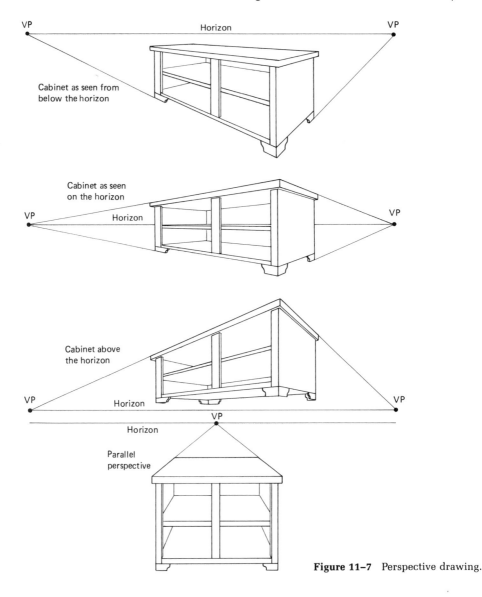

Figure 11–7 Perspective drawing.

1. Vanishing Points (VPs) along the horizontal at the base of a cabinet reveal only one end and front.
2. VPs along the horizontal through the center of the cabinet reveal only one end and front.
3. VPs along the horizontal which is below the cabinet reveal details of the cabinet base, one end, and front.

4. VPs along the horizontal which is above the cabinet reveal details of the cabinet top, one end, and front.

5. VPs along the horizontal above the cabinet and centered reveal only the front and top.

Summary

The types of drawings suitable for cabinetmakers to use in first establishing a way of incorporating the owner's desires and later converting these to shop drawings have been discussed and illustrated. Each was shown to have a purpose. The order of their presentation in this chapter, beginning with the sketch, is the usual way they occur in real-world situations. The most detailed and important for construction purposes is, of course, the working drawing. In the next section we identify some of the techniques and tools that make these drawings communicate to others the details they need to understand.

11.2 DRAFTING TOOLS AND TECHNIQUES

Drafting Tools

Figure 11–8 shows a sample of the tools usually needed to draw cabinets. Each is labelled in the figure. Overall, the cost of these is minimal considering that most last a lifetime.

Figure 11–8   Drafting tools.

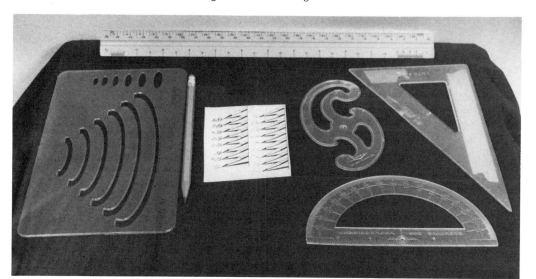

Drafting Techniques

Numerous books in any public library could provide pages and chapters on drafting techniques. Some are really basic, while others include geometry and other forms of higher math. What we provide here is sufficient to meet the needs to draw almost any cabinet or piece of furniture.

1. Lines and curves are shown in Figure 11–9.
2. Lettering is shown in Figure 11–10. Notice that the arrow indicates the direction the pencil or pen is moved to create a line or curve in the letter.
3. Detailing a drawing is shown by examples in Figure 11–11. The rise of both dimension and extension lines are very evident in detail drawings.

Since arrowheads on the dimension line are about $\frac{1}{8}$ inch long, there will be many times where the dimension lines will be drawn outside the main drawing area. Fractions of an inch, inches, or millimeters would be written adjacent to the end of one of these dimension lines. Some illustrators use a short exten-

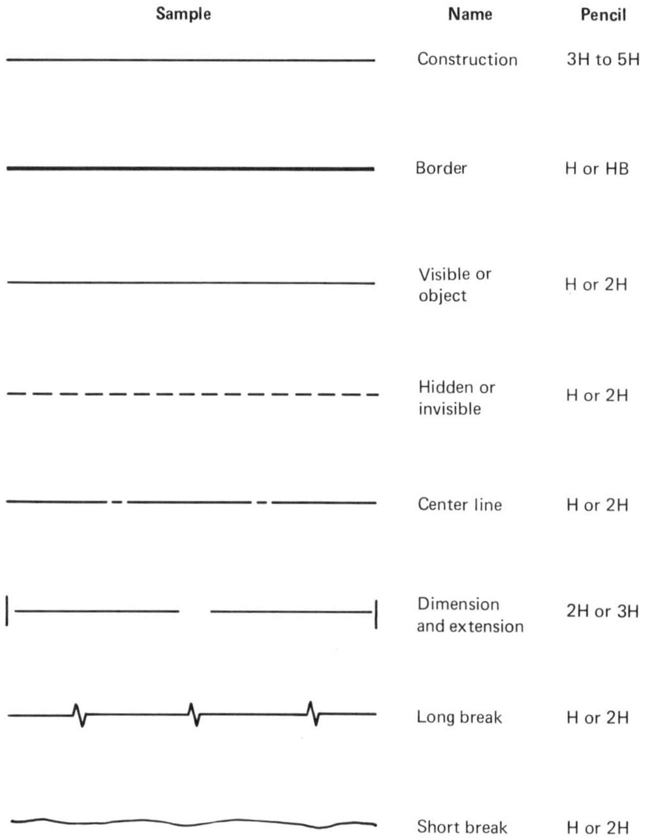

Sample	Name	Pencil
	Construction	3H to 5H
	Border	H or HB
	Visible or object	H or 2H
	Hidden or invisible	H or 2H
	Center line	H or 2H
	Dimension and extension	2H or 3H
	Long break	H or 2H
	Short break	H or 2H

Figure 11–9 Lines and curves.

*1▾ Indicates direction and number of strokes   **Figure 11–10**   Lettering.

sion line to ensure that the measurement is associated with the proper dimension line. One difference between cabinet details and house or commercial blueprint details is that the measurements are written horizontal to the position of the page or drawing, whereas on blueprints the measurements are in line with the dimension line.

Several rules should be followed in making detail drawings.

1. Gradually work outward with extension and dimension lines. The outermost dimension line should contain the longest measurement.
2. Attempt to center the measurement within the dimension line.
3. Make sure that extension lines are clear where they start but do not touch object lines, and that they extend $\frac{1}{16}$ in. or so beyond the point of the arrowhead.
4. Make extension and dimension lines finer (less bold) than object lines.
5. Scale the drawing.

It is a rare situation where a cabinetmaker would draw a set of working drawings in a scale of 1, where 1 inch on the drawing equals 1 inch of the cabinet. If this were done a 5-foot-long cabinet would require a 5-foot-long drawing. What we do instead is select a scale that provides a set of drawings only as large as needed to comfortably read the details and measurements and understand the parts of the cabinet being displayed. An architect's scale is an excellent tool to use for the job, along with the T-square and angles to make the drawing.

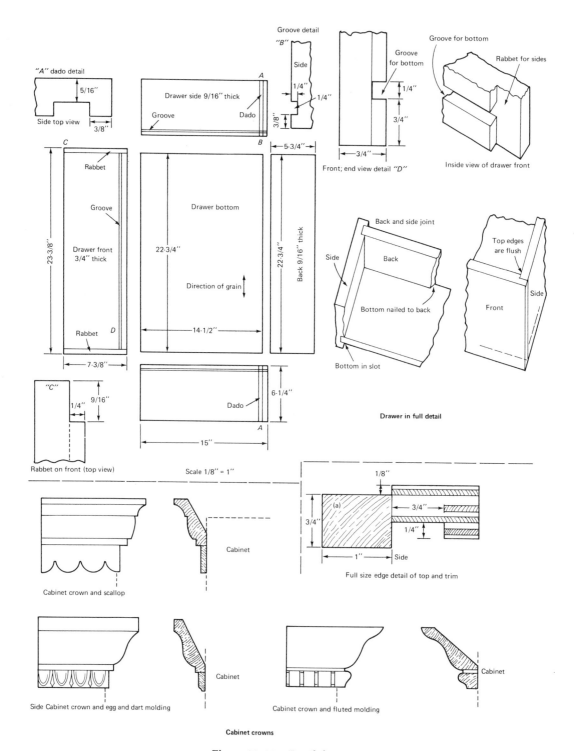

"A" dado detail

5/16"

Side top view

3/8"

Groove detail

"B"

Side

1/4"

1/4"

3/8"

Front; end view detail "D"

Groove
for bottom

1/4"

3/4"

3/4"

Groove for bottom

Rabbet for sides

Inside view of drawer front

Drawer side 9/16" thick

Groove

Dado

A

B

5-3/4"

C

Rabbet

Groove

23-3/8"

Drawer front
3/4" thick

Rabbet

D

7-3/8"

Drawer bottom

22-3/4"

Direction of grain

14-1/2"

22-3/4"

Back 9/16" thick

Back and side joint

Side

Back

Bottom nailed to back

Bottom in slot

Top edges
are flush

Front

Side

Side

Drawer in full detail

"C"

9/16"

1/4"

Rabbet on front (top view)

Dado

6-1/4"

A

15"

Scale 1/8" = 1"

Cabinet

Cabinet crown and scallop

1/8"

(a)

3/4"

3/4"

1/4"

1"

Side

Full size edge detail of top and trim

Cabinet

Side Cabinet crown and egg and dart molding

Cabinet

Cabinet crown and fluted molding

Cabinet

Cabinet crowns

Figure 11–11   Detail drawing.

An architect's scale is slightly longer than 12 inches because the ends tend to get scratched. The beginning of a scale is about $\frac{1}{4}$ inch from the end, so it is protected. Triangular scales have a variety of different scales to select from. These include:

1. A 12-inch ruler graduated in sixteenths of an inch.
2. A 1 inch = 1 inch scale on the left end, and a $\frac{1}{2}$ inch = 1 inch scale on the opposite end.
3. A $\frac{3}{4}$ inch = 1 inch scale on the left end, and a $\frac{3}{8}$ inch = 1 inch scale on the opposite end.
4. A $\frac{1}{8}$ inch = 1 inch scale on the left end, and a $\frac{1}{4}$ inch = 1 inch scale on the opposite end.
5. A $1\frac{1}{2}$ inches = 1 inch scale on the left end, and a 3 inches = 1 inch scale on the opposite end.
6. A $\frac{3}{16}$ inch = 1 inch scale on the left end, and a $\frac{3}{32}$ inch = 1 inch on the opposite end.

Figure 11–12 provides several scales for our next discussion. Let's say that we want to make a drawing of a cabinet that we have sketched. The length of the cabinet is 60 inches, the height is 32 inches, and the depth is 16 inches. We would like a drawing of the front and end views on a piece of drawing paper 24 inches long. Using the table below, determine the scale that would provide the largest working drawing.

Scale	Paper Length Needed for Front View Only
1″ = 1″	60″
3/4″ = 1″	45″
1/2″ = 1″	30″
3/8″ = 1″	$22\frac{1}{2}$″
1/4″ = 1″	15″
3/16″ = 1″	$11\frac{1}{4}$″
1/8″ = 1″	$7\frac{1}{2}$″

The most acceptable scale would be the $\frac{1}{4}$″ = 1″ scale. With the larger scales, both views would not fit. The $\frac{3}{16}$″ = 1″ scale would work, but the larger scale would be easier to work with. We reject the $\frac{1}{8}$″ = 1″ scale because the drawing would be much too small for practical use.

Now let's look at the $\frac{1}{4}$-inch scale (Figure 11–13) and find some of the measurements we need.

If you have never used an architect's scale, a little orientation is needed. First, notice that there is a zero beginning reference point that is *not* on the

Figure 11–12 Architect's scale.

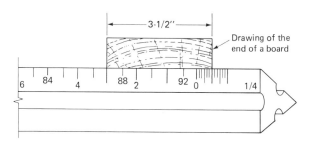

1/4 inch scale drawn twice as large to show detail

Figure 11–13 Quarter-inch scale.

right end of the scale, but rather $\frac{1}{4}$ inch from the end. All markings (graduations) to the left are spaced $\frac{1}{4}$ inch apart and represent 1 inch of actual cabinet dimension. Since our example cabinet is 60 inches long and the longest mark is 48 inches, we would need to continue from the right again and add 12 more graduations to obtain 60 inches. As long as all cabinet dimensions are in whole-inch increments, we never will use the markings to the right of the zero reference. However, we know that the cabinet base will be $3\frac{1}{2}$ inches high and the top will be $\frac{3}{4}$ inch thick. To read and determine the vertical height of the base, we would use graduations to the left and right of the zero reference. The ones to the left provide whole values of an inch on a $\frac{1}{4}$-inch scale [Figure 11–12(b)]. Each graduation to the right of zero represent $\frac{1}{12}$ of an inch. Therefore, $3\frac{1}{2}$ inches would be represented by three graduations to the left of zero and six graduations, or $\frac{1}{2}$ inch, to the right on a $\frac{1}{4}$-inch scale. To scale the dimension of the top, no full graduations would be used, but only the fractional notations to the right of zero [Figure 11–12(c)].

This simple explanation should suffice for all similar drawings. The technique of using a scale is a constant repetition of the same procedure.

11.3 SYMBOLS, PATTERNS, AND DESIGNS USED
IN EUROPEAN STYLED FURNITURE AND CABINETS

The figures on the next several pages illustrate several characteristics, features, and patterns of objects and designs that are included in European styled cabinets and furniture. Figure 11–14 shows hardware details, Figure 11–15 shows leg details, and Figure 11–16 shows some common adornments.

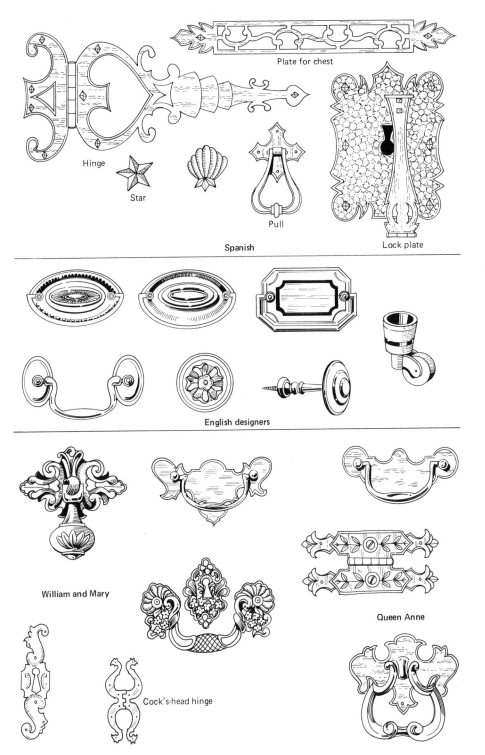

Figure 11–14 Hardware details for European cabinets.

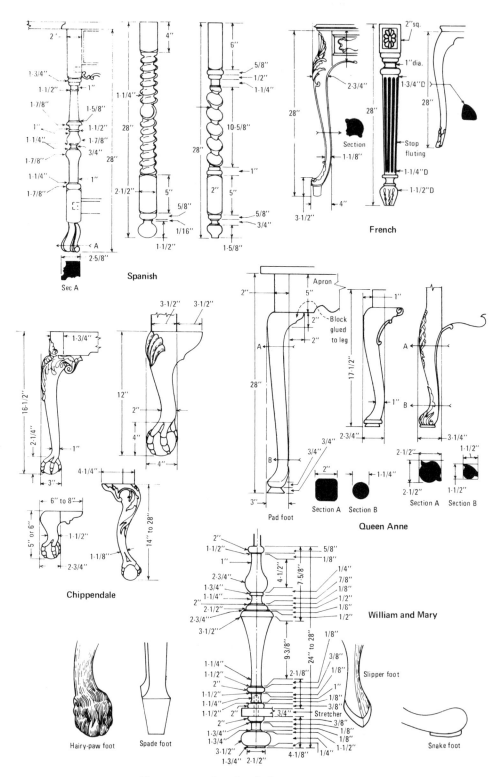

Figure 11–15 Leg details for European cabinets.

198

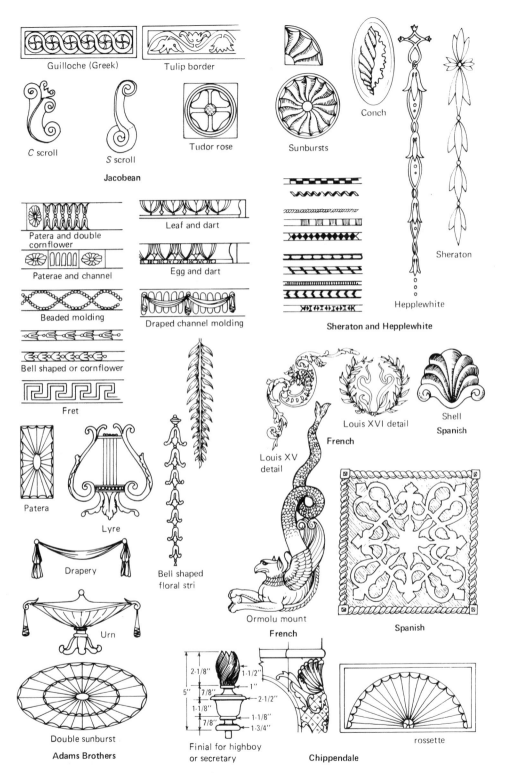

Guilloche (Greek)

Tulip border

C scroll

S scroll

Tudor rose

Jacobean

Conch

Sunbursts

Patera and double cornflower

Paterae and channel

Beaded molding

Bell shaped or cornflower

Fret

Leaf and dart

Egg and dart

Draped channel molding

Sheraton

Hepplewhite

Sheraton and Hepplewhite

Patera

Lyre

Drapery

Bell shaped floral stri

Louis XVI detail

French

Louis XV detail

Shell

Spanish

Urn

Double sunburst

Adams Brothers

Ormolu mount

French

2-1/8″
1-1/2″
1″
5″ 7/8″
2-1/2″
1-1/8″
1-1/8″
7/8″
1-3/4″

Finial for highboy or secretary

Chippendale

Spanish

rossette

Figure 11–16 Adornments for European cabinets.

REVIEW EXERCISES

1. The type of drawing most suitable for cabinetmakers to use when designing is the perspective type. (T/F)

2. Sketches serve to illustrate in picture form the details and characteristics of a cabinet. (T/F)

3. Rule 1 in sketching suggests that a 12-inch dimension be drawn narrower than a 36-inch dimension. (T/F)

4. As a standard procedure in sketching, all lines are drawn alike, even when hidden parts are shown. (T/F)

5. A working drawing is like a floor plan, elevation plan, and a detail plan all in one. (T/F)

6. In making a cabinet drawing, the oblique angle is always:
   a. 30 degrees.
   b. 45 degrees.
   c. 60 degrees.
   d. none of the above.

7. In making a cabinet drawing, the oblique dimension is always _____ the actual dimension.
   a. one-eighth of
   b. one-quarter of
   c. one-half of
   d. equal to

8. When making an isometric drawing, the oblique lines are usually _____ from the horizontal reference.
   a. 15 degrees
   b. 30 degrees
   c. 45 degrees
   d. 60 degrees

9. When using the architect's scale, and specifically the $\frac{1}{4}'' = 1''$ scale, what dimension would you use to mark a cabinet whose height is 39 inches?
   a. 9.75
   b. 14.625
   c. 19.5
   d. 39

10. If you wanted to illustrate a detail larger than the actual size, what architect's scale would you use?
    a. $\frac{1}{2}'' = 1''$
    b. $\frac{3}{4}'' = 1''$
    c. $1'' = 1''$
    d. $1\frac{1}{2}'' = 1''$

ESSAYS

11. Explain the advantage of using the cabinet drawing to draw a cabinet.
12. Making a working list of the types of lines used in drawing and the best pencil for making each.

ANSWERS

1F, 2T, 3T, 4F, 5T, 6b, 7c, 8b, 9d, 10d

12

Cabinet Joinery

In this chapter we provide examples of the various joints used by cabinetmakers of European furniture and cabinets. The details provided are only those essential for a basic understanding of their characteristics and uses. Specific details for making each joint with specific tools such as hand tools, portable power tools, or bench power tools are not provided. For that level of detail, refer to a book on the principles of joint making, such as *Cabinetmaking: From Design to Finish*, published by Prentice Hall, Inc. The detail provided in this chapter captures the essential functionality, applicability, and quality of the various joints, with illustrations provided for visual recognition.

Objective

1. Identify the applications and qualities of each type of cabinet joint.

12.1 BUTT JOINT

The butt joint is by far the most basic of woodworking joints. It is extremely functional and serves many purposes, and can be a very easy joint to make. As with any joint used in woodworking, when the pieces to be joined are properly prepared and proper glues are used, the results are very good.

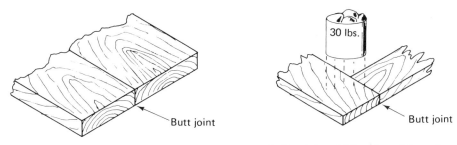

a. Butt joint (parallel joint)

b. Butt joint with boards at right angles

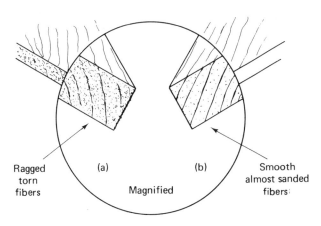

Ragged torn fibers

(a)

(b)

Smooth almost sanded fibers

Magnified

c. End cuts for butt jointing

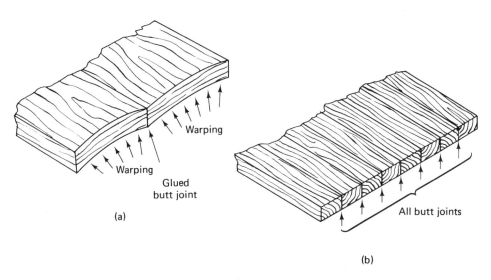

Warping

Warping

Glued butt joint

(a)

All butt joints

(b)

d. How to eliminate warping with butt joints

Figure 12–1   Butt joint.

Applications and Qualities

The butt joint, as shown in Figure 12–1, provides a means for making a wide surface. Since the two boards are in complete contact over their entire length, the joint should have good strength once the glue dries.

A right-angle butt joint is frequently used on cabinet frames, especially in kitchen cabinets. This joint has less quality than the parallel joint, as can also be seen in the figure. The joint is essentially a weak one, but very functional, and when it is built carefully, it is quite adequate. Our example shows (by use of the weight) the way the joint is weak. When cutting the board, if you use a saw with many teeth—a No. 12 or No. 14 handsaw, or a planer blade with upward of 200 teeth in a power machine—your joint will hold better and will be stronger. Why? Look at Figure 12–1 again, which shows two boards cut off. One (a) has been cut with a Standard No. 8 handsaw, the other (b) has been cut with a planer saw. The No. 8 handsaw, although classified as a crosscut saw, actually makes a very ragged cut. You can see by the figure that the edges are coarse and torn and that the interior fibers are torn as well. The result is a very porous end cut. Now look again at board (b). Notice how smooth the edges are and how little the inner fibers are torn.

When large, wide surfaces are needed and plywood is not to be used, the butt joint works well. When picture frames are cut, their miters are usually butted together and glued. The butt joint is commonly used for facing kitchen cabinets, but it is also useful for applying edge molding, plant-ons, or base molding to occasional tables or cabinets.

12.2 RABBET JOINT

The rabbet joint has been in use for hundreds of years. This joint can be made relatively easily with a specially designed hand plane called a side rabbet plane (see Figure 12–2). It can also be made with a handsaw and a chisel, with a router, using a dado or rabbet bit, or with a table saw, radial arm saw, and jointer.

Figure 12–3 shows a rabbet joint. Notice how an L-shaped cut is made into the piece of wood across the end and along the side. This cut is never made arbitrarily—it always conforms in size to the dimension of the piece it will join. For example, if a rabbet joint is used to join the sides of a box made from $\frac{3}{4}$-inch stock lumber, one dimension of the rabbet will be $\frac{3}{4}$ inch and the other will be a selected depth. Refer to Figure 12–3 and note how the dimensions are cut to allow for an exact fit of an end piece.

A joint made with a rabbet is functionally stronger than a butt joint. In the first place, there are two gluing surfaces, as opposed to one in the butt joint. Figure 12–3(b) shows these as views a and b. Second, if nails and screws can be used, they can be driven from both sides [Figure 12–3(c)].

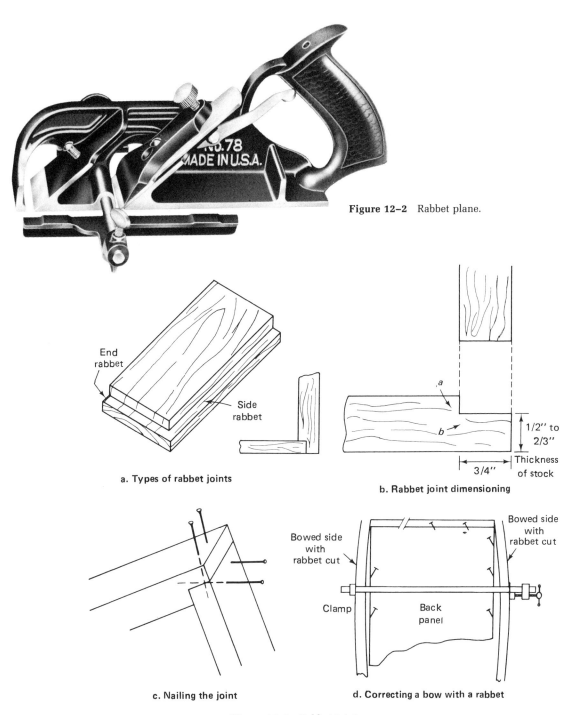

Figure 12–2 Rabbet plane.

End rabbet

Side rabbet

a. Types of rabbet joints

a

b

1/2'' to 2/3''

Thickness of stock

3/4''

b. Rabbet joint dimensioning

c. Nailing the joint

Bowed side with rabbet cut

Bowed side with rabbet cut

Clamp

Back panel

d. Correcting a bow with a rabbet

Figure 12–3 Rabbet joint.

Another important feature of the rabbet joint is that it is easier to make a square corner. After the rabbet is cut across the end of a board and the second piece used in the joint is tightly glued or butted to surfaces a and b, a square joint results. Another quality feature of the joint is that the piece being fitted into the rabbet cut will not have an end showing, and the piece with the rabbet cut will only have approximately half its end thickness showing.

The rabbet joint is used extensively. Wooden windows have rabbets where the glass fits, as do picture frames. To hide cabinet backs from side view, a rabbet is made into the side pieces and top piece. Box fronts and backs and certain cabinets have all four sides rabbeted.

12.3 DADO JOINT

The best workmanship is often accomplished when time is spent making strong joints in the wood. The time involved in machine setting or hand cutting a dado joint definitely pays off in an excellent product. In almost any cabinet you build, the use of the dado joint will play an important part in its total design and strength.

Figure 12–4 shows the two basic dado joints. The one on the left, view (a), is a straight dado joint. Notice how the dado (cutaway stock) is made from edge to edge of the stock. In the other example, view (b), the dado is stopped back from the face edge. This variation is called a "gain" joint or blind dado. The stock that will fit into the dado must have a notch cut into it to complete the joint. This method is excellent to use when no facings are to be used on the cabinet.

Of all the types of joints used in cabinetmaking, the dado joint creates the strongest joint. The principle in making the joint is to remove a section of wood from one of the pieces in the exact dimensions of the piece to fit into the dado. The stock that is dadoed is weakened by the dado, but when the other piece is inserted and glued, full strength is restored.

From the illustration in Figure 12–4, you might have already guessed that the dado cut is usually made into a vertical section of a cabinet. This is true; usually shelves are dadoed into the sides pieces. However, a dado joint can be used in horizontal pieces as well. You might also note that no additional bracing is required to hold the shelf. To illustrate just how good this joint is study view (b) of the figure.

Figure 12–4(b) illustrates the difference between cleating a shelf and dadoing a shelf. As shown in the figure, the shelf is actually inserted into the vertical side piece. Because the shelf stock replaces the original stock that was removed to make the dado, total strength is restored. In addition to the functional quality, the clean lines created by the joint and its inherent squaring ability are advantages.

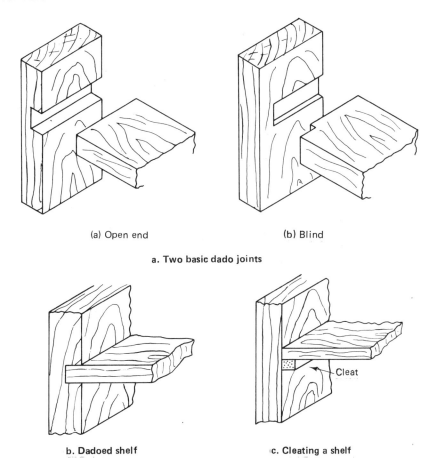

(a) Open end   (b) Blind

a. Two basic dado joints

b. Dadoed shelf   **c. Cleating a shelf**

Figure 12–4   Dado joint.

The cleating method is a poor substitute for the dado. In Figure 12–4(b), note that a cleat has been fastened to the vertical side piece. Then the shelf is laid on top and glued or nailed/screwed and glued. Actually a butt joint is created. Inherent weaknesses exist: (1) the cleat is the main support and it is held in place by screws and glue, and (2) the only bond the shelf has with the side of the cabinet is the glue bond. When the shelf is loaded with books, a great strain is placed upon the joint and separation can and often does occur.

If no facings are to be used on the cabinet, or if narrow facings are to be used, the cleat presents a problem. How can it be finished to look neat? It really cannot. Not only is the cleat unsightly, but it creates a nuisance. The book that is stored next to the side of the cabinet must be short enough to fit under the cleat. The end grain of the cleat shows when the facings are narrow.

12.4 MORTISE

Making a mortise goes hand in hand with making a tenon. The two pieces fit together to make a very strong cabinet joint. However, a mortise can be used by itself with a mortise lock and a mortise (butt) hinge. Some texts discuss the mortise and tenon as one subject. However, there is a particular series of steps that must be performed when making the mortise.

Figure 12–5 shows the two basic types of mortises, a closed mortise and an open mortise. There are other variations of the mortise, but they all fall in these two categories.

Some of the variations of the mortise, along with their tenons, are shown in the figure. View (c) shows a haunched mortise-and-tenon joint. You should recognize that this is a dado in the mortised piece of stock. For the tenon to fit snugly, a piece of its stock (the haunch) is left. When the two pieces are clamped together, the haunch replaces the dadoed section.

View (d) shows a concealed haunch mortise-and-tenon joint. This joint is more difficult to make because of the angle of the haunch. The effect that is obtained when using this joint is that the full end of the mortised piece is intact.

View (e) shows a standard blind mortise, but one made with auger or router bits. Note the rounded corners. The tenon must also have rounded corners.

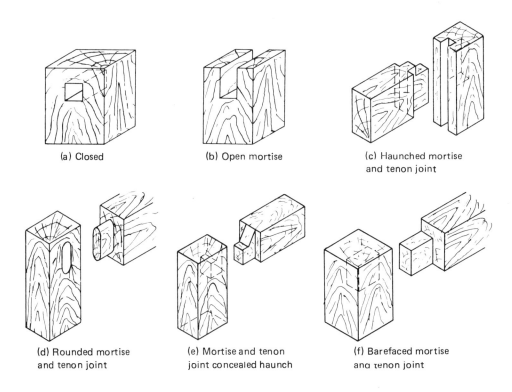

(a) Closed

(b) Open mortise

(c) Haunched mortise and tenon joint

(d) Rounded mortise and tenon joint

(e) Mortise and tenon joint concealed haunch

(f) Barefaced mortise and tenon joint

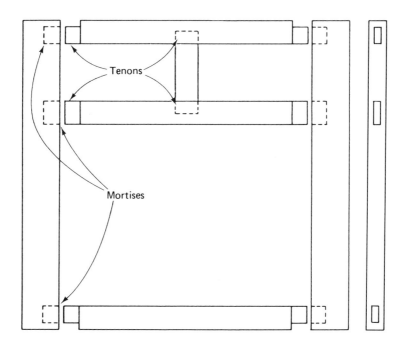

View (f) illustrates a bareface mortise-and-tenon joint. This joint is frequently used in table manufacturing. One side of the tenon is flush with the outside of the stock, but the mortise is usually centered in its stock.

The mortise combined with the tenon makes one of the strongest joints used in woodworking. With no glue at all and exceptionally well-fitted pieces, the joint is self-sustaining. However, with the addition of glue, the joint is almost indestructible.

Cabinet facings, as shown in Figure 12–6, are frequently joined at the corners with the mortise-and-tenon joint. The vertical pieces, called stiles, usually—but not always—have the mortise. The horizontal pieces, called rails, usually have the tenons. Doors made by the frame-and-panel method usually are made using the mortise and tenon. This is where the haunch style is found as well. Tables and chairs are made from stock materials as a rule. Their pieces must be made rigid and there are very few pieces to work with. Therefore, the mortise-and-tenon joint is frequently used. The table rail just below the table top fits into the table leg with this type of joint. The mortise-and-tenon joint can be found in every style of European cabinet and furniture.

To show how many applications of the mortise there are, take a look at any door in your home. The door has stiles and rails and is made rigid by the use of the mortise and tenon. The stiles and rails of a wooden screen door are also joined by the mortise and tenon. Door locks made and used today often require the mortise so that the main portion of the lock can be inserted into the door. The open-shelf type of bookcase, in which the ends are made to resemble a ladder, is another excellent example of the use of the mortise and tenon. The rails in this type of bookcase provide the shelf supports.

12.5 TENON

Whereas a mortise may be used alone for several purposes, the tenon is usually used together with the mortise. Hence, the shop methods presented in this chapter show how to lay out a tenon from a previously made mortise. If a set of plans is being used to make a project, the layout for a tenon may be shown from the side view, or a top view may also be shown if, for instance, a haunch is to be cut. The total thickness of the stock is given on the drawing, as is the thickness of the completed tenon and whether the tenon is centered or offset.

For the shop method, laying out a tenon can be simplified if the tenon is made as long as the width of the stock that has the mortise. Figure 12–7(a) shows an example. Notice how the flanges of the tenon are shown equal to the inside edge of the stile. The total depth of the mortise (shown as the dashed area) is less than the width of the stile. Therefore, additional cuts are required on the tenon. First, the tenon length is cut to fit the depth of the mortise. Second, the top edge of the tenon is cut, thereby completing the tenon. This method results in some wasted stock, but it has a very important benefit: its use eliminates almost all chance for error.

Suppose that a panel and frame must be made as shown in Figure 12–7(b). The parts are labeled as follows: a, rails (top and bottom); b, styles (sides); and c, panel (center piece). The stiles are mortised to a depth of slightly more than half their width. The rails are cut the full width of the panel. After the full tenon is made, the finishing length of the tenon will equal half the width of the stile. The little space remaining between the end of the tenon and the bottom of the mortise is important. Excess glue and chips or sawdust are sometimes trapped by the tenon and forced into the bottom and into this small space.

To further illustrate how this method minimizes the chance for error, let's explore the view of the panel and frame in Figure 12–7(b) and Figure 12–7(c). In this figure, a slight modification was made to the actual finished pieces of the frame. The tenons are shown as they are before final fitting (reaching to the outer edge of the stiles). This is where the chance for error is eliminated. The frame is 24 inches wide, so the rails are precut to 24 inches (the total width of the frame).

The next step would be to lay out a tenon on each end of the rails, then cut and trim the tenon to fit the mortise. Notice that it was necessary to use a ruler only once during the layout. Since the tenon was made for the full width of the stock and then cut off, the completed panel and frame will be 24 inches wide.

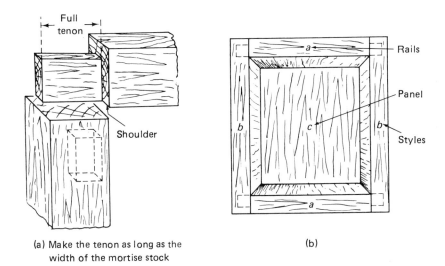

(a) Make the tenon as long as the width of the mortise stock

(b)

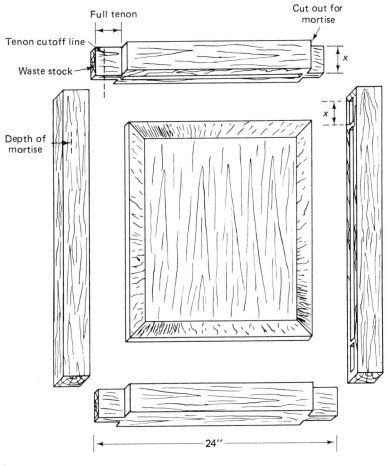

(c) Panel and frame

Figure 12–7 Tenon joint.

An alternative method can be used, but it is a bit more tricky. A mistake can easily be made, especially during the cutting stage. Again, use Figures 12-7(b) and 12-7(c) as examples. This method requires you to calculate the distance between the stiles (total width 24 inches less the width of each side). Next you add the length of each tenon (one-half the width of the stile times two stiles). This total plus the first figure (intermediate length) results in the exact length of the rail pieces.

You see that the method is not too difficult. However, errors are easily made while making the calculations and later while using the machines or hand tools. A cut on the wrong side of a pencil line, for instance, results in a panel that is smaller by $\frac{1}{8}$ inch. There are occasions when this mortised piece has a width over 4 inches. The waste (using the full-length-mortise method) may be too costly, especially where many pieces are being cut. For a rule of thumb, use the following table when determining which method is best for the job:

Stile 1 to 4 inches with a mortise	Use full-length-tenon method
Stile 4 inches and over with a mortise	Use intermediate-length plus two-tenon-length method
Depth of mortise 1 to 4 inches stock width	Use 30 to 55 percent of the width of stock
Depth of mortise on over 4 inches stock width	Use 2 inches to 50 percent of the width of the stock

The tenon is usually used with the mortise. The two pieces join to make a very strong and secure joint. The strength that the tenon gives to the joint comes from the fact that the piece having the tenon reaches almost the full width of a frame, or under the full length of the table top, or across the full width of a door. Although these examples indicate that the tenon is usually used with the rail, it is not restricted to this use. On many case fronts (cabinet facings), a vertical piece of stock is mortise-and-tenoned to provide the framework for drawers. In modern cabinet facings, single doors are used in preference to double doors. A stile will be tenoned into the center of the opening at the top and bottom, thereby making a separation for the two doors.

12.6 DOWEL JOINT

The doweled joint is simpler for a manufacturer to make. All the pieces to be joined can be treated as if they were butt joints. A double-doweling drill press is manufactured that will drill two holes at one time. By using this machine alone a worker can prepare both pieces for the dowel. The process is simple and cheap, but what strength and other properties are lost, if any?

Applications and Qualities

The functional quality of two boards reinforced with dowels is much greater than in the simple butt joint. More than just the bond of glue is added to the joint when dowels (usually made of hardwood) are inserted across the grain. If a series of dowels is used in joining the two parallel sides of boards, it would require breaking the dowels to break the joint.

The dowel is an alternative for the tenon that basically provides the same characteristics. When two or more dowels are used rather than a single mortise and tenon, a reasonable substitution is accomplished, but inherent weakness does result. The dowel must be inserted into the end grain of one of the two pieces being joined. Even though glue has strength, it is not quite the same as having a tenon from the same piece. Another limiting factor is that the amount of wood in a dowel does not equal the amount of wood normally found in a tenon. Therefore, there has to be a slight decrease in the quality of the joint as compared to the mortise and tenon joint.

There are, of course, some applications for which it is more desirable to use the dowel than to use a mortise and tenon or a simple butt joint. We have already mentioned the ease with which the dowel joint can be made in the factory. More important, though, are situations in which two or more boards are joined at a common point, as they are when a chair is being made—such a situation is the joining of the rails of a chair to the stiles. If two tenons were inserted into two mortises cut in the stile, the stile would be very weak at that point. By using doweling and by offsetting the dowels, very little material is removed from the stile.

We have already mentioned that doweling is fairly easy. One of these devices is the dowel centering pin [Figure 12–8(a) and (b)]. It acts like a pilot, letting you know exactly where to center the drill bit. The other device, shown in Figure 12–8(c), is the dowel centering tool. It is more complex but very easy to use. Merely clamp it to the stock to be doweled, adjust the scale according to its instructions, and drill through the pilot sleeve.

Several materials may be used for dowels. The best is shown in Figure 12–8(d). Pins such as this one can be purchased in different thicknesses and lengths. Some of the more common thicknesses are $\frac{1}{4}$, $\frac{5}{16}$, $\frac{3}{8}$, and $\frac{1}{2}$ inch. Some of the common lengths are 1, $1\frac{1}{2}$, $1\frac{3}{4}$, 2, and $2\frac{1}{2}$ inches. The dowel pin shown has a few characteristics that are important. First, notice the scoring that goes around the pin. This is designed to allow air and glue to escape from the hole the dowel is being inserted into. Another feature is the rounding off of the edges (normally square) on each end of the dowel.

A dowel may be made from maple, birch, oak, or any other wood of great strength. A plastic dowel is also available in some hardware stores. If you must make your own dowels, buy dowel sticks at any hardware store or lumberyard and cut them to the length you need. Round the ends with a pocket knife or

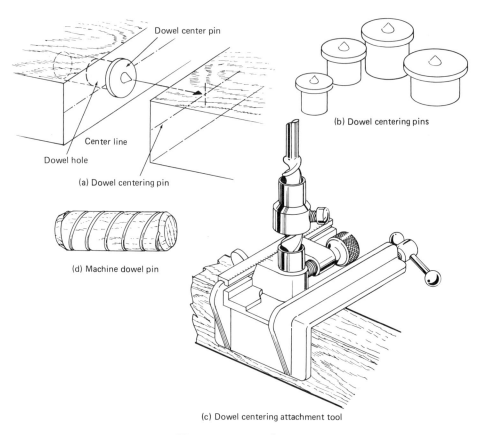

(b) Dowel centering pins

(a) Dowel centering pin

(d) Machine dowel pin

(c) Dowel centering attachment tool

Figure 12–8   Dowel joint.

on the sander. Add flutes to the dowel to allow air and excess glue to come up around the outsides of the dowel.

Doweling may be used to strengthen a miter joint. It is especially useful when joining miters on large picture frames. We have already said that it is extensively used in making chairs. It is also useful in making tables. Even well-made cutting boards have doweling all the way through them.

12.7 FRAME AND PANEL

The frame and panel is the first in a series of types of woodworking joinery that combines basic joints to create another joint or product. A number of basic joints can be used to make the frame and panel: some are the mortise, the tenon, and the dado. In this chapter we shall provide procedures used to make the frame and panel.

The frame and panel provides a cabinetmaker with a lightweight, sturdy, decorative assembly that has many uses. The advantage of the lightweight feature is understood when comparison is made with a panel of the same size made from solid wood of the same kind and thickness. Usually the panel in the frame is quite a bit thinner than the usual stock lumber.

Because several pieces are used to make a frame and panel, well-fitted joints must be made in well-seasoned lumber. If these conditions are met, the strength usually needed when frame and panel are used approaches the strength of a solid panel of equal thickness.

A great variety of designs can be incorporated into a frame and panel without the skill of a woodcarver, as Figure 12–9(a) shows. When solid panels were used, woodcarvers might spend many weeks carving one panel. Today, lumberyards and hardware stores provide a variety of moldings and plant-ons or escutcheons that can be incorporated into frame-and-panel construction.

Some of the most frequent uses for the frame and panel are the end panels on cabinets, dust covers between drawers in chests and dressers, and as doors on any and all varieties of cabinets. Within the styles of furniture examined earlier, almost every style, at one time or another, used some version of the frame and panel.

Last, but certainly not least, the frame and panel is a boon to cabinetmaking because it minimizes the chance for splitting, which can often occur if solid wood panels are used.

Figure 12–9(b) through 12–9(i) show the variety of techniques that can be used to make the frame and panel.

12.8 LAP JOINT

The lap joint has been used extensively in construction for centuries. Because of its variety of types, it is also used in the manufacture of furniture and in cabinetry.

By definition, a lap joint is a type of joint wherein one member of wood laps over the other. Figure 12–10 shows an end lap, probably the simplest of all lap joints to make. Notice how the definition accurately describes the joint.

The lap joint falls within the category of joints that are combined to make a new structure. It does so because the dado, rabbet, tenon, dovetail, scarf, key, and tongue and groove can be used to make lap joints. In the figure, each type of joint is shown in combination with another.

The lap joint provides many opportunities for use in cabinetmaking. Where supports are needed for open shelving, the lap joint is made from the dado and rabbet or dado and half-tenon [Figure 12–10(b)]. If a strengthened corner joint is needed where a butt joint would prove weak, the lap joint shown in Figure 12–10(a) would provide the added strength needed.

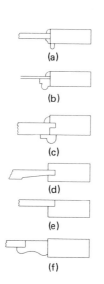

(a)

(b)

(c)

(d)

(e)

(f)

a. Molding to hold panels in frames and panels

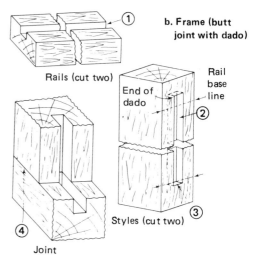

b. Frame (butt joint with dado)

Rails (cut two)

End of dado

Rail base line

Styles (cut two)

Joint

Preferred sequence

① Dado rails

② Dado (blind) styles

③ Clean corners of styles with chisel

④ Glue joint with panel inserted and clamp

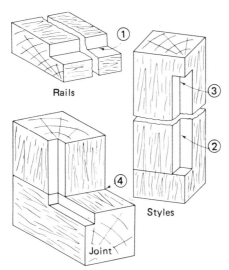

Rails

Styles

Joint

Preferred sequence

① Rabbet rails

② Blind rabbet styles

③ Clean out corners with chisel

④ Glue and clamp frame. (Fit and insert panel after gluing or when glue has dried)

c. Frame (butt joint with rabbet)

Preferred sequence

① Cut two styles with dado

② Cut two rails with haunch at each end to fit dado in style

③ Dado rails

④ Glue joints with panel inserted clamp

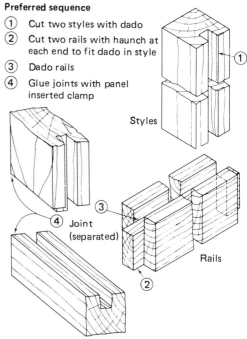

Styles

Joint (separated)

Rails

d. Frame (haunch with dado)

Figure 12–9 Frame and panel.

216

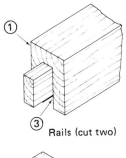

Rails (cut two)

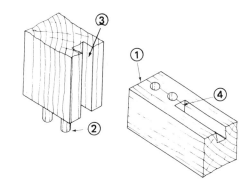

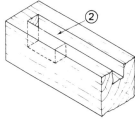

Styles (cut two)

Preferred sequence

① Make blind mortise and tenon

② Make dado run into mortise on styles

③ Make dado run full length or rails

e. Frame (mortise and tenon and dado)

Preferred sequence

① Butt cut styles and rails to correct dimensions

② Dowel rail ends and style surfaces using dowel centering jig

③ Dado rails full length

④ Blind dado styles (both ends); make dado extend into end equal to rail dado depth

f. Frame (dowel and dado)

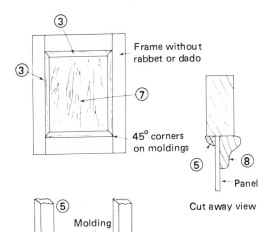

Frame without rabbet or dado

45° corners on moldings

Panel

Cut away view

Molding

Preferred sequence

1 Make frame using any joint desired; glue; let dry

2 Sand both sides of frame

③ Precut molding 1 inch longer than needed

④ Precut one end of each piece of molding on a 45° angle

⑤ Measure and cut the other end of each piece of molding (back pieces first)

6 Install back pieces

⑦ Cut and install panel (have grain run as shown)

⑧ Install face molding

g. Panel (with molding)

Figure 12–9 Continued

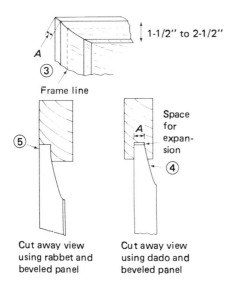

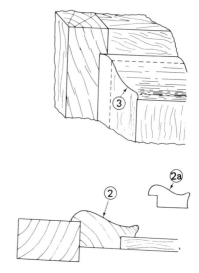

Cut away view
using rabbet and
beveled panel

Cut away view
using dado and
beveled panel

Preferred sequence

1   Make a frame

2   Cut panel to fit frame

③   Using radial saw, table saw, or
    shaper, bevel panel so that the
    thickness is equal to *A*

④   Insert panel into frame

⑤   Install panel into rabbet

6   After fitting all pieces, glue
    and clamp

NOTE: If rabbet method is used,
frame may be glued and dried
before inserting panel

7   Sand

Preferred sequence

1   Make and glue frame

②   Buy or make molding. Molding
    can be bought as shown in ②a
    Rabbet back side for panel

③   Cut molding pieces 1″ longer
    than needed and cut a 45° angle
    on one end of each piece

4   Mark the other end for cutting
    and cut a 45° angle

5   Glue in molding; let dry

6   Cut and fit panel; make sure
    grain is as shown; glue

h. Panel (rabbet or dado and beveled panel)   **i. Panel (molding and rabbet)**

Figure 12–9   Continued

In instances in which a restriction of thickness is a requirement, the lap
joint can be used. This might be when a dust cover is needed or in some cases
when a frame for a frame and panel is made. Because each member has one-
half of its stock removed, the resultant joint retains the same thickness as the
original member.

Not all lap joints are made on the plane as shown in Figure 12–10(a). They
are made on edge, an illustration of which is provided later in the chapter.

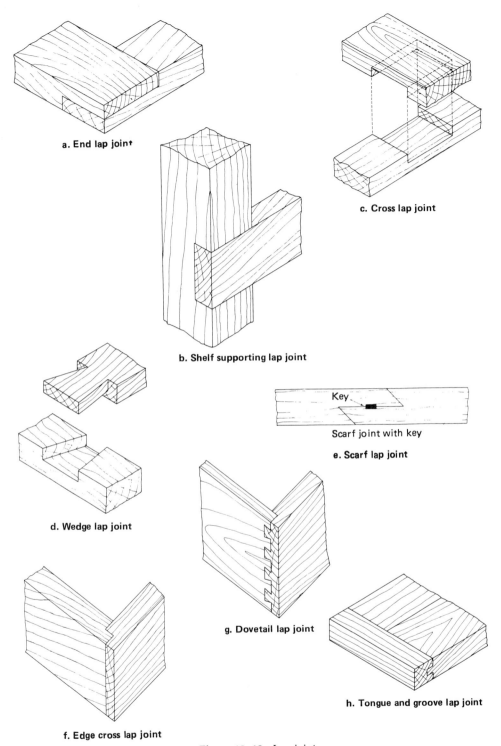

a. End lap joint

b. Shelf supporting lap joint

c. Cross lap joint

d. Wedge lap joint

Key

Scarf joint with key

e. Scarf lap joint

f. Edge cross lap joint

g. Dovetail lap joint

h. Tongue and groove lap joint

Figure 12–10 Lap joint.

However, the edge lap joint is used many times in cases where a band is installed around a table [see Figure 12–10(b)]. It is also used when making workbenches, shop tables, and stools. Many pieces of lawn furniture, such as chaise lounges, tables, and rolling serving carts, use the edge lap joint.

Some of the methods that can be used to make the lap joint are shown in Figures 12–10(c) through (j), along with concise directions for their manufacture.

12.9 THE MITER AND OTHER CUTS

The most universal of all cabinet joints is the miter. It has the most variety of application of all the joints. It is often used in the basic construction of a cabinet. The ends, tops, sides, and front are frequently mitered at 45-degree angles to make a cabinet joint. The miter is used in doors when mitered corners are desired for effect. It is used consistently when moldings are installed on cabinets, as a band around the top of the cabinet, as decorative trim on the face of a cabinet door, or as base molding.

In addition to the uses stated above, the miter is used in combination with other joints, such as the lap joint, dowel, and of course the butt joint, since the miter joint is a variation of the butt joint.

Used by itself, the miter has as much or little (depending upon one's point of view) strength as a butt joint. If, for instance, the two mitered pieces are 45 degrees and joined, the relative strength is greater than two miters of 30 or $22\frac{1}{2}$ degrees because of the slant of the cuts. The 30-degree and $22\frac{1}{2}$-degree cuts have more end fibrous material than the 45-degree cut and hence less holding strength.

When the miter is used in combination with the dowel, however, it takes on the strength of a doweled joint. The same is true when the lap joint is combined with the miter by using it with the end lap or tongue and groove.

Functionally, the miter is very effective as a means for joining two members of the same width and thickness and of varying widths and the same thickness. For instance, as shown in Figure 12–11(a), two members of unequal width are to be joined to effectively make a right angle. Notice that to make the corner, each piece is cut at a different angle. This is not difficult to figure out or cut. A simple shop method is shown in Figure 12–11(b). Notice how the one member is laid on top of the lower member and a mark made. Connecting the mark with a line to the adjacent corner results in making a miter layout. Reverse the members' positions, and a miter layout can be made on the narrower member.

Several adaptations are illustrated in Figures 12–11(c) through 12–11(f). Each is a complex joint that requires a great deal of skill to make.

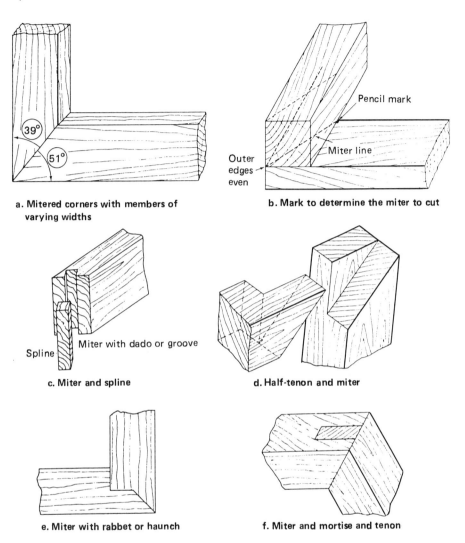

a. Mitered corners with members of
   varying widths

b. Mark to determine the miter to cut

c. Miter and spline

d. Half-tenon and miter

e. Miter with rabbet or haunch

f. Miter and mortise and tenon

Figure 12–11   Miter and other cuts.

REVIEW EXERCISES

1. For a butt joint to be effective, the joining surfaces must have absolute contact. (T/F)

2. For a butt joint with one end surface, the crosscut should be made with a No. 8 saw. (T/F)

3. The rabbet cut is a "C" shaped cut along the edge of a board. (T/F)
4. The rabbet joint is stronger than a butt joint because of the two bonding surfaces on each board. (T/F)
5. A dado that does *not* extend to the outer surface or edge is called:
    a. open.
    b. closed.
    c. blind.
    d. flush.
6. The joint in a stile that provides bonding surfaces for a tenon is called a
    a. dado.
    b. tenon.
    c. lap joint.
    d. mortise.
7. What is the purpose for the grooves in a dowel?
    a. It permits the dowel to rotate while being installed.
    b. It permits air to escape from the dowel hole.
    c. It permits the glue to escape from the bottom of the hole.
    d. Both b and c above.
8. Which of the following types of joints are *not* used in making a panel and frame?
    a. Mortise
    b. Dado
    c. Tenon
    d. Shiplap
9. A lap joint is all of the types listed below except:
    a. dado
    b. rabbet
    c. mortise and tenon
    d. dovetail

ESSAYS

10. Prepare a report on the relative advantages of the mortise-and-tenon joint over the miter joint in making a panel and frame.
11. Explain how to make a blind dado and also list some of the places in a cabinet where the joint is used.

ANSWERS

1T, 2F, 3F, 4T, 5c, 6d, 7d, 8d, 9c

13

Bonding Materials
and Techniques

A relatively wide variety of bonding materials are manufactured that are particularly adaptable to cabinetmaking. They include two broad categories, adhesive materials and mechanical fasteners. The adhesive materials include a variety of glues and cement. Mechanical fasteners include nails, screws, bolts, and dowels. In this chapter we examine the properties of both bonding and fastening materials, and then discuss various bonding techniques and some of the problems that occur when mistakes are made.

Objectives

1. Identify the single type or combination of bonding materials for a given purpose in cabinetmaking.
2. Identify how proper use of bonding materials avoids problems and reduces material waste.

13.1 BONDING MATERIALS

Adhesives

Two broad catagories of adhesive materials are *glues* and *cements*. Types of glues include casein, animal and vegetable proteins, and natural and synthetic resin products. Cements are either natural or synthetic, but natural cements are not, as a rule, used in furniture and cabinetmaking. Both glues and cements require setting or curing periods. Most have thermosetting properties, which means that the presence of heat within the material creates its hardening capacity.

Vegetable (protein) glue. This type of glue is generally prepared from organic chemical compounds which are altered to form a resin that is able to bond wood and wood products through thermosetting action. This type of glue is usually sold in liquid form in a conveniently designed plastic dispensing container. The glue is easy to apply, easy to control, and is easily cleaned up with water before the setting action has finished. It sets up quite rapidly, but much more slowly than hot glue. It is one of the forms of glue used most frequently by cabinetmakers.

Animal glues. Animal glues are made from hides and hooves of animals and are available in powder, chip, flake, and block form. These glues are generally used in hot gluing operations. When used in cabinetmaking, they are especially useful in frame making and subassembly construction, where the operation must be completed in a short span of time.

Casein glues. Casein and casein protein glues are obtained from milk and cheese and are alkaline. They are available in powder, liquid, or emulsified forms. If the glue is purchased in powder form, it is mixed with water and will set in temperatures at 40 degrees to 100 degrees F or higher through thermosetting action. Wood with up to 20 percent moisture content can be glued satisfactorily with these products.

Casein glues are used extensively in cabinet and furniture making since in these applications they are generally protected from weather conditions and excessive moisture. They are not reliable for joints in pieces that will be used outside or in damp, warm areas.

By the inclusion of various additives, the casein glues can have various useful properties: mold resistance, fast and slow setting speeds, easy mixing, low pressure requirements, long shelf life, and others.

Contact cement. Contact cement may be solvent- or water-thinned, and is applied to both surfaces to be bonded. Contact cement may be sprayed, brushed, rolled, or applied with a spatula. On each surface to be bonded, the coating should be uniformly applied and heavy deposits avoided. When edge veneers are applied with this adhesive, 100 percent coverage is a must; but when wood or plastic veneer sheets are laminated over a substrata, 80 percent coverage usually is adequate. A serrated trowel is usually used in shop applications of veneers, whereas spraying techniques are commonly used in factory production. Figure 13–1 shows the process of edge veneering with contact cement.

Contact adhesives are usually made of resins and other chemicals. Although the resins themselves have low flammability, the thinners used in them, such as toluene and acetone, have very low flash points and should be treated carefully. Fumes from these adhesives are strong and somewhat toxic, so proper ventilation must be used. Contact adhesives for cabinet and furniture making purposes are used to bond both wood to wood and plastic to wood.

Resorcinol (waterproof) resin glues.   Glues made from these materials are durable under all conditions of exposure and are moldproof as well. They are available in both powder and liquid forms. Shop and on-site gluing is usually performed by mixing the powder with water and applying a cream-consistency coat to one of the two surfaces being glued. Clamps or strategically placed nails hold the glued pieces together under pressure until the glue sets and cures.

Where resorcinol resin glues provide waterproof bonding, phenol-resorcinol resin glues provide resistance to abnormally high heat in addition to waterproof bonding. Generally, residential cabinets and furniture have no need of this type glue, but some commercial cabinets and furniture may require these

Figure 13–1 Edge veneering with tape and contact cement.

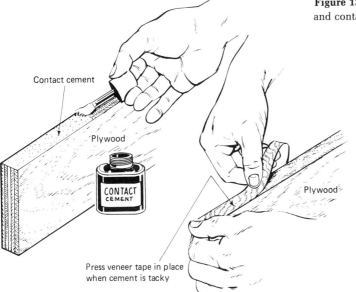

Contact cement

Plywood

CONTACT CEMENT

Plywood

Press veneer tape in place when cement is tacky

properties. This glue is composed of a liquid resin and powdered catalyst which are mixed just before use.[1]

Urea and urea-formaldehyde resin glues.   These glues have high heat resistance, will stand some degree of soaking, and are also moldproof. Generally these glues are used for interior cabinets and furniture and not in pieces that will be exposed to the weather. Urea glues are thermosetting at room tempertures and need to be applied only to one of the surfaces to be bonded. For best results, both surfaces are coated, and clamps or strategically placed nails provide the pressure treatment of glued members which is recommended.

Certain physical properties may be given to urea glues. Urea-formaldehyde resin may be craze resistant, which improves gluing capability of rough or ill-fit surfaces such as mortise-and-tenon joints, finger joints, scarf joints, and other applications where gap-filling properties are needed. These glues may be extended with recommended quantities of either wheat or nutshell flour. However, extending the resin reduces its ability to sustain moisture without adverse effects. This adhesive may be used within four hours of mixing, and has good speed in setting and curing. Catalysts and water are added to the powder resin, along with flour if extended resin is required. Catalysts speed the setting time, and water is used to emulsify the powder and begin the setting process.

Polyvinyl acetate resin emulsion.   This is a name applied to a family of emulsions which provide for a specific bonding characteristic suited to the two materials being bonded. These glues may be applied with roller or spray. The primary purpose of these adhesives is to bond a variety of plastics to wood, other plastics, steel, or paper. There are only limited applications of this adhesive for general cabinetmaking purposes; more often they are used in commercial applications.

Mechanical Fasteners

Nails.   A variety of nails made from steel, aluminum, bronze, and copper are made for use in cabinetmaking. Each has a variety of sizes, thicknesses, and shapes. As shown in Figure 13–2, they include common wire, box (the same general shape as common), finish, and brads.

Physical dimensions of nails are also listed in Figure 13–2. However, there is a great deal more to study on nails as a cabinetmaking fastener. Extensive testing of the holding power (withdrawal resistance) has been done on a variety of nails driven into woods of different kinds and in end and side grain. Those woods with high specific gravities (fir, oak) hold nails more firmly and there-

---

[1]Commercial Standard CS 171-58, U.S. Department of Commerce.

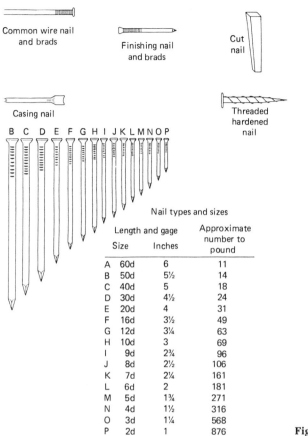

Figure 13–2 list:

	Size	Inches	Approximate number to pound
A	60d	6	11
B	50d	5½	14
C	40d	5	18
D	30d	4½	24
E	20d	4	31
F	16d	3½	49
G	12d	3¼	63
H	10d	3	69
I	9d	2¾	96
J	8d	2½	106
K	7d	2¼	161
L	6d	2	181
M	5d	1¾	271
N	4d	1½	316
O	3d	1¼	568
P	2d	1	876

Figure 13–2   Nails.

fore have higher withdrawal resistance than lighter woods (ponderosa pine). Consider the differences between a 6d common nail driven into Douglas fir and a 6d common nail driven into Idaho white pine:

Wood	Specific Gravity	Withdrawal Resistance
Douglas fir	0.51	29 lb/in.
Idaho white pine	0.40	16 lb/in.

Notice how much less holding power the pine has as opposed to the fir. For a complete description of the properties of nails, one should obtain a copy of "National Design Specifications for Wood Construction," published by the National Forest Products Association.

Screws.　Wood screws, lag screws, and metal screws are produced to satisfy a variety of bonding needs for both wood and metal products. Screws are made from unhardened steel, stainless steel, aluminum, or brass. Screws made with anodized finishes that represent old English and antique bronze are very common for cabinetmaking needs. Most wood screws are threaded to approximately two-thirds the length of the screw, as are lag screws. Others have threads from the tip to the flange for applications where more holding power is needed. Metal screws, although infrequently used on cabinets, are threaded to the head (Figure 13–3). There are also specialty screws such as oval-headed screws, screws that simulate ancient hammered nails, and several other kinds. Screw heads best for cabinetmaking purposes include the common slotted, cross point, and Phillips-head types. A new specialty screw used on computer cabinets and other cabinets subject to frequent teardown and reassembly have a very flat surface and an hexagon screw inset in the head. The bolt is installed with a hex key set.

Bolts.　Figure 13–4 shows the most commonly used bolts, which are the carriage, stove, and machine types. Carriage bolts fall into three categories: square-neck bolt, finned-neck bolt, and ribbed-neck. Their lengths and diameters are shown in Figure 13–4. Machine bolts are made with cut national fine or national coarse threads extending specified distances from the end. Selection of the bolt is made on the basis of head style, length and diameter, number of threads per inch, and coarseness of threads. Stove bolts are less precisely made than machine bolts and may have threads extending the full length of the body. Bolts are infrequently used in cabinetmaking, but are more frequently used in furniture making. Tables, beds, chinas, and other furniture items of large dimensions are often made in sections and then bolted together. The turnbuckle form of bolt is also used in cabinetmaking when there is a possibility of sagging.

Pegs and dowels.　Pegs and dowels are also commonly used for mechanical holding and fastening. Pegs are tapered rather than round as a rule. They act as a wedge when hammered into a pilot hole. Glue holds them in place, although the pressure exerted on the sides of the hole by the peg is usually sufficient. Sometimes the style dictates that the peg be hand-trimmed with a knife and not sanded smooth. When this technique is used, the exposed body of the peg is shaped like facets in a diamond. As a rule dowels are serrated to permit the air to escape while the dowel is being forced into the hole. Dowels are made from wood and plastic. Their diameters and lengths range from very small ($\frac{3}{16}$″) to large (1″), and in length from 1″ to 2″ or more. Plastic dowels are also available in right-angle style for use in reinforced mitered joints.

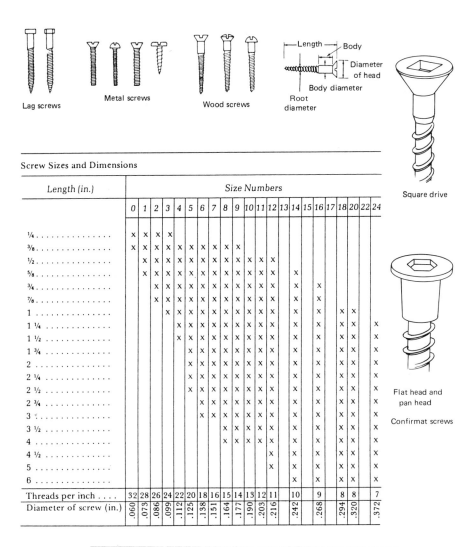

Lag screws

Metal screws

Wood screws

Length — Body
Diameter of head
Body diameter
Root diameter

Square drive

Flat head and pan head

Confirmat screws

Screw Sizes and Dimensions

Length (in.)	0	1	2	3	4	5	6	7	8	9	10	11	12	13	14	15	16	17	18	20	22	24
¼	x	x	x	x																		
⅜	x	x	x	x	x	x	x	x	x	x												
½		x	x	x	x	x	x	x	x	x	x	x	x									
⅝		x	x	x	x	x	x	x	x	x	x	x	x		x							
¾			x	x	x	x	x	x	x	x	x	x	x		x		x					
⅞			x	x	x	x	x	x	x	x	x	x	x		x		x					
1				x	x	x	x	x	x	x	x	x	x		x		x		x	x		
1 ¼					x	x	x	x	x	x	x	x	x		x		x		x	x		x
1 ½					x	x	x	x	x	x	x	x	x		x		x		x	x		x
1 ¾						x	x	x	x	x	x	x	x		x		x		x	x		x
2						x	x	x	x	x	x	x	x		x		x		x	x		x
2 ¼						x	x	x	x	x	x	x	x		x		x		x	x		x
2 ½						x	x	x	x	x	x	x	x		x		x		x	x		x
2 ¾							x	x	x	x	x	x	x		x		x		x	x		x
3							x	x	x	x	x	x	x		x		x		x	x		x
3 ½								x	x	x	x	x	x		x		x		x	x		x
4								x	x	x	x	x	x		x		x		x	x		x
4 ½												x	x		x		x		x	x		x
5												x			x		x		x	x		x
6													x		x		x		x	x		x
Threads per inch	32	28	26	24	22	20	18	16	15	14	13	12	11		10		9		8	8		7
Diameter of screw (in.)	.060	.073	.086	.099	.112	.125	.138	.151	.164	.177	.190	.203	.216		.242		.268		.294	.320		.372

Lag screws, Sizes and Dimensions

Lengths (inches)	1/4	Diameters (inches)		
		3/8, 7/16, 1/2	5/8, 3/4	7/8, 1
1	x	x	—	—
1½	x	x	x	—
2, 2½, 3, 3¼, etc., 7½, 8 to 10	x	x	x	x
11 to 12	—	x	x	x
13 to 16	—	—	x	x

Figure 13–3 Screw types and sizes.

229

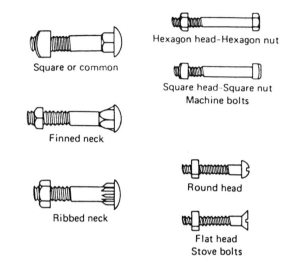

Square or common

Hexagon head–Hexagon nut

Square head–Square nut
Machine bolts

Finned neck

Round head

Ribbed neck

Flat head
Stove bolts

Carriage bolts – dimensions

Lengths (inches)	Diameters (inches)			
	$\frac{3}{16}$ $\frac{1}{4}$ $\frac{6}{16}$ $\frac{3}{5}$	$\frac{7}{16}$, $\frac{1}{2}$	$\frac{9}{16}$ $\frac{5}{8}$	$\frac{3}{4}$
$\frac{3}{4}$ -------------------	.x	----	----	----
1 -------------------	x	x	----	----
$1\frac{1}{4}$ -------------------	x	x	x	----
$1\frac{1}{2}$, 2, $2\frac{1}{2}$, etc., $9\frac{1}{2}$, 10 to 20	x	x	x	x

Screw, cap (machine bolts – dimensions

Lengths (inches)	Diameters (inches)				
	$\frac{7}{16}$	$\frac{1}{2}$, $\frac{9}{16}$, $\frac{5}{8}$	$\frac{3}{4}$, $\frac{7}{8}$, 1	$1\frac{1}{8}$, $1\frac{1}{4}$
$\frac{3}{4}$ -----------	x	----	----	----	----
1, $1\frac{1}{4}$ --------	x	x	x	----	----
$1\frac{1}{2}$, 2, $2\frac{1}{2}$ -----	x	x	x	x	----
3, $3\frac{1}{2}$, 4, $4\frac{1}{2}$, etc., $9\frac{1}{2}$, 10 to 20.	x	x	x	x	x
21 to 25_____	----	----	x	x	x
26 to 39_____	----	----	----	x	x

Figure 13–4 Bolts.

13.2 BONDING TECHNIQUES

Gluing

The first and foremost rule of gluing is to ensure that both surfaces are extremely smooth so that (1) the glue mixture maintains its own bond, (2) the surface cells are uniformly coated, and (3) the cell walls are clear and therefore able to absorb the glue mixture. Whether using an emulsified liquid or mixed powder, the bond will take well only if the surfaces being glued are very smooth and fit very closely. For example, as shown in the magnified view in Figure 13–5, coarse sanding or sawed edges in the two surfaces being glued together causes the joining members to stand apart. This causes the glue to separate so that some of the glue seeps into deep cell areas and some of it lays on the ridges. Although some bonding takes place, there is no uniform surface area and hence an uneven bond. However, two smooth surfaces, as also shown in the figure, allow complete bonding of both surfaces, provided a thin layer of glue evenly coats the surface area. It does not matter which glue is used—emulsified, powdered, or contact; the entire surface should have a uniformly thin coat of glue.

Another method of gluing is called spot gluing, where spots or ribbons of glue are applied to a surface, and when the members are clamped together the glue is forced to spread. Unfortunately, the spread is uneven and the areas of the surfaces that remain dry provide no strength to the joint. The main reason for using the spot or ribboning technique is that it prevents overflow of the glue onto surfaces that will be finished later. As shown in Figure 13–6, any glue that runs from within a joint and is allowed to dry on wood surfaces could cause serious problems during the finishing phase, since those surfaces will not take stain. Severe sanding (Figure 13–7) may be required to remove the glue from the wood.

Figure 13–5   Glue bond, uniform and nonuniform.

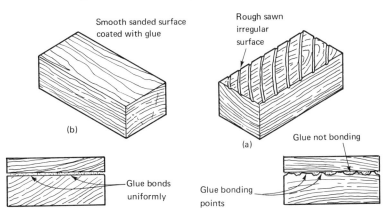

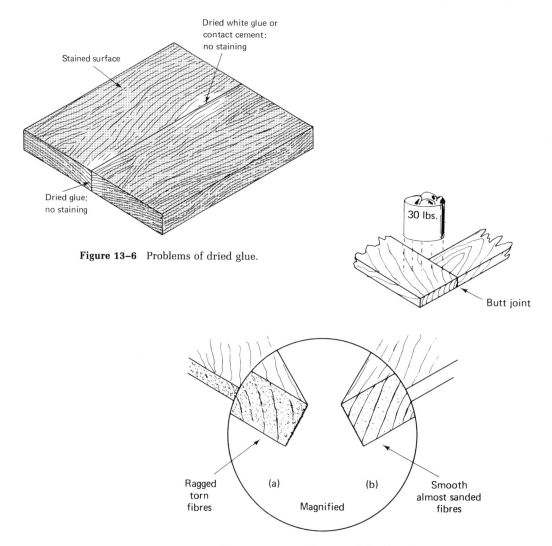

Figure 13–6 Problems of dried glue.

Figure 13–7 Bonding parallel and end surfaces with glue.

Fortunately, both protein (white or cream) and brown glues that spill out beyond the glue line may be cleaned away before hardening. Two techniques are useful. One method is to use a damp rag or towel immediately to dilute and remove the glue outside the glue line, taking special care to avoid disturbing the glue in the gluing line. In the other method, the glue outside the glue line is left to become rubbery (partially dried), and then lifted from the wood with a chisel, knife, or putty knife.

Applying Contact Cement

Contact cement is applied to both surfaces to be glued. It should be applied with a brush on edge surfaces and they should be coated thoroughly. On flat or curved surfaces, it should be applied with a serrated trowel. In both applications the cement must be allowed to surface-dry until tacky, then the pieces may be joined. It must be done correctly, because once in contact the pieces cannot be pulled apart. This is the main reason for making the veneer about $\frac{1}{8}$- to $\frac{1}{4}$-inch wider than the substrata. When the veneer is laid onto the substrata, it should be rolled onto it rather than allowed to fall flat. This rolling action eliminates air pockets that would otherwise form. Next, a roller should be used to ensure bonding as well as to remove any small air pockets that may have formed. The rolling operation on flat surfaces should begin in the middle and work to the ends and edges.

Nailing

Fasteners, as we already know, include nails, screws, staples, and pegs. Of the four, nails, screws, and staples may be driven through wood, whereas pegs always require predrilling. There is a way to insert these fasteners that ensures a successful joining, and there is also a way to insert them that causes an irreversible problem—splitting. Nails and screws—especially nails—should be installed as far away from the board's end as practical. This reduces and often eliminates the chances for splitting the board. Figure 13–8 shows the different effects of driving a nail through a board close to its end, and at a safe distance back from the end. Questions one might reasonably ask here are what causes splitting and what is a safe distant back from a board's end? A split occurs because the nail's thickness causes stress in the wood cells. If this stress exceeds the holding strength of the cell walls, they tear, resulting in a split on both sides of the nail in the direction of the grain at the board's end. As previously stated, a split is irreversible. In answer to the second question, the safe distance from the end at which a nail can be driven varies with the type of wood. In the industry, testing is performed by many agencies to establish the degree of elasticity of different types of wood. Certain hardwoods—oak, birch, pecan, maple, mahogany, and elm, among others—and several softwoods—yellow pine, fir, and hemlock—have tremendous cell strength. These woods resist bending extremely well. Other woods, such as bass, white or ponderosa pine, and spruce do not have this strength and bend quite easily. Hence when deciding where to drive the nail into the board, follow these general guidelines:

1. Because of its stiffness, hardwood tends to split easily when a nail is driven through it.
2. Softwood is less likely to split, but may do so occasionally.

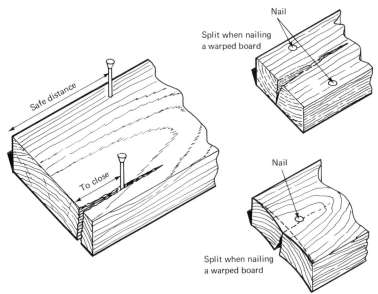

Figure 13-8 Proper and improper nailing.

3. Hardwood does not bend easily, so nails placed 2, 3, or even 4 inches back from the board's end have the same holding power as nails placed close to the ends.

4. Softwood, because of its tendency to bend, needs to have nails driven closer to the board's end. These nails should be driven $1\frac{1}{2}$ to $2\frac{1}{2}$ inches from the end to prevent splitting.

Now that we know how splits can occur, let us understand fasteners' varying holding power. The brad nail, for instance, has adequate holding power for thin boards nailed to other boards side-grain to side-grain and for some toe-nailing operations. The finish nail and casing nail have greater relative holding power because they are longer and contain more steel. However, if improperly used, they will have very little holding power. The general rule for nailing,

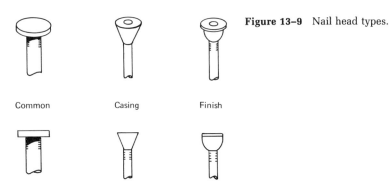

Figure 13-9 Nail head types.

Common   Casing   Finish

whether through a board or in toenailing, is to select and use a nail whose length is 2 to $2\frac{1}{2}$ times the board's thickness. For example, use a 4d finish nail ($1\frac{1}{2}$ inches long) to nail boards up to $\frac{3}{4}$ inches thick to other boards; use a 6d finish nail (2 inches long) to nail $\frac{3}{4}$- to $1\frac{1}{8}$-inch boards to others; use an 8d finish nail ($2\frac{1}{2}$ inches long) to nail $1\frac{1}{8}$- to $1\frac{1}{2}$-inch-thick boards to others.

The shape of the nail head also aids in holding. As depicted in Figure 13–9, the flat-head common nail (not used in cabinetmaking) has a great deal of holding power; the casing nail head has less but still considerable holding power; and the finish nail has less than the others but does have some holding power. These nail heads provide holding power for the board being nailed in that the head prevents the board from lifting.

In many cases, nails can be used in the assembly of a cabinet. There are restrictions, though.

1. They cannot be placed where the heads will show after the job is finished.
2. They must be the right size for the job.
3. They must be the right type of nail for the job.

Face nailing can be used if a piece of trim will cover the nails. Toenailing is usually very desirable since it allows for nailing at angles where nails seldom show. Two usual places for toenailing are under shelves, into sides, and at the end of the board. Face nailing is used into the bottom shelf through the dado, and toenailing is used through the top of the end and side pieces through the rabbet and into the cabinet top. In both cases, the nails will be covered by trim. The bottom nails will be covered by the base, and top nails will be covered by the edge trim that is glued on later.

Screwing

Driving screws entails the same problems as nailing, but the problems are more severe. Whereas a nail is generally uniform in thickness throughout its length, a wood screw is cone shaped. Its diameter increases from its point to its head. This, as you can imagine, adds considerable stress to a board's cells if the screw is driven into hardwood and some softwood species without predrilling. Therefore, predrilling a pilot hole with drill and bit is essential to satisfactory screwing. The pilot hole may be fairly close to the board's end, provided it is of a diameter that will result in very little stress on cell walls when the screw is driven through. Notice in Figure 13–10 that a pilot hole may also be used for nailing.

Here is a tip on installing screws: After you have drilled the pilot hole and recessed head area for the screw, put ordinary bar soap on the screw before inserting it into the hole [Figure 13–10(b)]. The soap lubricates the hole and screw and makes driving easier. Any soap that spills out should be washed away thoroughly.

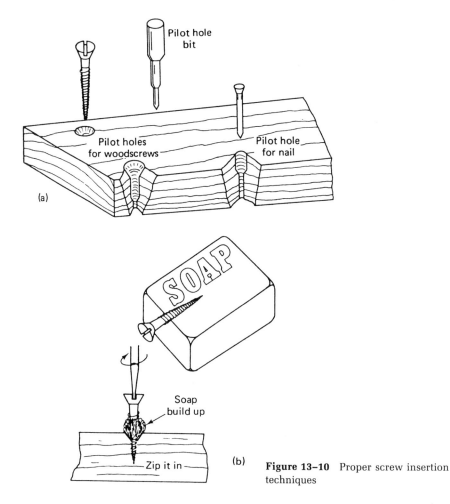

Figure 13–10 Proper screw insertion techniques

If a nail head provides holding power, obviously a screw head does also. The larger the screw head diameter, the greater the holding power. In addition, round-head screws provide a flat contact with the wood surface and a great deal of holding power. In contrast flat-head screws, with their tapered under-surface, provide considerable holding power even though the force is oblique.

Bolting

A variety of bolts that are useful in cabinetmaking have already been identified. Some techniques for their use are provided here. Subassemblies, such as upper and lower sections of breakfronts, china cabinets, mirrors for dressers, and bed frames, all require the use of bolts. No part of the bolt should show when the finished product is ready for use and display. In the case of china cabinets, a carriage bolt painted the same color as the stained cabinet must be used, and each bolt must be located in a discreet place, such as a corner. All bolts must be inserted into holes just large enough to permit free passage. Lag bolts, commonly called lag screws, need holes slightly smaller than their diameter so that the threads bite into the surfaces of the hole. Where possible, a flat washer should be used under the head of the bolt and below the nut. This arrangement provides the greatest holding power. The turnbuckle bolt is used to rack a cabinet in such a way to prevent sagging. This type of bolt is used on long dressers, sideboards, and china cabinets.

We have touched briefly on the various bonding techniques. Since only the basic ones have been discussed, you will need to make adaptations of these techniques to particular needs as they arise. A point to remember is that wood can be stressed just so much—beyond that point something must give, and it is always the wood. Be careful, and learn to deal with fastening wood correctly and successfully.

REVIEW EXERCISES

1. Two broad categories of bonding materials are glues and pastes.   (T/F)
2. Most liquid bonding agents used in cabinetmaking rely on thermosetting properties to effect the bond. (T/F)
3. One of the most readily used forms of glues used by cabinetmakers is the vegetable protein glue.   (T/F)
4. Casein glues generally are used where moisture is a problem.   (T/F)
5. To be effective, only a single surface must be coated with a contact cement, but 100% of that surface must be covered.   (T/F)
6. A very efficient method of bonding veneer tape to a board's edge is with:
   a. casein glue.
   b. liquid protein glue.
   c. contact cement.
   d. resorcinol glue.
7. Which of the glues listed below is waterproof?
   a. Casein
   b. Vegetable protein
   c. Urea-formaldehyde
   d. Phenol-resorcinol
8. Which glue is heat resistant and moldproof, but generally not used where moisture is a problem?
   a. Casein
   b. Urea
   c. Phenol-resorcinol
   d. Vegetable protein

9. In which wood would a nail have better holding power?
   a. Oak
   b. Ponderosa pine
   c. White pine
   d. Spruce

ESSAYS

10. Provide a well-written paper of 30 to 50 words that explains the problem of end-gluing pieces together and what must be done to make a sound bond.

11. List and explain the ways of dealing with surface-dried glue (spillover).

12. Explain why nails can be driven closer to the end of a piece of pine than a piece of maple. Be technical.

ANSWERS

1F, 2T, 3T, 4F, 5F, 6c, 7d, 8b, 9a

14

Sanding Materials and Techniques

Once a cabinet is constructed, considerable effort must be spent in sanding so that the finished product will be a beautiful piece of work. This chapter provides an understanding of the principles of sanding and the materials required to do the job.

The sanding phase involves a three-step decision process which determines how to properly sand a cabinet.

Objectives

1. Select the type of grit for the job. This includes deciding what size grit is required and whether the sandpaper should be the open-coated or closed-coated variety.
2. Select the weight and type of sandpaper backing material that is best for the job.
3. Decide what type of operation should be used—hand, vibrator, belt sander, disk, drum, or all methods, but at different times and for different purposes.

Several terms need to be understood before these decisions can be made:

Hardness. Hardness is defined as the factor that determines the ability of the abrasive to penetrate the object to be ground or sanded. If the abrasive is not sufficiently hard to penetrate a surface, the only result would be heating, through friction, which would result in a burnishing or polishing operation.

Toughness. An abrasive mineral must have sufficient resistance to shearing or breaking down so that it will penetrate and continue to penetrate for an extended period. This property is called toughness. If a mineral is hard enough to cut into the material but because of its brittleness wears away rapidly, its use would not be economical.

Fracture. Of no less importance than hardness and toughness is the shape and type of sharp edge formed after the crude mineral is fractured or broken down through crushing to a desired grading. Abrasive mineral fractures and forms sharp edges that produce a cutting action. The cutting edges left after crushing play an important part in the use of the abrasive. Each type and class of mineral has a natural formation or shape when crushed. The irregular sides of surfaces are generally dish-shaped, allowing for chip clearance.

The relative hardness, toughness, and type of fracture of the five distinctly different minerals are shown in Table 14–1.

TABLE 14–1   TYPE OF COATING ABRASIVES

Abrasives	Hardness	Toughness (%)	Fracture
Flint	6.8–7.0	20	Light wedges
Garnet	7.5–8.5	60	Light wedges
Emery	8.5–9.0	80	Round and blocky
Aluminum oxide	9.4	75	Heavy wedges
Silicon carbide	9.6	55	Sharp wedges and silvers

Note: The measurement of toughness is based on a percentage table that shows the percentage of resistance toward breakdown under a given pressure.

14.1 SELECTING THE TYPE OF GRIT FOR THE JOB

As Table 14–1 shows, there are five distinct and different minerals used in the manufacture of coated abrasives. They are flint, emery, and garnet (all natural minerals), and aluminum oxide and silicon carbide (both synthetic minerals). These are shown in Figure 14–1. Flint, garnet, and emery are natural abrasives mined from the earth's surface. Aluminum oxide and silicon carbide are produced in an electrochemical furnace. Bauxite ore is processed to make aluminum oxide, and silica sand is processed to make silicon carbide.

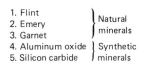

1. Flint ⎫
2. Emery ⎬ Natural minerals
3. Garnet ⎭
4. Aluminum oxide ⎫ Synthetic minerals
5. Silicon carbide ⎭

Flint
This mineral is quartz, white in color. Its appearance is similar to white sand.

Emery
Dull black in color. It is hard and blocky in structure.

Garnet
A reddish brown colored mineral of medium hardness with good cutting edges.

Aluminum oxide
An off-white to gray-brown colored mineral that is extremely tough, durable and resistant to wear. It is capable of penetrating almost any surface.

Silicon carbide
It is shiny black in color and due to its brittle qualities fractures into sharp, sliver-like wedges.

Figure 14–1   Abrasive minerals.

Flint

Flint or quartz mineral, which is white in color and similar to white sand, is the mineral used on ordinary sandpaper—flint paper, as it is known in the trade. Its type of fracture is well adapted in the fine grades to the finishing of cabinets. Flint sandpaper is used by master cabinetmakers. Obviously, due to its lack of hardness and toughness, it is not an abrasive that will stand up under hard production usage.

Emery

Emery, a dull, black natural mineral, is found in large deposits in both the United States and Turkey. Although of sufficient hardness to penetrate most objects, even those of extreme toughness, its fracture is the poorest of all the abrasives. It is round and blocky with poor cutting edges and has a total lack of concave sides for chip clearance. Owing to its lack of sharp fracture, it will produce a higher polish when used with lubricants than will artificial minerals. With lack of free cutting, emery sandpaper will generate heat and therefore a luster or color. Obviously, emery's dull fracture and lack of chip clearance mean it could not be used satisfactorily for woodworking purposes. However, when it is used with oil and under pressure, it does produce a lustrous finish on a well-sanded surface.

Garnet

Garnet is a reddish-brown colored mineral of medium hardness. Garnet, being harder and tougher than flint, would be excellent for sanding wood, especially since it has a better cutting surface or fracture. Through the treatment of garnet grain by heat, the grain is toughened beyond its natural state and has just sufficient brittleness to break or refracture when in use, forming new but smaller cross sections of cutting edges. Garnet is primarily a woodworking product, but it is also used in quantity for sanding between coats of finishing materials, such as enamel, paint, varnish, shellac, and lacquer.

Aluminum Oxide

Aluminum oxide, an off-white gray to brown colored mineral, fourth in hardness to the diamond, is capable of penetrating practically any type of wood or finish. It is extremely tough and therefore resistant to wear. However, these qualities in themselves defeat to some extent the possibility of developing a type of fracture with elongated edges and cupped sides. The crystals come from the electrochemical furnace as a dense mass, and when crushed for use in sandpaper manufacture, form blocky or regular heavy wedge-shaped crystals. Such shapes are ideal for cutting and tooling. The heavy shoulder supporting the short edges gives the mineral its toughness. The peculiar qualities of this mineral make it more effective than garnet for heavy-duty, high-speed machine sanding of wood.

Owing to the greater hardness and toughness of this mineral, even though it is less sharp in fracture, it is capable of standing up without refracture or breakdown under mechanical pressure or high speeds on belt, drum, disk, and other mechanical woodworking sanding devices. On hardwoods, the positive pressure of drum sanders can be met better with aluminum oxide grain than with garnet.

From this we may conclude that aluminum oxide, although more expensive than garnet, has found a definite place in the woodworking industry, where it is possible to carry the abrasive product to the full length of its cutting efficiency or life. Where it is not possible to do this, as, for example, in sanding softwoods, in sanding with machines running at low speeds, or wherever the nature of the work is such that the full life or production cannot be obtained, garnet is the more popular choice.

Silicon Carbide

Silicon carbide is shiny black in color, third only to the diamond in hardness, and fractures into crystals or grit sizes that have the longest edges of all minerals and the best dish shape (concave sides). The crystals are very brittle, however, and although capable of penetrating any object other than diamond and boron carbide, their relative brittleness allows them to wear down rapidly. Nevertheless, it is an excellent abrasive for most low-tensile materials, such as softwoods and hardwoods. Since these materials are not resistant enough to break it down, the life of the coating is dependent upon its ability to resist filling or clogging.

Silicon carbide is also used in sanding or surfacing hard-finishing materials such as lacquers or undercoats. The hardness and sharpness of the mineral enable these media to be cut down smoothly with the least amount of time and without excessive refracture of the mineral itself.

14.2 SELECTING THE BACKING MATERIAL FOR THE JOB

Combining the abrasive material with a particular type of backing results in a variety of papers for a variety of applications. The following paragraphs examine the various materials used for sandpaper and identify the types of sanding operations usually performed with them.

The backings used for coated abrasives can be classed under the following four headings: paper, cloth, a combination of paper and cloth, and fiber.

The type of backing is as important in many respects as the proper mineral in the selection of the product for a given job. If the work to be performed is on a flat, even surface, a paper or combination-type backing may be the best choice, since these are lower in price. Where the greater tensile strength is required, cloth should be used. Accordingly, for mechanical sanding of flat surfaces on woodwork, a paper or combination-type backing is generally used, especially if there is no tendency toward strain that would rip or tear the product from its side edge.

For mechanical sanding of irregular surfaces, curved shapes, and other applications where the backing must be flexible to conform to the surface outline, cloth is used. The basis for the selection of the proper type will be explained later.

Where an abrasive product is used by hand on regular and irregular surfaces, paper or cloth is used, depending on the type of work. In light sanding on woodwork for turning, moldings, flutes, and for flat surfaces, paper is generally used in preference to cloth. Where, in general, heavier pressures are exerted due to the hardness of the wood, as in polishing wood stock in lathes, and the abrasive is used by hand on these mechanical operations, cloth is used. A cloth backing is a better all-around medium for shop requirements, since it can be used interchangeably for hand or machine sanding operations. However, because of its lower price, paper is used quite often, especially for light sanding.

For the multitude of sanding operations in shops, selection of the correct type of backing for the job can be determined after better understanding of the backings themselves.

Paper

Papers are classified according to weight, as follows:

- A *weight* is known in the trade as finishing paper.
- C *and* D *weights* are known in the trade as cabinet paper.
- E *weight* is known in the trade as roll stock.

Two kinds of fibers are used in making paper for coated abrasives. They are: (1) wood-pulp base fiber, of which there are two classes, kraft and alpha-cellulose; and (2) hemp base (rope) pulp.

Pulp can be processed into two types of paper construction, Fourdrinier or cylinder. Fourdrinier paper is one in which all the fibers from the sheet have been laid out in a single layer, then calendered and dried. Cylinder paper is one in which five separate thin sheets are formed from the pulp, combined in the wet state, then properly calendered and dried.

Kraft paper (Fourdrinier) wood pulp is used for flint and emery sheet paper only. It is a cheaper product and is not as strong or as pliable as a refined grade of wood pulp or rope stock paper.

Rope stock, as the name implies, is generally a cylinder paper having thousands of tiny hemp fibers. This paper has great lengthwise tensile strength, which makes it very desirable for endless abrasive belts and drum sanding covers. It also has a necessary shear strength and crosswise tensile strength to overcome brittleness and prevent tearing.

Several grades of alpha-cellulose paper, a wood pulp paper, have been developed since 1935. These papers have resulted in backings for cabinet and finishing paper that are equal or superior in all respects to the rope stock Fourdrinier paper formerly used for these abrasive items.

A-weight finishing paper is a lightweight, flexible alpha-cellulose Fourdrinier paper used chiefly for sanding by hand on finishing materials. The cabinetmaker often needs to feel the imperfections of the surface as he or she is sanding, and the thinness of the paper allows this. Flexibility is desired in order that the backing conform to moldings, grooves, flutes, and narrow surfaces under light pressure without breaking up.

C- or D-weight alpha-cellulose Fourdrinier backing abrasive paper has a heavier and less flexible backing. It is used for hand sanding on wood where greater pressures are used for stock removal and are coated with coarser grits than is the case with finishing paper. Accordingly, it must be stronger than finishing paper and have more body, as it must lie flat without buckling when being used. It must be flexible enough to follow the contour of irregular, rounded, molded, or fluted surfaces.

E-weight or roll-stock cylinder paper is a heavy paper with great strength lengthwise to withstand the tensile strains developed by motor-driven belt sanders and drum sanders. This paper also has an adequate crosswise strength, which tends to eliminate shearing or tearing across its width. Cloated abrasives made on this type of backing are not flexible enough to be used on curved surfaces.

Cloth

There are two classifications of cloths:

> *Jean* is a lightweight and flexible cloth.
> *Drill* is a heavyweight cloth.

Abrasive cloth in sheet form is largely used for hand-sanding operations. It must be flexible enough to conform to irregular surfaces under hand pressure. Accordingly, it is made on a suitably filled jean or drill cloth in the fine and coarse grits, respectively, and is given enough body so that it does not wrinkle or buckle when put into use. Improperly filled cloth, that is, too ragged, would allow the sheet to wrinkle and buckle and tear with a poor edge when used in narrow torn strips.

Where flexible cloth is desired and needed in roll form, jean (coded J) should be used because of its flexibility. Being a lightweight cloth, it will stretch under excessive tension developed in heavy-duty sanding operations. However, the bond will break, and thus will not give the cutting life of a heavier-weight cloth.

Drill is a medium-weight, strongly woven, filled canvas cloth backing. It is made in roll form and is used for belts, disks, or in any place where mechanical sanding is required without a flexible backing. Although lacking sufficient flexibility to sand or grind intricate or narrow curved, molded, or fluted surfaces, its greater strength and greater resistance to stretch under high pressure and tension make it the product to use and recommend for medium- and heavy-duty grinding. Its lack of flexibility gives it greater body and a heavier and stronger foundation for the abrasive mineral.

Combination Backings

Combination or laminated backings are made of two materials. There are two types of combination backings:

- Paper combined with lightweight cloth.
- Cloth combined with fiber.

For the paper combination type of backing, a thin cloth, not unlike cheesecloth, is laminated to E-weight paper, with the mineral being coated on the cloth side. This product is stronger than paper and less expensive than cloth, and is used where the stress and strain is greater than E-weight paper is capable of withstanding. It is available as garnet combination, silicon carbide combination, and aluminum oxide combination.

Fiber combination disks for flexible-shaft machines must be flexible and yet have enough body to eliminate any tendency for the edges to wrinkle or buckle, or else the unsupported edges would catch and tear on the work. To meet this requirement, thin but extremely strong fiber is laminated to drill cloth backing on top of which the mineral is coated. This product is known as fiber combination and is furnished only in disk form.

Fiber

The newest addition to the backing types are the fiber backings. These backings are made of specially prepared rag stock which in the initial stages is made into a paper. Several layers of paper are often combined and are put through washing and drying operations. The resulting sheet is quite dense, relatively hard, and stiffer than ordinary papers.

14.3 SELECTING COATINGS OF BACKING MATERIAL

Open-Coated and Closed-Coated Papers

There are two types of mineral coatings: full or closed-coated, and spaced or open-coated. The difference between them is in the distance between the spacings of the bonded abrasive grits. In closed-coated paper, as the name implies, the mineral is closely coated, each grit being adjacent to the other or fully coating the backing. Open-coated paper has coating in which each mineral grit stands by itself with a spacing or void between.

Open coatings allow the material sanded to free itself without filling or clogging the surface. Closed coatings, with little spacing, form tight pockets that collect the material sanded and therefore fill more rapidly, especially on materials of low tensile strength.

Accordingly, for applications that call for light pressure and quick sanding, especially on soft, gummy, plastic surfaces, the open-coated products are used. The reasons for using open-coated products in sanding varnish, shellac, and enamels are obvious. This type of coating will eliminate rapid filling, and, since the medium itself presents a comparatively soft surface where light pressure is used, the coating will support the wear. It can be readily appreciated that open-coated grain on cloth allows a more flexible material than the full-coated type; consequently, this type of material is used for operations that require extreme flexibility, such as sanding moldings, where the mineral grain cuts fast and smooth without burning. In sanding hardwood, closed-coated abrasives are best adapted. As these materials have high tensile strength, they do not fill or clog rapidly, and because of their heavier mineral coat, the abrasive will last longer. Where heavy pressures are used or when sanding nonfilling materials for rugged stock removal for which a constant continuous cut is desired, full-coated types are used.

Open-coated abrasives are used for sanding finishing materials whose gum content would quickly clog a closed-coat material. They are also used for buffing and for stock-removal purposes in cabinetwork. Open-coated aluminum oxide fiber combination disks are recommended for paint removal in the refinishing of cabinets and other furniture.

One of the most important methods used to apply the abrasive coating is the electrostatic method. This is a patented process of coating minerals through the use of electricity. In the past, abrasive material has been coated to the backing by dropping it on the sheet coated with glue, but because the mineral chips landed haphazardly, their cutting edges were not oriented uniformly with regard to the item to be sanded. In the electrostatic method, the grains stand on the sheet with their cutting edges oriented in the direction of the work. This makes for greater uniformity and a faster, longer-lived product than it was formerly possible to make. Both open and closed coats can be electrostatically applied.

The following materials are coated electrostatically: aluminum oxide metalworking cloth sheets and utility rolls, aluminum oxide woodworking paper, combination rolls and cabinet and finishing paper, aluminum oxide woodworking cloth (jean and drill), silicon carbide combination and finishing paper, and garnet finishing paper.

Bond or Adhesive Used for Applying Coating to Backing

The adhesive or bond used to hold the mineral on a coated abrasive sheet is of several types, identified so that the cabinetmaker may select the proper type when polishing the cabinet:

1. Water-soluble bonds:
   a. Glue bond
   b. Glue with filler bond
2. Partly water soluble bond:
   a. Resin over glue bond
3. Water-insoluble bonds:
   a. Resin bond (resin bond on nonwaterproof backing)
   b. Waterproof (resin bond on waterproof backing)

Only the highest quality animal-hide glues are used on glue-bond abrasives. The glue is of higher quality than glues used for joining in the woodworking trade and for other commercial uses. For glue-with-filler-bond abrasives, the same grades of hide glue are used, with the addition of a carefully prepared filler that will modify the glue to produce a harder film, more heat resistance, and less effect by moisture than glue that is not so modified.

In the second group, the partly water soluble bond, there is construction resin over glue. Most abrasives have two coatings of adhesive, one on the backing into which the mineral coating is initially anchored, and the other a sizing over the abrasive particles. Resin-over-glue materials are meant to be used only in dry sanding operations. They are more heat resistant and perform consistently over a wider range of humidity.

The water-insoluble group of adhesives is divided into two groups: resin bond and waterproof. The term "resin bond" is generally associated with a phenolic resin adhesive coated on a backing that has not been waterproofed, as, for example, types C and D disks. Waterproof materials are designed to be used where wet sanding is desired. The backings on these products are waterproofed. The primary use for waterproof paper is for rubbing or sanding out surfaces, undercoats, lacquers, varnishes, and enamels. It is used extensively in rubbing out lacquer finishes on furniture and works well in polishing the new plastic varnishes. Waterproof cloth is used in the metal, glass, ceramics, and plastic industries for wet sanding to eliminate dust, filling, and heating. Examples of water-insoluble products are waterproof silicon carbide paper, waterproof aluminum oxide cloth, and waterproof silicon carbide cloth.

From the foregoing, an effort to select the proper and most economical abrasive for the type of work on which the abrasive is to be used has been examined. The limitations of the various abrasive materials, their backing, their coatings, and their bond type have been reviewed, and only by coordinating these conditions with the job can the proper sandpaper be selected. This foundation, added to your own experiences in use of the product, should result in a well-sanded product.

14.4 SELECTING THE SANDING METHOD

Once decisions are reached about the various types of papers best for a particular phase of sanding a cabinet, the next step is to select the proper sanding method. Will it be the hand method or a machine method? If both methods are to be used, when should each be used?

Hand Method

For hand sanding, a sanding block is often used to exert a uniform area of force on the surface being sanded. A sanding block is either a commercial type that is available in local hardware stores, or the handmade variety consisting of a scrap piece of board $1\frac{1}{4} \times 3 \times 9$ inches around which the sandpaper is wrapped. When other than flat surfaces are sanded by hand, the block identified above may be shaped to the curve in the cabinet or table. For smaller areas and trim, the sandpaper may simply be folded and held with palm and fingers. The A-type papers are best for this operation, since a feel for the finish, curves, and angles is usually desirable.

Machine Method

Various sanding machines are available to the part-time or full-time cabinet-maker.

Belt sander.   The portable belt sander is used primarily for heavy-duty operations. There are a variety of types of papers available for different jobs. The following list will help determine when to use the belt sander and what weight of paper and grit to use:

Stock lumber	Coarse (30–60); medium (80–100); fine (100–150)
Plywood	Medium (80–100); fine (100–150)
Veneers	Fine (120–150)

Vibrator sander.   The vibrator sander is a finishing sander. On most operations, smooth finish paper is installed. There are three separate operations for which this machine is especially useful: for sanding before staining, for sanding between finishing coats of varnish or lacquer, and for polishing, which is usually performed after the last coat of finish has dried.

Disk sander.   The disk sander is usually an attachment to an electric drill or flexible shaft. This type of sander is used in some wood-sanding operations, for instance, where materials are curved and hard to get at. The disk is limited to a few operations because of the circular marks the paper makes in the grain of the wood.

Another type of disk sander is the fixed or stationary type. It is usually mounted on the same machine base as the stationary belt sander (home work-shop variety). This type is ideal for the edge sanding of curved materials and ends of boards, 45-degree miters, and such. The variety of grit available for various operations is as follows:

Heavy stock removal	36–50 grit
Medium stock removal	60–100 grit
Light stock removal/polishing	120–150 grit

Drum sander.   The drum sander may be either a stationary machine, where the drum or spindle rotates and oscillates up and down, or it may be an attachment for an electrical drill. This attachment may be installed in either a portable electric drill or a bench or floor-model electric drill.

The usefulness of this type of sander lies in its ability to be used in sanding inside curves that have small radii. The various operations that can be performed require paper of the same grit as that used in disk sanders.

Surface sander.   Several surface sanders are available to cabinetmakers, but seldom are found in shops of novices or small-business cabinetmakers. One type uses a large belt. The surface to be sanded is placed on a movable table under the revolving belt. The cabinetmaker uses a block like an iron for pressing clothes. As the belt slides over the piece to be sanded, the cabinetmaker presses the back side of the belt down onto the wood surface. He or she moves both the block and table to smooth all parts of the surface. The second is a wide drum, usually wider than the surface to be sanded. This machine works like a surface planer.

14.5 SANDING FOR A FINISH

There are three decisions that must be made during the finishing process:

- First, select the proper paper to smooth irregularities that occur during staining and finishing operations.
- Second, select the proper combination of sandpaper and liquid that will create a smooth surface.
- Third, select the proper sandpaper for polishing to a glossy, satin, or dull finish.

The proper paper.   It is necessary to sand a cabinet after it has been stained and dried because the liquid in the stain caused the fibers in the wood to swell and become erect. With the use of 180- or 220-grit type-A paper and very gentle pressure, these fibers will be sanded away. A very gentle pressure is used, because heavy or uneven pressure will sand away some of the stained wood and result in unevenly colored areas.

At all times, sand with the grain in a forward and backward motion. Be especially careful when sanding near the edges—the stain could be sanded away with one stroke. While sanding or after sanding, wipe the entire cabinet with a cloth to find all the rough spots. Resand these until they are smooth. Repeat this operation between coats of finish material. After the last coat of finish material is dry, the polishing may begin.

The proper paper and liquid for polishing.   The first sanding should be with water, so a water-insoluble-bond type of paper should be selected. The weight should be very light so that no scratching occurs. The grits range from 220 to 600.

The water tends to make the paper cut more smoothly and keeps the surfaces cooler, so that no burning takes place. A substitute for water is paraffin oil. It is used the same as water. Liberally apply the oil to the surface to be sanded, then sand with the grain. Wipe away the excess oil when finished. Let the cabinet dry thoroughly (24 hours), and then polish it with wax.

Polish with sandpaper.   Polishing can be performed with sandpaper and a solvent such as paraffin oil. By proper selection of grit, the addition of lubricant, and proper pressure and velocity, any desired effect can be obtained. The finer grits (400, 500, 600) result in more polishing and little cutting, for a highly polished finish. The coarser grits (220–320) result in a more satin appearance, because more of the sheen is removed from the top dressing.

In summary, in the decisions needed to sand a cabinet, a variety of types of sandpapers is needed. There are different types for use in the various machines. There are different grits, 60–80 for coarse work to 500–600 for finishing polish work. There are lightweight, wet/dry, and heavyweight papers.

Sanding stock lumber must be done in a series of steps, starting with the rougher papers and progressing to the finer papers. Between coats of finish and after the final coat, other sandings must be done with finer grades of paper and lubricants such as water or oil.

A beautiful cabinet will result by proper selection and application of sandpaper.

REVIEW EXERCISES

1. One of the first decisions to make about sanding is the selection of grit size.   (T/F)
2. Hardness is defined as the ability of an abrasive mineral to resist shearing and breakdown while sanding. (T/F)
3. A properly fractured mineral coating on sandpaper will have irregular sides of a dish-shape to allow for chip clearance. (T/F)
4. The mineral with the hardest rating is garnet. (T/F)
5. If selecting a sandpaper for its toughness, you would select emery. (T/F)
6. Which sandpaper mineral coating has round and blocky shaped abrasive?
    a. Flint
    b. Garnet
    c. Emery
    d. Aluminum oxide
7. Which type of backing on sandpaper is most adaptable for belt sanders?
    a. Paper
    b. Cloth
    c. Alpha-cellulose
    d. Fiber

8. Which paper weight is known in the trade as cabinet paper?
    a. A
    b. C
    c. C and D
    d. E
9. Which combination of names below is correct?
    a. Full or open-coated
    b. Full or closed-coated
    c. Spaced or closed-coated
    d. Open-coated or deposit-coated

ESSAYS

10. Write a paper on the advantages of open-coated and closed-coated sandpaper.
11. Prepare a report that explains the relative importance, if any, of the type of backing sandpapers have.
12. In a short paper of 50 to 75 words, tell how you would sand for a finish.

ANSWERS

1T, 2F, 3T, 4F, 5T, 6c, 7b, 8c, 9b

15

Finishes and
Finishing Techniques

The final major phase of constructing a cabinet is to apply the finishes. The tasks performed in this phase are not easy ones. In fact, many cabinets have been reduced to storage bins in the garage because of a poor finishing job. In this chapter, the five basic sub-phases—filling, sealing, staining, intermediate and final coating, and polishing—and the four finishing methods—lacquer, oil rub, shellac and wax, and varnish—are first presented in overview. Then each sub-phase is covered in detail including descriptions of the materials required and instructions in their use.

Objectives

1. Identify the characteristics of finishes used on cabinets and furniture.
2. Understand which finishing techniques are used with each other to completely finish a cabinet.

15.1 OVERVIEW OF THE FINISHING PROCESS

There are two principles to consider when finishing cabinets: the sub-phases to follow and the methods to be used. Illustrated in Figure 15–1 are the phases

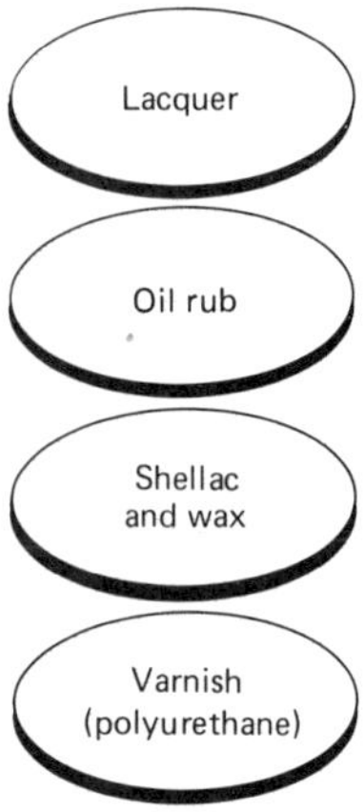

Figure 15–2 Finishing methods.

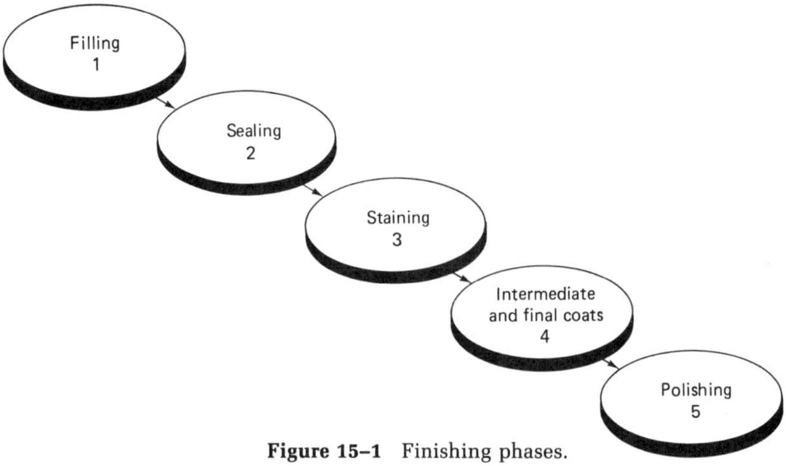

Lacquer

Oil rub

Shellac and wax

Varnish (polyurethane)

Filling
1

Sealing
2

Staining
3

Intermediate
and final coats
4

Polishing
5

Figure 15–1 Finishing phases.

usually performed in each finishing task. The operations are listed sequentially, but there may be certain cases in which some of the them are combined.

Figure 15–2 illustrates four of the frequently used methods for finishing cabinets: the lacquer method, the oil-rub method, the shellac and wax method, and the varnish method. Each method is briefly explained in the next few paragraphs. This information is essential to understanding the information in the following sections.

The Lacquer Method

Lacquer, although available in both brush and spray varieties, is generally considered a spray finish. Lacquer is available commercially in dull, satin, and high-gloss sheens. Tinted lacquer may be purchased, but it is generally used in the clear state. When used with a sprayer at pressures between 25 and 50 pounds per square inch, lacquer is very easy to apply.

Lacquer's primary advantage is its quick drying. Depending upon the amount of retarding agent used, the drying time varies from a few minutes to 20 minutes. This means that the entire finishing job for a small to medium-sized cabinet will take from 2 to 4 hours. Another advantage is that lacquer may be used for wash coating, sealing, and top dressing, thereby reducing the variety of equipment and supplies that would be needed if another finish were selected.

Lacquer is a tough, durable finish that does not mar easily. If special conditions must be controlled, such as moisture, mildew, or fungus, special additives may be added that make lacquer more desirable.

A build-up of lacquer can result in the orange-peel effect, which is a stippled effect that resembles the rough peel of an orange. If this happens during a spraying operation, the excess lacquer must be removed by rubbing and cleaning. The orange-peel effect results from insufficient thinner in the mixture being sprayed, or using too much air pressure while spraying.

Another element to consider when using lacquer is its tendency to cause bleeding of the stained wood. If the lacquer is not mixed with a retarder, it dries too fast and traps moisture, causing the stains to interfere with the lacquer and creating streaking effects.

Lacquers are usually finished by rubbing with pumice, followed by polishing with rottenstone and oil, and a good cleaning. For the French polish effect seen on pianos, start with a high-gloss lacquer. Do not use pumice unless to correct cases of orange peel. Burnish with rottenstone and an oil-soaked felt pad. Finish with a good application of wax.

The Oil-Rub Method

Oil-rubbed finishing brings out the natural beauty of wood. The oil is allowed to penetrate the pores or cells of the wood until they become saturated and hardened. The process is a continuing one which starts with a daily application of boiled linseed oil, drier, and turpentine. After one week the applications are spaced at weekly intervals, then graduated to monthly applications. From then on, the applications are dependent upon the use—or abuse—the cabinet receives. An inherent characteristic of this type of finish is its darkening. The older the finish gets, the darker it becomes.

Boiled linseed oil is diluted with turpentine, after which spar varnish and/ or a drier may be added. A mixture of two parts boiled linseed oil to one part turpentine is the basis to which 10 percent varnish may be added. To work properly, the mixture must be at room temperature or slightly warmer. Saturate a cloth with the mixture and rub small sections of the cabinet for periods of 10 to 15 minutes. Or brush on generously, let stand 5 to 10 minutes, then rub another 10 to 15 minutes. The oil must penetrate the cells. Pressure usually speeds the penetrating process. Wipe off excess oil and let dry 24 hours between coats.

If the oil-rub finish is used, no paste wood filler is usually required, except on end-grain woods. The oil mixture will fill the pores.

After the basic coats have been applied, with sanding done between coats, the surface may be rubbed with rottenstone and an oil-soaked felt pad to bring additional sheen and luster to the surface.

The Shellac and Wax Method

In the shellac and wax method, shellac, denatured alcohol, sandpaper, pumice, rags, a good brush, and wax are needed. Where a shellac finish is selected, avoid using spirit stains and non-grain-raising stains, as these stains contain alcohol.

Apply three to four coats of shellac, each one thinned with a mixture of shellac and alcohol in equal parts. Follow each coating with sanding. Because it dries quickly, shellac must be applied rapidly. Avoid overlapping strokes by having the second brushful start before the first brushful has begun to set. Be fast in applying the shellac, and be sure to cover the entire surface only once. Shellacking edges, turned moldings, and legs should be no problem because these areas are relatively small, and a single stroke of the brush from bottom to top usually will cover the piece. If spraying, be careful not to overspray.

Shellac can be treated like any of the other finishes during the rubbing operations. In the final polishing you may use fine sandpaper, pumice, and rottenstone. It is suggested that large flat areas be rubbed first. Then the stiles, rails, panels, and turned areas can be rubbed to match the flat surfaces. Clean off the slurry of pumice or rottenstone, and oil with benzine or naphtha and a soft rag. Do all wiping with the grain. Follow these operations with washing with water and drying with soft, lint-free rags. Water should not be used when polishing with pumice or rottenstone. The results will be a too-dull surface finish. Follow the cleaning with a waxing.

The Varnish Method

The polyurethane varnishes are much better to work with than ordinary spar varnish. They dry better, are lighter, and are easier to work with. The varnish method described here will explain how to use this type of varnish.

Polyurethane varnishes cannot, as a rule, be applied over shellac; therefore, shellac is not acceptable as a seal coat. The best method, according to several manufacturers of this product, is to seal the surface with a diluted solution of the same varnish.

There is a distinct difference in finishing with varnish. Varnish takes quite a long time to dry because the resins and oils in the varnish must harden after the thinner has evaporated. Both the turpentine and the humidity will vary the drying conditions.

Of the various finishing materials, varnish is one of the best methods of obtaining a satin-sheen finish. Because of its body, it covers completely and relatively thickly, thereby creating a suitable surface for rubbing with pumice. One precaution should be observed: allow the varnish to dry thoroughly before beginning the rubbing and polishing operations.

Of necessity, a dust-free workroom or booth should be used when varnishing. A day before you are going to varnish, clean and vacuum the shop. Do not do any additional dusting on the day you are varnishing, or raise any dust by using machines.

For most cabinets, three coats of varnish will provide adequate coverage. These may be applied with a spray gun or with a $1\frac{1}{2}$- to 3-inch soft bristle brush. The soft bristles are needed to minimize the brushmarks. Sand the sheen from each coat before applying the next coat to ensure a good binding surface.

15.2 THE FILLING PHASE OF THE FINISHING PROCESS

The pores or cells in certain wood used in making cabinets are very large. For wall paneling and certain other materials, applying a direct finish without filling would be satisfactory. However, in the finishing of most cabinets, a porous, uneven finish is not desirable. Therefore, a filler is applied that, when dried and sanded, creates a smooth, even surface for the application of top dressings.

For a filler to appropriately perform its function, it must contain particles that will readily fill the minute pores and cracks in stock, plus an agent that will evaporate and allow the filler to harden.

Paste Wood as a Filler

Most commercial paste wood fillers are adequate for the job of filling stock, but there are a few brands, classified as liquid fillers, that contain little body and hence have little use. Paste wood fillers, whether bought commercially or homemade, have a silicon base. The silicon is combined with linseed oil, japan dryer, and turpentine in varying quantities, depending upon the type of application. As a base reference point, combine one quart of turpentine with one pint of japan dryer and two to three pounds of fine silex. For a heavier-bodied paste, decrease the volume of turpentine and japan dryer proportionally or increase the silicon content. For a lighter, thin base, increase the turpentine base. One quart of paste wood filler will cover approximately 70 square feet of board.

The filler may be applied to previously stained wood and to bare wood in its natural creamy color, or a color pigment may be added to tone it. If coloring is added, it should be slightly darker than the actual color of the stain that is to be used. This feature will cause the pores being filled to be slightly darker than the surrounding wood surfaces, thereby creating a pleasant effect. Use the following table as a suggestion for tinting the filling.

Cabinet color/Wood	Pigment
Mahogany	Burnt umber
Walnut	Van Dyke brown
Oak	Touch of burnt umber
Maple	None required

If a lightener or darkener is needed, use zinc oxide to lighten the filler or ground lamp black to darken the filler.

Finally, prepare paste wood filler to the consistency of cream, heavy or light depending upon the type of wood being filled and whether it is the first or second coat. If, as happens in some cases, the first coat does not completely do the job, a thinner mixture of the same paste can be applied as a second coat.

The prepared paste should be liberally applied to the cabinet surface. Use a stiff bristle brush 2 to 4 inches wide with medium-length bristles to vigorously rub the paste into the grain. This is usually accomplished by holding the brush perpendicular and using circular motions. After this brushing operation is complete, the paste may be left as it is, or stroked with the grain, or brushed across the grain to prevent lifting the filler from the grain until dull.

The paste will dull to a flat finish within 10 to 20 minutes. When this happens, the paste must be wiped away from the surface. Take a piece of burlap cloth or wood wool and vigorously wipe away the excess wood filler by stroking across the grain. If the filler has hardened too much to permit easy removal, soften it by adding thinner to the rag. A dowel tapered to a flat tip is very effective for removing excess filler from moldings and inside corners.

After you have gently (but firmly) removed the excess filler, wipe a final time with a smooth, soft cloth. Wipe with the grain. If the filler has been properly embedded, the rag will not pull it from the wood.

The filler can be applied most easily and thoroughly when the surface is horizontal. Once the filler has been applied, the position of the surface is relatively unimportant.

Allow the filler to dry thoroughly (24 hours is generally sufficient), then sand with paper of 180 to 220 grit. If there are pores or uneven places (hollows) within the grain that are not filled, a second coat of filler may be needed. If so, use either the same consistency as before where heavy coating is needed, or thin the filler and apply a light-bodied coat where it is needed.

Shellac as a Filler

On some not-so-porous woods, a liquid filler usually provides a good base for sealing the pores and evening the surface. Where this is the case, a coating of white shellac usually solves the problem nicely. The shellac should be reduced to one part shellac to six parts denatured alcohol. When using this type of filler, the stain is frequently applied first, but if you want to control the stain, using filler first, and then smoothing the surfaces will reduce the penetration of the stain.

Cellulose Fiber (Wood Dough) as a Filler

Commercially prepared cellulose wood fillers are available in most of the standard wood types and colors. There are natural, bleached, maple, oak, and walnut tones, to mention just a few. These fillers dry extremely fast and may be applied in more than one coat. Their usefulness is limited to cracks, pits, and filling between joints. In some instances, coarsely end-cut materials are filled with this type of filler.

There are two theories regarding when to apply this wood filler. Some people feel that there is less discoloration and better blending if the filler is applied after staining and the stain is sealed. If this method is used, the filler must be tinted before application. Other people apply natural color or tinted filler directly to unfinished wood, believing that this method allows more freedom for sanding after the filler dries.

15.3 THE SEALING PHASE OF THE FINISHING PROCESS

Sealing provides two important functions: it protects the stain or wood from discoloration when the finishing material is added, and it provides a base for controlling stains where a limited penetration of stain is desired or top staining is to be used.

Shellac as a Sealer

One of the cheapest sealers is shellac. To use shellac as a sealer, reduce its strength by mixing it with four to six times its volume of denatured alcohol. The porousness of the wood and the amount of control desired will dictate the desired reduction.

Lacquer as a Sealer

Lacquer can also be used as a sealer. An effective sealing coat is composed of one part lacquer to three parts lacquer thinner. Lacquer sealers are especially useful where lacquer will be the top dressing.

Sanding Sealers

A fairly new product on the market is sanding sealer. This product usually can be purchased in clear form or in a variety of stain colors. It has a varnish base, so caution should be exercised where the final coats of finish are to be something other than varnish. This product requires good presanding and considerable postsanding. It is very much like a varnish stain, except that it has some additional sealing qualities. There is very little control over tone and texture when using this product or any type of finishing product that combines steps of the finishing process.

Varnish Wash Coat as a Sealer

Varnish may be used as a wash coat. When it is, it is reduced in strength so that the open pores of the wood to which it is applied will be partially filled. In this way the stain is restricted from penetrating very deeply. Varnish wash coats should be used when varnish is to be the final topcoating material.

15.4 THE STAINING PHASE OF THE FINISHING PROCESS

Although a variety of types of stain can be purchased commercially, such as oil, water, and varnish stains, oil stain is the most popular for use on cabinets. Oil stain can be purchased in a variety of colors to match every type and color of furniture built for American homes, old or new. Certain precautions should be exercised when staining, and these will be discussed.

Pigment Oil Stains as Coloring Agents

Pigment oil stains are usually made from a mixture of ground powders soluble in naphtha or turpentine. The pigments are made from a mixture of various oxides and silicates. The vehicle contains varnish, mineral spirits, and driers such as japan drier. These are combined with various oils such as linseed and tall oil and are added to mineral spirits, which makes up 80 percent of the volume of the container.

Oil stains should be applied to scrap pieces of all materials to be stained to give a quick, reliable gauge of how the stain will appear on the cabinet. Since all woods take color differently, the various shades, depths, and tones will show on the scrap piece.

Stain can be applied with a soft bristle brush $1\frac{1}{2}$ to 3 inches wide or with a soft cotton rag. There are two ways to stain: (1) apply the stain across the grain first and then with the grain to even it up, or (2) brush or wipe with the grain at all times.

After the stain is applied, let it set briefly, from 2 to 10 minutes, until the desired depth of color is achieved. Wipe the end grain immediately; if the stain is allowed to remain it will become extremely dark (unless presealed with a wash coat). Begin to wipe the stain with a clean, dry, soft cloth, starting with those pieces that take stain most easily. Continue wiping the surfaces until all the excess stain has been removed. Let dry 4 to 24 hours, depending upon the weather and the type of stain used. Penetrating oil stains are very similar to pigment oil stains but tend to react more quickly. Therefore, a wash coat of shellac mixed with four to six parts alcohol is usually applied to the cabinet before staining. The method of application is the same as that of the pigment oil stain.

Spirit Stains as Coloring Agents

Spirit stains are composed of aniline powder, are soluble in alcohol, and are very difficult to use. Because they dry quickly, the colors may not be even. When shellac is added as a retarding agent, more control is obtained. This type of stain, however, is ideal for touch-up work when refinishing.

Water Stains as Coloring Agents

Water-soluble powder made from aniline dyes is the most desirable stain to use on a cabinet that will be exposed continuously to direct sunlight. It is the most penetrating of all stains, especially when used on base wood. The stain is sold in small packets as dry powder. The best results are obtained when the powder is added to very warm water, as it will then dissolve completely and mix more easily.

Since all colors are not available in powdered form, variations will have to be made by combining various water-soluble dyes. The amount of dye added to a basic color will have to be determined on a trial-and-error basis. Therefore, when making a mixture, be sure to make enough for the entire job. Some basic water-soluble dyes are: red (crimson), brown (tobacco), standard walnut, auramine yellow (lemon), nigrosine crystals (jet black), fusciasine red (scarlet), and malachite green (blue-green). As an example, a lighter brown can be obtained by adding yellow to standard walnut, a darker brown by adding nigrosine crystals, a reddish brown by adding crimson or fusciasine red. If a light walnut color is desired, just add more water, diluting the color.

Water stain is best applied with a brush that has long, fairly stiff bristles. Apply the stain in a sweeping motion back and forth with the grain. Continue brushing and staining until the entire surface is completely covered and appears to have the same density or volume of stain. As a last step before the stain sets, brush the entire surface with a clean brush until the stain is distributed evenly and the surface has a dull appearance. The best position for the surface to be stained is horizontal.

It is difficult to control the color because of the rapid penetration of the stain. Therefore, *do not* add additional coats of stain or double brush near the ends of each stroke. There is no way to correct a double dose of stain.

Be sure to seal the container if you wish to store any leftover stain. To recover the dyes, which may be used again, allow the water to evaporate, and recover the stain. When needed again, bring the water to a boil, add the dried dyes, and stir until dissolved.

Touch Staining and Restaining

As the name implies, touch staining is a technique that is used to color small areas rather than the entire surface. Apply stain with a brush or rag to the areas desired, being careful not to overlap the other surfaces. Allow the stain to set for several minutes, then wipe off the excess. Repeat this step as often as needed to bring out the desired color. Should the stained area become too dark, moisten a clean rag with mineral spirits and gently wipe the area, removing as much of the stain as needed.

Restaining, in contrast, means that the entire surface is to be stained. Standard staining applications should be performed. However, the possibility exists that some color still remains from the original staining, so care must be used. The exact color you want very likely will not result in restaining because of previous staining, but experience has shown that lighter stains applied over stripped surfaces frequently produce the desired shades. Experiment with a small area in a place that is not easily seen.

If you use a combination of the two techniques described, you can control and develop a uniformly colored surface. It is better to apply coats of stain and use very short penetration times than to allow stain to set for 10 minutes or more. After a coat has been wiped and left to dry, make observations in bright daylight. Incandescent or fluorescent lighting plays tricks on colors because of shadow effects.

15.5 THE INTERMEDIATE AND FINAL COATING PHASE OF THE FINISHING PROCESS

The most foolproof method of applying finish coats is to start and finish with the same product. This will always assure compatibility because there will be no conflict in chemicals. In certain cases chemicals of different products react with each other, and lifting, softening, opaquing, and dissolving are apt to result. A product that works well as an undercoating for certain finishes is shellac.

Shellac as an Intermediate and Final Finishing Material

Properly diluted, shellac is frequently used in finishing operations as a wash coat and an undercoat. If light-colored cabinets are being finished, white shellac is the better choice. If dark cabinets are to be finished, orange shellac is better. In either case, the shellac must be diluted with denatured alcohol.

Since shellac is a derivative of varnish, it follows that the product will work well under most varnishes. Before using shellac, always refer to the instructions on the can of varnish. For instance, polyurethane varnish cannot be applied over shellac. However, when diluted properly (one part shellac to four parts denatured alcohol), shellac can be used as a base coat for a lacquer-finished cabinet.

Shellac is ideal as a base coat because of its filling qualities and quick-drying capabilities. Some types of stain, such as oil and spirit stains, may bleed into the final finish and cause clouding or uneven coloring. By using shellac (when compatible with the final finish), a complete seal can be achieved, thereby preventing bleeding. Shellac also provides a quick method for preparing for the final coat, because when thinned it will dry in 30 minutes to 2 hours, depending upon the drying conditions. Some cabinets may require 10 to 15 coats before the desired depth and luster are obtained.

Lacquer as an Intermediate and Final Finishing Material

If lacquer is used as a final topcoating, it may also be used as a sealer and undercoat. Start with a very thin application of lacquer (one part lacquer to three parts thinner) and watch for bleeding. The mixture will dry in seconds. Check the surface for any ill effects; if none, apply a second coat.

If you use a brushing lacquer, make sure that the lacquer dries slowly enough to permit even brushing. When thinning brushing lacquer, follow the manufacturer's suggestions by adding a retarding type of lacquer thinner.

After one, two, or three coats have been successfully applied and are dry, sand the surface with a very fine paper (220 grit) using gentle strokes. It usually requires seven to nine coats of lacquer before adequate body and depth are achieved.

Polyurethane Varnish as an Intermediate and Final Finishing Material

Plastic varnishes usually cannot be applied over previously sealed surfaces because of chemical reactions. Therefore, if the cabinet is to be finished with a polyurethane type of varnish, an undercoat of the same material is most suitable. Thin the varnish to about 50 percent strength and apply with a brush or spray. When dry (usually 4 to 18 hours), sand with fine paper. Apply a second coat and subsequent coats with a stronger concentration of varnish. Sand after each coat dries.

Wax as an Intermediate and Final Finishing Material

Prepare special-purpose furniture waxes and apply each succeeding coat when the previous coat is thoroughly dry. Sufficient coats must be applied to build up a sheen. Water and alcohol are harmful to wax finishes, so care must be used.

Oil as an Intermediate and Final Finishing Material

Liberally apply the mixture of oil (linseed usually) and brushing lacquer to the surface and rub well into the surface with even-pressure strokes. Wipe off the excess and let dry. Repeat oil applications until the surface is completely saturated and the desired depth is achieved.

15.6 THE POLISHING PHASE OF THE FINISHING PROCESS

The final phase in the finishing of a cabinet is the polishing. The purpose of polishing is to develop a final sheen and to remove any imperfections that may have occurred the final coats.

Sandpaper with a grit from 240 to 600 may be used. The finer the grit, the more polishing and the less cutting will occur. In addition, rubbing abrasives such as pumice stone and rottenstone are used to develop special sheens. Finally, waxes are available that will produce a specific sheen and texture.

The topcoats can be polished, rubbed, and cleaned. Each operation has a different purpose. They are:

- *Rubbing* is an operation designed to remove irregularities that may have developed during the topcoating.
- *Polishing* is a burnishing action that removes or blends fine scratches so they cannot be seen with the naked eye.
- *Cleaning* is an operation that removes all foreign matter that results from polishing or rubbing.

Rubbing Materials

Rubbing may be performed with fine sandpaper and/or pumice or a combination of sandpaper and pumice. Following are instructions for obtaining the various sheens:

Dull finish.   To achieve a dull finish, sand the cabinet with a grade 360 to 400 paper until the entire finish has been dulled, then follow with a good cleaning. Afterward, no shine should be visible.

Satin-sheen finish.   To achieve a satin-sheen finish, sand the cabinet with a grade 360 to 500 paper, then hand rub with a fine grade (type F or FF) pumice mixed with water or oil.

High-satin-sheen finish.   To achieve a high-satin-sheen finish, sand the cabinet with grade 500 to 600 paper until smooth, then follow with a rubbing of fine to extra fine (type FF or FFF) pumice mixed with oil. Clean.

Rubbing is usually required regardless of the type of top dressing. There is no practical way to prevent dust in the air from settling onto the surface, and there is no way to prevent foreign matter from entering the topcoat, no matter how much filtering is done.

Machine rubbing may be very satisfactory for flat panels and surfaces. Generally, in-line sanding is required because scratching results from across-the-grain sanding. Pumice, which is almost always rubbed by hand, should always be rubbed in-line. For those hard-to-get-at inside corners and moldings, a slurry mixture of pumice and oil applied and rubbed with a rubbing brush or stick generally is effective. Sometimes a toothbrush is ideal. Pumice cuts fairly fast, so caution must be used. Occasionally, wipe the surface clean and dry it so that an examination can be made. Usually, though, two separate rubbings of pumice are required before the rubbing phase is complete. When wiping, be sure to wipe with the grain.

Polishing Materials

Polishing, which we have defined as a burnishing action, is the next-to-last phase in the finishing operation. Polishing may be performed to achieve a desired appearance but it is designed primarily to blend the slight imperfections created by the brush or sprayer into a glass-like surface. A smooth, extra fine pumice may be used on satin-sheen surfaces. If a higher gloss is desired, a mixture of rottenstone and oil is used instead of pumice. Rottenstone, unlike pumice, will not scratch. Its cutting power is negligible. The polishing effect is achieved by the friction and heat generated during the rubbing. Heat will soften the top dressing sufficiently to allow the rottenstone to blend the slight imperfections and create a polish. The same precautions apply when polishing as when rubbing. Two separate polishing steps are desirable, with a good cleaning between operations.

Cleaning Materials

The purpose of cleaning is to permit examination of the surfaces previously rubbed or polished. Various substances may be used to clean: dry, lint-free, soft rags; water and a rag; mineral spirits and a rag. If water was used along with the pumice or rottenstone, then water can be used to wash down the cabinet after rubbing. Be careful that no wiping is done across the grain, or scratching may result. Wipe dry with a soft, lint-free rag.

 If a slurry of oil and pumice or rottenstone was used in rubbing or polishing operation, wipe away all excess slurry with a clean rag. Follow this initial wiping with another wiping, using a rag and mineral spirits. Finally, wash with water and wipe dry. Be cautious when using the spirits—do not select a type that could affect the top dressing.

Waxing Materials

After the cabinet has been cleaned, examined, and the desired finish achieved, a good grade of furniture wax should be applied. Any of a number of commercial paste waxes and liquid waxes can be used for this operation. If desired, a wax mixture can be made from beeswax and turpentine. When the beeswax is thoroughly dissolved (usually in 2 days), color may be added to the wax.

 Color pigment, such as burnt umber, should be added to any clear wax when the wax is to be applied to any cabinet that has color (not bleached). The addition of color may prevent the possibility of wax smudges and discoloration in corners and crevices after the wax dries.

 Apply a liberal coat of wax evenly with a small pad of soft cloth. Let it stand long enough to penetrate and give the finish an opportunity to show the proper luster. To do this, the wax must not harden before it is buffed, so it must be applied at moderate temperatures (68° to 80°F).

REVIEW EXERCISES

1. The finishing process as described in this chapter consists of five sub-phases, the first of which is the sealing. (T/F)

2. The principal advantage in using the lacquer method of finishing is its variety of colors. (T/F)

3. For a satin finish, lacquer finishes are first rubbed with pumice then rotten-stone. (T/F)

4. Boiled linseed oil is one of the materials used in the oil-rub finishing method. (T/F)

5. A good quality spirit stain should be used under a shellac finish. (T/F)

6. For a varnish finish, the seal coat should be made from a diluted mixture of varnish and thinner. (T/F)

7. In which phase of the finishing process might one use silicon and japan dryer?
   a. Filling
   b. Sealing
   c. Staining
   d. Topcoating

8. A mixture of how many parts of shellac and how many parts of denatured alcohol, respectively, is correct for sealing?
   a. 1, 1
   b. 1, 2
   c. 1, 4
   d. 1, 8

9. Which is the proper vehicle to mix with a powder to produce an oil stain?
   a. Varnish, mineral spirits, and dryers
   b. Alcohol and shellac
   c. Water

ESSAYS

10. In a paper of 50 to 75 words, explain how to finish a cabinet with one of the finishing methods.

11. Explain what *touch staining* is and under what circumstances you could recommend its use.

12. Prepare a graph which illustrates where the polishing phase fits into the finishing process.

ANSWERS

1F, 2F, 3T, 4T, 5F, 6T, 7a, 8c, 9a

Index